FESTIVAL AND SPECIAL EVENT MANAGEMENT

IAN McDONNELL • JOHNNY ALLEN • WILLIAM O'TOOLE

John Wiley & Sons Australia, Ltd

BRISBANE • NEW YORK • CHICHESTER • WEINHEIM • SINGAPORE • TORONTO

First published 1999 by
John Wiley & Sons Australia, Ltd
33 Park Road, Milton, Qld 4064

Offices also in Sydney and Melbourne

Typeset in 10.5/12 pt New Baskerville

National Library of Australia
Cataloguing-in-publication data

McDonnell, Ian.
    Festival and special event management.

    Includes index.
    ISBN 0 471 33934 2.

    1. Festivals — Management. 2. Promotion of special events
    — Management. I. Allen, Johnny. II. O'Toole, William.
    III. Title.

394.26068

Cover photograph: Australian Picture Library

Printed in Singapore
10 9 8 7 6 5 4 3 2

PREFACE

Each year in January, February and March, events occur in New South Wales and Victoria that dominate the media, fill airline seats and hotel rooms, colour the streets, and help shape the identity of their host cities all year round.

The Sydney Gay and Lesbian Mardi Gras was born out of a street march and protest against police discrimination in Sydney's Oxford Street in 1978. It quickly grew into a celebration attracting interest well beyond the gay community, as it captured the spirit of cheeky extroversion and in-your-face hedonism of Sydney. The original Mardi Gras street parade has now grown into the month-long Sydney Gay and Lesbian Festival, which the organisers justifiably tout as the largest gay and lesbian event in the world. It has become a major community event, as gay clubs and societies, travel agents, hairdressers, costume designers, dancers and satirists combine to put on the city's biggest annual street parade and party. A crowd estimated at more than 500 000 people lines Oxford Street to view and cheer the parade, which is followed by an all-night dance party at the old Sydney Showgrounds.

Organisers have not been slow to tout the event's economic and tourism significance to Sydney. An economic impact evaluation study (Marsh & Greenfield 1993) revealed 3511 interstate visitors, 2158 international visitors and a total impact on the New South Wales economy of more than $12 million. The festival is not without its detractors, most famously the Reverend Fred Nile, but it is an undeniable feature of Sydney's cultural life and international tourist profile.

Meanwhile, in almost the same time frame, Sydney's rival Melbourne plays host to a very different event, both in style and conception. The Australian Formula One Grand Prix was lured away from Adelaide in 1992 with the backing of Victorian Premier Jeff Kennett, ambitious for his State to dominate the Australian events scene and for Melbourne to make its mark by hosting a major international event. It forms part of the international formula one racing circuit, with a global television audience of 500 million (Kyriakopoulos 1996).

The grand prix track has taken over a section of Albert Park on the edge of the city, which has not pleased everyone and has created a significant strand of community opposition to the event. However, the distinctive black and white check insignia of the race has dominated Melbourne's streets and restaurants for the event; in 1996, 154 000 spectators spilled out into the surrounding streets and suburbs of Melbourne. Overall, the event has been judged a success by the organisers, the public and the media:

> ■ Motor racing is quintessentially macho, loud and fast, with an abundance of ornamental women on hand. It is a celebration of the politically incorrect: precious fossil fuels are burnt by the gallon and the whole event is sponsored for the most part by tobacco companies and, this year, Melbourne's toll freeway project. Yet the crowd lapped it up, and the protestors, whose rallies outside the arena were overwhelmed by the enormity of the event, faded away without incident (Kyriakopoulos 1996). ■

A few weeks earlier, in mid-January, another event takes place in the northern New South Wales city of Tamworth. The Australasian Country Music Festival and Awards began in 1972 as an awards ceremony in Tamworth Town Hall. Locals still recall the days when a bell had to be rung outside in the street to round up a sufficient audience to stage the awards ceremony. The festival now attracts an estimated 50 000 visitors and contributes $40 million to the city's economy. For example, motels and restaurants on the New England Highway from Newcastle to the Queensland border share in the tourism bonanza. Attractions such as the Country Collection Wax Museum, Roll of Renown, Hands of Fame, the giant golden guitar and the guitar-shaped swimming pool demonstrate Tamworth's status as the country music capital of Australia. Recording studios, syndicated radio programs, and publications such as *Capital News* and the *Country Music Directory* help to support an economy based on country music. A series of monthly concerts, the Tamworth Country Theatre, caters for the busloads of tourists arriving throughout the year for the Tamworth country music experience. They even arrive at a guitar-shaped visitor centre. The organisers' original goal was to create an identity for an otherwise undistinguished town and to reverse the summer flow of Tamworth's residents to the coast. Through the dedicated and professional development of the event, they have certainly achieved these goals and, in the words of local festival observer Nick Erby, 'Tamworth now has a second Christmas every January'.

These three events, which are discussed in later chapters, illustrate in various ways the power of events to raise the profile of their host cities, attract visitors, deliver economic benefits and create jobs. They also illustrate the various origins of events, ranging from a community celebration growing out of protest, to an international event supported for political and economic ends. They all raise issues of costs and benefits, and of the impact on their host communities. They also serve as models for event management, development and marketing.

Festival and Special Event Management examines these and other aspects of events in the Australian context. In part one, 'Event creation and development', the reasons human societies create events and the events culture that has evolved in contemporary Australia are examined, as are the range and types of events and their impacts on their host communities, environment and economy. In part two, 'Event marketing and management', a methodology for the strategic management of events is illustrated by an examination of the processes involved in developing, planning, implementing and marketing events. The third part of the book, 'Event administration', examines sponsorship and other sources of funds, and provides guidance on budgeting and financial control mechanisms. Information is also provided on general administrative issues such as contracts, payments, taxation, insurance, copyright and risk management. Part four, 'Event coordination', covers such topics as operations, stage management, and the process of monitoring and evaluating events and reporting back to stakeholders.

The book is amply illustrated throughout with Australian case studies, which assist the reader to relate the theory of events management to the real world of events practice, with all its challenges, frustrations and rewards. The book provides the reader with both a tool for greater understanding of events management and a framework for planning and implementing events.

By its very nature, events management is a creative process, and by drawing on the body of knowledge in the field, it is hoped that the reader will in turn contribute to the future of this young and exciting industry.

REFERENCES

Kyriakopoulos, Vikki 1996, 'And the winner is… Melbourne', *The Bulletin*, 19 March, p. 86.

Marsh & Greenfield 1993, *Sydney Gay and Lesbian Mardi Gras: An Economic Study*, Sydney Gay and Lesbian Marid Gras Ltd, Sydney.

ABOUT THE AUTHORS

Ian McDonnell, MA, is a lecturer at the University of Technology, Sydney's School of Leisure and Tourism Studies, and specialises in the management and marketing of tourism and leisure services. Prior to becoming an academic, Ian held a managerial position for many years with Qantas. In this position he lived and worked in northern and western Australia, south-east Asia, the south Pacific and Europe.

Johnny Allen's lifelong career in events ranges from being codirector of the original Nimbin Aquarius Festival in 1973, to events manager for Sydney's Darling Harbour, and devising an events strategy for the New South Wales Government as Special Events Manager for Tourism New South Wales. Johnny currently teaches events management at the University of Technology, Sydney, where he has established a centre for events management training and research.

William O'Toole has been involved in creating and organising events for more than 20 years. His interest has always been in the use of events and festivals to create a unique Australian environment and culture. His primary field of work is in Australian music, including concert promotion and music festivals. William created and manages the music group Sirocco and, over 15 years, has toured with the group to most major festivals in Australia and throughout Asia. William is currently teaching event management at both the University of New South Wales and the University of Technology, Sydney.

CONTENTS

ACKNOWLEDGEMENTS

William O'Toole wishes to thank the following people for their assistance: Reno Dal, Roger Foley, John Pinder, Port Fairy Folk Festival, Victor Harbour Folk Festival, Woodford Folk Festival, Mark Cavanagh, Di Henry, Musica Viva Australia, Australia–India Council, Luci Rafferty, Northern Rivers Folk Festival.

The authors and publisher wish to thank the following people and institutions for permission to reproduce material covered by copyright.

Figures

P. 59 (figure 4.1): *Management*, 5th edn by Robbins/Coulter, © 1996. Reprinted by permission of Prentice-Hall, Inc., Upper Saddle River, NJ; p. 60: S. P. Robbins, *Management*, 1997, Prentice Hall of Australia ©; pp. 66, 68: James A. F. Stoner, *Management in Australia*, 1985, Prentice Hall of Australia ©; p. 85 (figure 5.1): *Australian Human Resources Management*, 2nd edn, R. Clark, McGraw-Hill Book Company, Sydney, 1992, p. 236; p. 85 (figure 5.2): Royal Botanic Gardens Sydney and Domain; p. 93: Reproduced from Robbins and Mukerji, *Managing Organisations: New Challenges and Perspectives*, 2nd edn, with the permission of Prentice Hall of Australia Pty Ltd. © 1994; pp. 113, 124, 128, 134: Michael Morgan, *Marketing for Leisure and Tourism*, Prentice Hall, 1996; p. 119 (figure 6.3): *Fundamentals of Marketing*, 3rd edn, Stanton, Miller and Layton, McGraw-Hill Book Company, Sydney, 1994, p. 97; pp. 121, 127 (figure 6.9): C. H. Lovelock, et al., *Services Marketing Australia and New Zealand*, 1998, Prentice Hall of Australia ©; pp. 191–2: Courtesy: Folk Federation of South Australia Inc.; p. 123 (figure 6.6): Ansoff, 1951, 'Strategies for diversification', *Harvard Business Review*, Sept.–Oct., pp.113–24; p. 202: Port Fairy Folk Festival; pp. 220–1, 223, 228: Woodford Folk Festival; p. 224: Northern Rivers Folk Festival, Lismore NSW; p. 238: A. Volders (1996) Port Fairy Folk Festival 1996 Audience Survey; p. 252: Roger Foley, Fogg Productions ©; pp. 282–3: Cultural Minister's Council, Statistics Working Group, *Measuring the Impact of Festivals*, National Centre for Culture and Recreation Statistics, Australian Bureau of Statistics, April 1997, pp. 11–12. Commonwealth of Australia copyright reproduced by permission.

Text

P. 32 (table 2.3): 'An economic evaluation of the Adelaide Grand Prix', in Syme, Shaw, Fenton, Mueller (eds) 1989, *The Planning and Evaluation of Hallmark Events*, Avebury, Aldershot, p. 183; p. 59 (table 4.1): *Management*, 5th edn by Robbins/Coulter, © 1996. Reprinted by permission of Prentice-Hall, Inc., Upper Saddle River, NJ; p. 160: *Hallmark Tourist Events: Impacts, Management and Planning*. Copyright John Wiley & Sons Limited. Reproduced with permission; p. 197: from 'Legal issues in sports marketing', by Lydia Dowse and Luci Rafferty in Mark Fewell (ed.), *Sports Law: A Practical Guide*, LBC Information Services, 1995, pp. 57–64. Reproduced with the permission of LBC Information Services.

PART 1

EVENT CREATION AND DEVELOPMENT

1

What are
special events?

LEARNING OBJECTIVES

After studying this chapter, you should be able to:

- define special events

- demonstrate an awareness of why special events have evolved in human society

- describe the role of special events in Australia, and the Australian tradition of special events

- describe the rise and effect of the community arts movement on special events

- understand the growth of State events corporations and the emergence of an events industry

- distinguish between different types of special events

- discuss the attributes and knowledge requirements of a special events manager

- describe the consolidation of the special events industry in Australia.

Historical events		Celebrations, festivals and events

Historical events | **Celebrations, festivals and events**

Arrival of the First Fleet — 1788

First Anniversary Day celebrations — Other States begin to celebrate their own Foundation days

Gold rushes 1850s — 1850, 1860

1861 — First Melbourne Cup

Development of country show circuit
Company and trade union picnics
Development of Australian Rules football

Federation — 1901 — Inauguration of Federation of Australia, Sydney

World War I 1914–18 — 1914, 1918

Development of surf lifesaving carnivals and test cricket matches; growth of Anzac Day

World War II 1939–45 — 1939, 1945, 1950

1954 — Visit of Queen Elizabeth II

1956 — Melbourne Olympic Games — Growth of civic festivals

1959

1960 — First Adelaide Festival of the Arts

Australian involvement in Vietnam War 1962–72 — 1970, 1971 — Early rock festivals

Whitlam Government 1972–75 — 1972 — First Tamworth Country Music Festival

1973 — Nimbin Aquarius Festival

1974 — Sydney Opera House opening

1975, 1976, 1977

Community arts movement
Multicultural festivals

1978 — First Gay and Lesbian Mardi Gras

1979, 1980, 1981

1982 — Commonwealth Games, Brisbane

1983

1984 — Victoria's Sesquicentenary

1980s economic boom — 1985 — First Adelaide Grand Prix

1986 — America's Cup defence, Fremantle

1987 — First Maleny (later Woodford) Folk Festival

Australia's Bicentenary
Tall Ships visit
Opening of Darling Harbour, Sydney
Expo 88, Brisbane
First Aboriginal Survival Day concert, Sydney

1988, 1989, 1990

1991 — First Gold Coast Indy

1992 — Opening of Southbank, Brisbane, and Southgate, Melbourne

1993, 1994, 1995

1996 — Australian Formula One Grand Prix moves to Melbourne

1997 — Opening of Crown Casino, Melbourne

1998 — Olympic Festival of the Dreaming

1999

2000 — New millennium celebrations and Sydney Olympic Games

2001 — Centenary of Federation celebrations

Figure 1.1
*Australian
event time
line*

SPECIAL EVENTS AS BENCHMARKS FOR OUR LIVES

Since the dawn of time, human beings have found ways to mark important events in their lives: the changing of the seasons, the phases of the moon, and the renewal of life each spring. From the Aboriginal corroboree and Chinese New Year to the Dionysian rites of ancient Greece and the European carnival tradition of the Middle Ages, myths and rituals have been created to interpret cosmic happenings. To the present day, behind well-known figures such as Old Father Time and Santa Claus lie old myths, archetypes and ancient celebrations. The first Australians used storytelling, dance and song to transmit their culture from generation to generation. Their ceremonies were, and continue to be, important occasions in the life of the community, where cultural meaning is shared and affirmed. Similarly in most agrarian societies, rituals were developed that marked the coming of the seasons and the sowing and harvesting of crops.

Both in private and in public, people feel the need to mark the important occasions in their lives, to celebrate the key moments. Coming of age, for example, is often marked by a rite of passage, examples of which are the tribal initiation ceremony, the Jewish bar mitzvah and the suburban twenty-first birthday.

At the public level, momentous events become the milestones by which people measure their private lives. We may talk about things happening 'before the recession', in the same way that an earlier generation talked of marrying 'before the Depression' or being born 'after the War'. Occasional events — Australia's Bicentenary, the Sydney Olympics and the new millennium — help to mark eras and define milestones.

Even in the high-tech era of global media, when many people have lost touch with the common religious beliefs and social norms of the past, we still need larger social events to mark the local and domestic details of our lives.

THE MODERN AUSTRALIAN TRADITION OF CELEBRATIONS

In the cultural collision between Aboriginal people and the first Europeans, new traditions were formed alongside the old. Probably the first 'event' in Australia after the arrival of the First Fleet was a bush party to celebrate the coming ashore of the women convicts in 1788:

> ■ Meanwhile, most of the sailors on *Lady Penrhyn* applied to her master, Captain William Sever, for an extra ration of rum 'to make merry with upon the women quitting the ship'. Out came the pannikins, down went the rum, and before long the drunken tars went off to join the convicts in pursuit of the women, so that, Bowes remarked, 'it is beyond my abilities to give a just description of the scene of debauchery and riot that ensued during the night'. It was the first bush party in Australia, with 'some swearing, others quarrelling, others singing' (Hughes 1987, pp. 88–9). ■

From these inauspicious beginnings the early colonists slowly started to evolve celebrations that were tailored to their new environment, so far from Georgian Britain. Hull (1984) traces the history of these early celebrations, noting the beginnings of a national day some 30 years later:

> ■ Governor Macquarie declared the 26th of January 1818 a public holiday — convicts were given the day off, a ration of one pound of fresh meat was made for each of them, there was a military review, a salute of 30 guns, a dinner for the officers and a ball for the colony society. ■

This may have been the first festival celebrated by the new inhabitants of Australia. Although 'Anniversary Day', as it was known, was not to become a public holiday for another 20 years, the official celebration of the founding of the colony had begun with the direct involvement and patronage of the government that exists to this day. In contrast to government-organised celebrations, settlers throughout the nineteenth century entertained themselves with balls, shows and travelling entertainments as a diversion from the serious business of work and survival.

At the turn of the century, the celebration of Australia's Federation captured the prevailing mood of optimistic patriotism:

> ■ At the turn of the year 1900–1 the city of Sydney went mad with joy. For a few days hope ran so high that poets and prophets declared Australia to be on the threshold of a new golden age... from early morning on 1 January 1901 trams, trains and ferry boats carried thousands of people into the city for the greatest day in their history: the inauguration of the Commonwealth of Australia. It was to be a people's festival (Clark 1981, p. 177). ■

At the beginning of the twentieth century, the new inhabitants had come to terms with the landscape of Australia, and the democratic ritual of the picnic had gained mass popularity. This extended to guilds, unions and company workers, as demonstrated by the following description of the annual picnic of the employees of Sydney boot and shoe manufacturers McMurtie and Company, at Clontarf in 1906:

> ■ 'The sweet strains of piano, violin and cornet... added zest and enjoyment to the festive occasion', said the *Advisor*. 'Laughter producers were also in evidence, several of the company wearing comical-looking hats and false noses so that even at the commencement of the day's proceedings hilarity and enjoyment was assured.' The enjoyment continued as the party disembarked to the strain of bagpipes, and the sporting programme began... The 'little ones' were provided with 'toys, spades, balls and lollies'. The shooting gallery was well patronised, and when darkness fell dancing went on in the beautiful dancing hall. Baby Houston danced a Scotch reel to the music of bagpipes. Miss Robinson sang *Underneath the Watermelon Vine*, and little Ruth Bailey danced a jig.

At 8 pm, the whistle blew and the homeward journey commenced with 'music up till the last' and a final rendering of *Auld Lang Syne* as the *Erina* arrived at the Quay (Pearl 1974). ■

However, Australians had to wait until after World War II before a home-grown form of celebration took hold across the nation. In the 1940s and 1950s, city and town festivals were established, which created a common and enduring format. Even today, it is a safe assumption that any festival with an Aboriginal or floral name, and that includes a 'Festival Queen' competition, street parade, outdoor art exhibition and sporting event, dates back to this period. Sydney's Waratah Festival (later replaced by the Sydney Festival), Melbourne's Moomba, Ballarat's Begonia Festival, Grafton's Jacaranda Festival, Bowral's Tulip Time, Newcastle's Mattara Festival, and Toowoomba's Carnival of Flowers all date back to the prolific era of local pride and involvement after World War II. Moomba and Mattara both adopted Aboriginal names, the latter word meaning 'hand of friendship'.

Holding such a festival became a badge of civic pride, in the way that building a School of Arts hall had done in an earlier era, or constructing an Olympic swimming pool would do in the 1950s and 1960s. These festivals gave the cities and towns a sense of identity and distinction, and became a focus for community groups and charity fundraising. It is a tribute to their importance to communities that many of these festivals still continue after half a century.

Alongside this movement of community festivals was another very powerful model. In 1947 the Edinburgh Festival was founded as part of the post-war spirit of reconstruction and renewal. In Australia, the Festival of Perth (founded in 1953) and the Adelaide Festival of the Arts (founded in 1960) were based on this inspiring model. The influence of the Edinburgh Festival proved to be enduring, as shown by the resurgence of arts festivals in Sydney, Melbourne and Brisbane in the 1980s and 1990s.

By the 1970s, however, with the coming to power of the Whitlam Government and the formation of the Australia Council, new cultural directions were unleashed which were to change the face of festivals in Australia.

The Community Arts Board of the Australia Council, under the leadership of Ros Bower, developed a strategy aimed at giving a voice to the voiceless and taking arts and festivals into the suburbs and towns of Australia. Often for the first time, migrants, workers and Aboriginal people were encouraged to participate in a new cultural pluralism which broke down the elitism which had governed the arts in much of rural and suburban Australia. Sensing the unique cultural challenge faced by Australia, Bower (1981) wrote:

■ In terms of our national cultural objectives, the re-integration of the artist into the community is of crucial importance. Australia lacks a coherent cultural background. The artist needs to become the spokesman, the interpreter, the image-maker and the prophet. He cannot do it in isolation or from an ivory tower. He must do it by working with the people. He must help them to piece together their local history, their local traditions, their folk-lore, the drama and the visual imagery of their lives. And in doing this he will enrich and give identity to his work as an artist. The arts will cease to be imitative, or preoccupied with making big splashes in little 'cultured' pools. They will be integrated more closely with our lives, our history, our unique environment. They will be experimental and exploring forces within the broader cultural framework. ■

The 1970s saw not only the emergence of multiculturalism and the 'new age' movement, but also the forging of the community arts movement and a new and diverse range of festivals across Australia. Some examples of the rich diversity spawned by this period are the Aquarius Festival staged by the Australian Union of Students at Nimbin in northern New South Wales, the Lygon Street Festival of Italian culture in Melbourne's Carlton, the Come Out young people's festival held in alternate years to the Adelaide Festival, the Carnivale celebration of multiculturalism across Sydney and New South Wales and Sydney's Gay and Lesbian Mardi Gras. Festivals became part of the cultural landscape, and became connected again to people's needs and lives. Every community, it seemed, had something to celebrate and the tools with which to create its own festival.

THE BIRTH OF AN EVENTS INDUSTRY

Through the 1980s and 1990s, certain seminal events set the pattern for the contemporary events industry as we know it today. The Commonwealth Games in Brisbane in 1982 ushered in a new era of maturity and prominence for that city and a new breed of sporting events. The Commonwealth Games also initiated a career in ceremonies and celebrations for a former ABC rock show producer, Ric Birch, which led to his taking a key role in the closing ceremonies at the Los Angeles and Barcelona Olympics. The Olympic Games in Los Angeles in 1984 demonstrated that major events could be economically viable. They managed to combine a Hollywood-style spectacular with a sporting event in a manner which had not been done before, but which would set a standard for all similar events in future. The production and marketing skills of the television industry brought the Olympics to an audience wider than ever before. Television also demonstrated the power of a major sporting event to bring increased profile and economic benefits to a city and to an entire country.

The entrepreneurs of the 1980s economic boom in Australia soon picked up on this, and the America's Cup defence in Perth and Fremantle in 1986–87 was treated as an opportunity to put Perth on the map and to attract major economic and tourism benefits to Western Australia. By 1988, there was a boom in special events, with Australia's Bicentenary seen by many as a major commemorative program and vehicle for tourism. This boom was matched by governments setting up State events corporations, thereby giving public sector support to special events as never before. In Brisbane, the success of Expo 88 rivalled the Bicentennial activities in Sydney, and Adelaide managed a coup by staging the first Australian Formula One Grand Prix.

The Bicentenary caused Australians to pause and reflect on the Australian identity. It also changed forever the nature of our public celebrations:

> ■ I would argue that the remarkable legacy of 1988 is the public event. It is now a regular feature of Australian life. We gather for fireworks, for welcome-home marches for athletes and other Australians who have achieved success. We go to large urban spaces like the Domain for opera, rock and symphonic music in our hundreds of thousands. The Sydney Festival attracts record numbers. The Gay Mardi Gras is an international phenomenon... Whatever the nature of debate about values, identity and imagery, one certainty is that Australians are in love with high-quality public events that are fun and offer to extend the range and experience of being Australian (McCarthy 1998). ■

The Bicentenary also left a legacy of public spaces dedicated to celebrations and special events and of governments supporting the social and economic benefits of such events. Sydney's Darling Harbour opened to welcome the Tall Ships on 16 January 1988, and provided the city with a major leisure centre. Darling Harbour incorporates dedicated celebrations areas, a festival marketplace and convention and exhibition centres, all adjacent to the Sydney Entertainment Centre and the Powerhouse and National Maritime museums. Likewise, Brisbane's riverside Expo 88 site was converted into the Southbank Parklands, and Melbourne followed suit with the Southgate development on the Yarra River.

Whatever the economic causes of it were, the recession of the early 1990s put a dampener on the party mood and the seemingly endless growth of events. That is, until 4.20 a.m. on 23 September 1993 when those memorable words were spoken by International Olympic President Juan Antonio Samaranch: 'And the winner is... Sydney!'

It was said by many that the recession ended the day Sydney was awarded the Olympic Games of the new millennium. Certainly it meant that the events industry could once more look forward with optimism, as though the recession of the 1990s had been a mere pause for breath. Events corporations formed in the late 1980s and early 1990s started to demonstrate that economic benefits could be generated through special events. This led to competition between the States for major events, with the Victorian Premier, Jeff Kennett, taking the Australian Formula One Grand Prix from Adelaide, the Australian Motorcycle Grand Prix from Sydney, and hosting, in Melbourne, the Three Tenors concert, the Bledisloe Cup and the Presidents Cup golf tournament. New South Wales fought back, with Sydney taking the AFI Awards from Melbourne and hosting the musicals *Showboat* and *The Boy From Oz*. Sporting and cultural events, always part of the landscape, had become weapons in an events war fuelled by the media. Australia was set to approach the end of the twentieth century with a competitive events climate dominated by the Sydney Olympics, the new millennium and the Centenary of Federation celebrations in 2001.

WHAT ARE SPECIAL EVENTS?

The term 'special events' has been coined to describe specific rituals, presentations, performances or celebrations that are consciously planned and created to mark special occasions or to achieve particular social, cultural or corporate goals and objectives. Special events can include national days and celebrations, important civic occasions, unique cultural performances, major sporting fixtures, corporate functions, trade promotions and product launches. It seems at times that special events are everywhere; they have become a growth industry. The field of special events is now so vast that it is impossible to provide a definition that includes all varieties and shades of events. In his groundbreaking work on the typology of events, Getz (1997, p. 4) suggests that special events are best defined by their context. He offers two definitions, one from the point of view of the event organiser, and the other from that of the customer, or guest:

1. A special event is a one-time or infrequently occurring event outside normal programs or activities of the sponsoring or organizing body.
2. To the customer or guest, a special event is an opportunity for a leisure, social or cultural experience outside the normal range of choices or beyond everyday experience.

Among the attributes that he believes create the special atmosphere are festive spirit, uniqueness, quality, authenticity, tradition, hospitality, theme and symbolism.

■ Figure 1.2
Categorisation of events

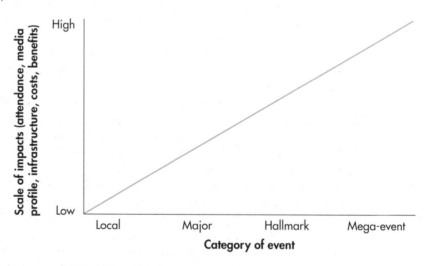

TYPES OF EVENTS

Special events are often characterised according to their size and scale. Common categories are mega-events, hallmark events and major events, though definitions are not exact and distinctions become blurred. Events are also classified according to their purpose or to the particular sector to which they belong, for example public, sporting, tourism and corporate events, which will be explored further in chapter 3. In this text, we will be examining all those 'events' that are being held by the emerging events industry, and we will use the term 'event' to cover all the following categories.

◾ Mega-events

Mega-events are those that are so large they affect whole economies and reverberate in the global media. They include Olympic Games and World Fairs, but it is difficult for many other events to fit into this category. Getz (1997, p. 6) defines them:

> ◾ Their volume should exceed 1 million visits, their capital costs should be at least $500 million, and their reputation should be of a 'must see' event ... Mega-events, by way of their size or significance, are those that yield extraordinarily high levels of tourism, media coverage, prestige, or economic impact for the host community or destination. ◾

Hall (1992, p. 5), another researcher in the field of events and tourism, offers this definition:

> ◾ Mega-events such as World Fairs and Expositions, the World Soccer Cup final, or the Olympic Games, are events which are expressly targeted at the international tourism market and may be suitably described as 'mega' by virtue of their size in terms of attendance, target market, level of public financial involvement, political effects, extent of television coverage, construction of facilities, and impact on economic and social fabric of the host community. ◾

By these definitions, the Sydney Olympic Games in 2000 may be Australia's first true mega-event. The Melbourne Olympics in 1956 belonged to an earlier era of far less extensive media coverage and smaller television audiences, although in relative terms it may well qualify as a 'mega-event' of its era. Even Brisbane's Expo 88 was officially a 'B' class Expo, and events such as the Commonwealth Games in Brisbane in 1982 and the America's Cup defence in Perth and Fremantle in 1986–87 would struggle to meet Getz's criteria. Australia's Bicentenary celebrations in 1988, if taken as a national event, would probably qualify, as may the Centenary of Federation celebrations to be staged in 2001.

◾ Hallmark *events*

The term 'hallmark events' refers to those events that become so identified with the spirit or ethos of a town, city or region that they become synonymous with the name of the place, and gain widespread recognition and awareness. Tourism researcher Ritchie (1984, p. 2) defines them as:

> ◾ Major one-time or recurring events of limited duration, developed primarily to enhance awareness, appeal and profitability of a tourism destination in the short term and/or long term. Such events rely for their success on uniqueness, status, or timely significance to create interest and attract attention. ◾

Classic examples of hallmark events are the Carnival in Rio de Janeiro, known throughout the world as an expression of the vitality and exuberance of that city, the Tour de France, the Oktoberfest in Munich, Germany, and the Edinburgh Festival in Scotland. Such events, which are identified with the very character of these places and their citizens, bring huge tourist dollars, a strong sense of local pride and international recognition. Getz (1997, pp. 5–6) describes them in terms of their ability to provide a competitive advantage for their host communities:

> ■ The term 'hallmark event' is used to describe a recurring event that possesses such significance, in terms of tradition, attractiveness, image, or publicity, that the event provides the host venue, community, or destination with a competitive advantage. Over time, the event and destination become inseparable. For example Mardi Gras gives New Orleans a competitive advantage by virtue of its high profile. Stratford, Ontario, has taken its tourism theme from the successful Shakespearean Festival. Increasingly, every community and destination needs one or more hallmark events to provide the high levels of media exposure and positive imagery that help to create competitive advantages. ■

Examples in Australia might include the Sydney Gay and Lesbian Mardi Gras, the Australasian Country Music Festival at Tamworth, the Melbourne Cup and the Adelaide Festival, all of which have a degree of international recognition and help to identify the ethos of their host cities.

■ Major *events*

Major events are events that, by their scale and media interest, are capable of attracting significant visitor numbers, media coverage and economic benefits. The Tall Ships visit, hosted by Sydney in 1988 and awarded to Hobart on the occasion of Bass and Flinders' Bicentenary in 1998, provided a focus on maritime heritage as well as attracting international prestige and media. The Grand Australian Sumo Tournament, staged in Melbourne and Sydney in 1997, attracted strong destination promotion in Japan for both host cities. Many top international sporting championships fit into this category, and are increasingly being sought after and bid for by national sporting organisations and governments in the competitive world of international major events.

Cultural events can also be contenders. The Victorian Government was keen to stage the Three Tenors concert in 1997, and major musicals such as *Phantom of the Opera* and *Showboat* reap considerable tourism revenue for their host cities. Betty Churcher, the former director of the National Gallery of Australia, enhanced the reputation of the gallery and helped create a tourism bonanza for Canberra through the staging of 'blockbuster' exhibitions of works by Rubens, Turner and the Surrealists, among others. South Australia has hosted Opera in the Outback and Womadelaide, and Canberra has initiated the National Opera Festival, each place with an eye to positioning itself in the tourism market as well as in the arts world.

In the area of meetings and conventions, international conferences are sought after and bid for by tourist bureaus with the same enthusiasm as major sporting and cultural events. Two major conferences alone — the World Congress of Chemical Engineers in Melbourne in 2001 and the World Congress of Cardiology in Sydney in 2002 — are expected to bring over 13 000 big-spending delegates to Australia.

CONSOLIDATING THE EVENTS INDUSTRY

The growth of events that have a wide variety of purposes and agendas means that the staging of events can now be considered an industry. Moreover, it is one that is capable of generating economic change, social and commercial benefits and employment.

Further indications of the emergence of an events industry, noted by Harris and Griffin (1997), are the formation of industry associations and the establishment of accreditation standards and events training courses. The International Special Events Society (ISES) and the Meetings Industry Association of Australia (MIAA) have both introduced accreditation schemes for members and professionals in the industry. The International Festivals and Events Association (IFEA) has not yet established such a scheme in Australia, but has affiliated branch organisations in most Australian States. A national competency standards study for festivals and events management is currently being undertaken by Culture Recreation Education and Training Australia (CREATE) as part of a project for the entertainment industry. Event modules within larger training packages have also been developed by Industry Training Advisory Boards (ITABS) in the fields of tourism and hospitality, and sport and recreation. The University of Technology, Sydney, and the Victoria University of Technology offer dedicated events management courses. Events units are included in other courses at these and many other educational institutions in Australia.

Harris and Griffin (1997) developed a profile of the education levels and event experience of event managers through a survey of 113 event organisers in Sydney and regional New South Wales:

> ■ As a group, event organisers are relatively highly educated with 56% of those sampled holding a postgraduate, undergraduate or TAFE qualification. The level of event related experience possessed by the sample group was high with 50% having played a significant role in the organisation of an event attracting 10,000 or more people, with a similar number (45%) being involved in organising two (2) or more different types of events. ■

Perry, Foley and Rumpf (1996) described the attributes and knowledge required by event managers based on a survey of the views of 105 managers who attended the Australian Events Conference in Canberra in February

1996. Seven attributes were frequently mentioned, of which vision was listed as the most important, followed closely by leadership, adaptability, and skills in organisation, communication, marketing and people management. Knowledge areas considered most important were project management, budgeting, time management, relating to the media, business planning, human resource management and marketing. The following graph shows some of the results of the survey. Respondents were asked to indicate how strongly they agreed or disagreed with a statement such as: 'An events manager requires skills in project management'. The numbers at the base of the graph show agreement and disagreement, with 1 being 'strongly disagree' and 5 being 'strongly agree'.

Figure 1.3
Knowledge required by event managers — respondents to survey

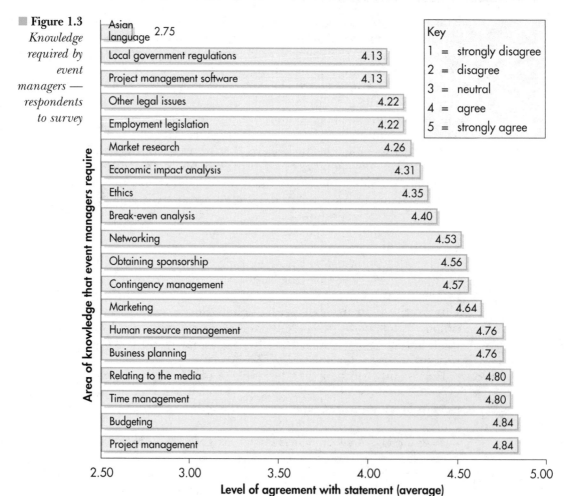

The results of this survey have also been incorporated into the planning of the postgraduate certificate in Events Management offered by Victoria University of Technology.

The emerging events industry, with its needs, challenges and opportunities, will be examined in the following chapters.

Special events perform a powerful role in society, and they have existed throughout human history in all times and all cultures. Aboriginal culture had a rich tradition of rituals and ceremonies prior to the arrival of the Europeans. The events tradition in modern Australia began in a primitive way with the arrival of the First Fleet, and developed through the late eighteenth and nineteenth centuries as the colony prospered and the new inhabitants came to terms with their environment. The ruling elite often decided the form and content of public celebrations, but an alternative tradition of popular celebrations arose from the interests and pursuits of ordinary people. During the twentieth century, changes in society were mirrored by changes in the style of public events. The post-war wave of civic festivals and arts festivals was strongly influenced by the community arts movement in the 1970s, along with multiculturalism and the 'new age' movement. Notions of high culture were challenged by a more pluralistic popular culture, which reinvigorated festivals and community events.

With the coming of the 1980s, governments and the corporate sector began to recognise the economic and promotional value of special events, and State events corporations spearheaded a new level of funding, profile and professionalism. The terms 'mega-events', 'hallmark events' and 'major events' are used to identify those events of large-scale significance and impact. With increasing expansion and corporate involvement, events are emerging as a new growth industry, capable of generating economic benefits and employment.

Questions

1 Why are special events created, and what purpose do they serve in society?

2 Do special events mirror changes in society, or do they have a role in creating and changing values? Give some examples to illustrate your answer.

3 Why have special events emerged so strongly in recent years in Australia?

4 What are the key political, cultural and social trends that determine the current climate of events in Australia, and how would you expect these to influence the nature of events in the coming years?

5 Identify an event in your city or region which has the capacity to be a hallmark event and give your reasons for placing it in this category.

6 What characteristics define an 'industry'? Using these criteria, do you consider that there is an 'events industry' in Australia?

7 Do you agree with the attributes and knowledge areas events managers believe they require? Create a list of your own attributes and skills based on these listings.

CASE STUDY

Resurgence of Australia Day
in New South Wales

In recent times Australia Day has become the nation's largest annual community celebration. The spectacular nature of Australia Day 1988 seemed to release in Australians the ability to express their emotions about their country. Prior to this, such emotion was usually reserved for national sporting events. It is important to note that although Sydney Harbour was the central focus of the world that day, more than 800 metropolitan, regional and rural communities across Australia also conducted outstanding events and in many cases their largest ever celebrations. Australia Day was transformed from a day of remembrance and reflection on the past, to a day of aspiration for the future, celebrating excellence and citizenship. Australia Day celebrations changed almost instantly from formal indoor 'afternoon teas' and speeches to large, outdoor, informal community-participation events, celebrating the land and its people. In Sydney, Darling Harbour and Sydney Harbour became focal points, and in more recent years the entire city and its institutions have become involved in a major way.

Meanwhile, local governments across New South Wales have become involved in a resurgence of Australia Day. In the country, Gunnedah helped initiate this change by conducting a national poetry competition for young people, sporting events, a parade, an Australia Day luncheon for 400 residents, and a flag-raising and citizenship ceremony. In 1987 its success attracted an ABC film crew to the area, resulting in a half-hour prime-time television program on Australia Day celebrations. In 1988, Warringah Shire encouraged its service clubs and organisations to become involved, and three large-scale breakfasts were commenced at Dee Why Beach, Newport Beach and Beacon Hill. More than 20 000 people now participate each year. Sutherland, with the assistance of corporate sponsorship, built its Australia Day celebrations into a huge three-day, three-night event. In 1998 the shire initiated an annual Opera on the Beach event for a large family audience at South Cronulla Beach. Cobar conducts a breakfast ceremony and a triathlon. Temora builds a beach for a beach volleyball competition, Hay holds a surf carnival, and Bourke holds its celebrations around a community swimming pool in the early evening twilight.

All ceremonies still have the participation of their State and federal politicians. However, the underlying theme is informality. The aim is to highlight citizenship and new citizens, to acknowledge excellence through the Citizen and Young Citizen of the Year awards (which are modelled on their national counterparts) and, of course, to provide a good time through entertainment and festive food.

The Ambassador Program has added to the success of Australia Day in New South Wales by including an outstanding Australian achiever in ceremonies held throughout the State. In 1997 more than 140 ambassadors, such as Fiona Coote, Vince Sorrenti, Margaret Whitlam, Laurie Daly and Peter Cousens, participated in more than 160 ceremonies. In 1998, seven of Australia's most famous artists, including Margaret Olley and Ginger Riley, painted their interpretation of Australia. The Australia Day Address has also been introduced in order to stimulate debate on Australia as a nation. The 1997 address was given by Thomas Keneally, and the 1998 address by Peter Garrett.

Local government has played an important role in the resurgence of Australia Day. Nearly all local governments have formed an Australia Day Committee, and value the role of Australia Day events in their local communities. Many have designated officers as Australia Day coordinators and special event organisers, who play a significant role in cultural and social change through the quality of their work and the events they produce.

The Australia Day Council of New South Wales has maintained strong links to government, through the Premier's Department, and to corporate Australia. Over $1 million in cash sponsorship and more than $3 million of in-kind sponsorship has been raised annually over the last five years. The Australia Day Council operates with a board of directors whose members each chair committees that draw on over 100 expert representatives. These representatives assist in the development of Australia Day activities statewide. As the new millennium approaches, Australia Day is a strong, broad-based day of community celebration. To continue to build Australia Day and to achieve a true national reconciliation, it may be important to change Australia Day to another date with the commencement of the twenty-first century.

John Trevillian, AM
Executive Director
Australia Day Council of New South Wales

Questions

1 Have you been aware of a resurgence in the celebration of Australia Day in your city or region? If so, provide details of the events held. If not, try to describe your community's attitudes to Australia Day.

2 What factors have contributed to Australia Day celebrations becoming less formal?

3 Devise an Australia Day program for your local community that will attract wide interest and participation.

4 What is the role of local government in the Australia Day celebrations in your area? What is the organisational structure of the group which plans the events, and how well does it represent the local community?

5 Do you think Australia Day should be moved from 26 January? If so, what other date would you choose, and why?

REFERENCES

Bower, Rosalie 1981, 'Community arts — what is it?', *Caper*, vol. 10, Community Arts Board, Australia Council, Sydney.

Clark, Manning 1981, *A History of Australia*, vol. 5, Melbourne University Press, Melbourne.

Getz, Donald 1997, *Event Management and Event Tourism*, Cognizant Communication Corporation, New York.

Hall, Colin Michael 1992, *Hallmark Tourist Events: Impacts, Management and Planning*, Belhaven Press, London.

Harris, Robert & Griffin, Tony 1997, *Tourism Events Training Audit*, prepared for Tourism New South Wales Events Unit, Sydney.

Hughes, Robert 1987, *The Fatal Shore*, Collins Harvill, London.

Hull, Andrea 1984, 'Feasting on festas and festivals', paper delivered to the Association of Festivals Conference at Caulfield Arts Centre, Victoria.

McCarthy, Wendy 1998, 'Day we came of age', *Sun-Herald*, 25 January, p. 46.

Pearl, Cyril 1974, *Australia's Yesterdays*, Readers Digest, Sydney.

Perry, M., Foley, P. & Rumpf, P. 1996, 'Event management: an emerging challenge in Australian education', *Festival Management & Event Tourism*, vol. 4, pp. 85–93.

Ritchie, J. R. Brent 1984, 'Assessing the impact of hallmark events: conceptual and research issues', *Journal of Travel Research*, vol. 23, no. 1, pp. 2–11.

The impacts of
special events

LEARNING OBJECTIVES

After studying this chapter, you should be able to:

- identify the major impacts which events have on their stakeholders and host communities

- explain how events can be used to strengthen community pride and values

- anticipate the social impact of events and plan for positive outcomes

- understand the management of crowd behaviour

- describe the physical and environmental impacts of events

- understand the political context of events

- describe the ways that events can be used to increase tourist visits and length of stay

- balance the economic costs and benefits of staging an event

- demonstrate an understanding of the role of the event manager in balancing the impacts of events.

BALANCING THE IMPACTS OF EVENTS

Events have a range of impacts — both positive and negative — on their host communities and stakeholders. It is the task of the event manager to identify and predict these impacts and then manage them to achieve the best outcome for all parties, so that in the balance the overall impact of the event is positive. To achieve this, all foreseeable positive impacts must be developed and maximised, and negative impacts countered. Often negative impacts can be addressed through awareness and intervention — good planning is always critical. Ultimately, the success of the event depends on the event manager achieving this positive balance sheet and communicating it to a range of stakeholders.

Great emphasis is often placed on the financial impacts of events, partly because of the need of employers and governments to meet budget goals and justify expenditure, and partly because such impacts are most easily assessed. However, the event manager should not lose sight of the full range of impacts resulting from the event, and the need to identify, describe and manage them. It is also important to realise that different impacts require different means of assessment. For example, social and cultural benefits play a vital role in calculating the overall impact of an event, but describing them may require a narrative rather than a statistical approach. Some of the complex factors that need to be taken into account when assessing the impacts of events are discussed in this chapter.

■ Table 2.1
The impacts of events

SPHERE OF EVENT	POSITIVE IMPACTS	NEGATIVE IMPACTS
Social and cultural	• Shared experience • Revitalising traditions • Building community pride • Validation of community groups • Increased community participation • Introducing new and challenging ideas • Expanding cultural perspectives	• Community alienation • Manipulation of community • Negative community image • Bad behaviour • Substance abuse • Social dislocation • Loss of amenity
Physical and environmental	• Showcasing the environment • Providing models for best practice • Increasing environmental awareness • Infrastructure legacy • Improved transport and communications • Urban transformation and renewal	• Environmental damage • Pollution • Destruction of heritage • Noise disturbance • Traffic congestion

Table 2.1
(continued)

SPHERE OF EVENT	POSITIVE IMPACTS	NEGATIVE IMPACTS
Political	• International prestige • Improved profile • Promotion of investment • Social cohesion • Development of administrative skills	• Risk of event failure • Misallocation of funds • Lack of accountability • Propagandising • Loss of community ownership and control • Legitimation of ideology
Tourism and economic	• Destinational promotion and increased tourist visits • Extended length of stay • Higher yield • Increased tax revenue • Job creation	• Community resistance to tourism • Loss of authenticity • Damage to reputation • Exploitation • Inflated prices • Opportunity costs

(**Source:** *Adapted from Hall 1989*)

SOCIAL AND CULTURAL IMPACTS

All events have a direct social and cultural impact on their participants, and sometimes on their wider host communities as outlined by Hall (1989) and Getz (1997). This may be as simple as a shared entertainment experience, as is created by a sporting event or concert. Other impacts include increased pride, which results from some community events and celebrations of national days, and the validation of particular groups in the community, which is the purpose of many events designed for seniors and disabled people. Some events leave a legacy of greater awareness and participation in particular sporting and cultural activities. Others broaden people's cultural horizons, exposing them to new and challenging people, customs, or ideas. The Grand Australian Sumo Tournament, held in Sydney and Melbourne in 1997, introduced the Japanese Sumo tradition, with its strong religious and cultural associations, to Australian audiences. It went beyond the bounds of a sporting event, and became a genuine Japanese–Australian cultural exchange, with strong awareness levels in both countries. In the same year, the ceremonies for the handover of Hong Kong from Great Britain to China had great symbolic importance for these countries. World media coverage of the ceremonies provoked emotions ranging from pride to sadness, jubilation to apprehension.

Events have the power to challenge the imagination and to explore possibilities. The greening of Swanston Street, implemented in Melbourne for Victoria's Sesquicentenary in 1984, offered a whimsical reminder of the pace of change in the urban environment. One evening, Swanston Street was closed to traffic and truckloads of turf were laid over the road surface to green the street. Workers arrived in the city the next morning to find the street was temporarily transformed into a green park, with people enjoying picnics on the grass as the trams plied their usual route through the centre of the street. This concept was innovative and fun, but also allowed participants the opportunity to explore potential changes to the environment in the unthreatening context of a temporary event.

Research suggests that local communities often value the 'feel-good' aspects of hallmark events, and are prepared to put up with temporary inconvenience and disruption because of the excitement which they generate, and the long-term expectation of improved facilities and profile. A study by Soutar and McLeod (1989) of Fremantle residents' views of the America's Cup indicated that the event was perceived as improving the quality of life in Fremantle, and providing the foundation for long-term improvement in the city's fortunes. Most residents said they would like to see another America's Cup or similar event in Fremantle in the future. The Australian Formula One Grand Prix in Adelaide was also popular among residents; Arnold et al. (1989) reported that 'The Grand Prix in 1985 set Adelaide alive... The spirit infected all of us, including large numbers of people who in "normal" times might be expected to be against the notion of this garish, noisy, polluting advertising circus.'

However, such events can have negative social impacts. Arnold et al. (1989) showed that in the five weeks around the 1985 Australian Formula One Grand Prix in Adelaide, there was a 34 per cent increase in the number of road accident casualties compared with the same period for the previous five years. Taking into account the rising trend of road accident casualties over those years, they calculated that about 15 per cent of these casualties were left unexplained, which they suggested could be due to the off-track emulation of Grand Prix race driving.

The larger the event and the higher its profile, the greater the potential for things to go wrong, generating negative impacts. The Sydney Festival in 1992 was responsible for the sixtieth anniversary celebrations of the opening of the Sydney Harbour Bridge. Arrangements were made to close the bridge to traffic, and to invite the public to walk across it from either end and experience a concert to be held at the centre of the bridge. Unfortunately, no-one had foreseen the effect of two very large crowds converging simultaneously from both north and south, and the result was chaos. The event became a negative experience for the participants, and was not a success from the point of view of the organisers.

Events, when they go wrong, can go very wrong indeed. Consider the Toohey's World's Biggest BBQ that ran out of food, and the Christmas Day riots at Bondi Beach in 1995. More seriously, the world was shocked by the bombing incident at the Atlanta Olympic Games in 1996, and the tragic collapse of the bridge at the entrance to the stadium for the Maccabiah Games in Israel in 1997. Such events have far-reaching negative impacts, resulting not only in bad press but damage or injury to participants, stakeholders and the host community.

Managing *crowd behaviour*

Major events can have unintended social consequences such as substance abuse, bad behaviour by the crowd and an increase in criminal activity (Getz, 1997). If not managed properly, these unintended consequences can hijack the agenda, and determine the public perception of the event. It has been necessary for events as diverse as the Australasian Country Music Festival at Tamworth and the Bathurst 1000 to develop strategies to handle alcohol-related bad crowd behaviour and protect their reputation and future. The case study at the end of this chapter will examine the Australian Motorcycle Grand Prix at Phillip Island in Victoria and the successful strategies it implemented to manage such unintended impacts.

Crowd behaviour can be modified with careful planning. Sometimes this is an evolutionary process. For example the management of New Year's Eve in Sydney has seen a series of modifications and adjustments over successive years. The impact of crowd behaviour on residents in The Rocks in the early 1980s caused the Sydney Festival to move the timing of the fireworks display forward to 9.00 p.m. This resulted in families leaving the city after the end of the fireworks. However, teenagers and much of the general audience remained in the city until well after midnight, transferring some of the problems to areas such as Kings Cross and Darling Harbour. By the early 1990s at Darling Harbour teenage alcohol abuse was resulting in bad crowd behaviour, confrontations with police, injuries and arrests. The Darling Harbour Authority had its regulations changed to allow it to prevent alcohol from being brought into the venue, and modified its program and marketing to create the expectation of a family-oriented celebration. The result was a turnaround in crowd behaviour, and a dramatic decrease in injuries and arrests. In recent years, Sydney City Council and its contracted event organisers Specktak Productions have orchestrated simultaneous celebrations across the city in different locations. This allows crowds to be spread out instead of concentrated in one area, facilitating better crowd management and a reduction in behaviour problems. Other Australian events, such as the New Year's Eve celebrations at Bondi Beach and Byron Bay, have been similarly transformed. This trend has continued overseas with initiatives like the First Night Program of alcohol-free celebrations which began in Boston and has been adopted by a wide range of communities.

Community ownership *and control of events*

Badly managed events can also have wider effects on the social life and structure of communities. These can include loss of amenities owing to noise or crowds, resentment of inequitable distribution of costs and benefits, and cost inflation of goods and services that can upset housing markets and impacts most severely on low income groups, as outlined by Getz

(1997). It follows that communities should have a major say in the planning and management of events. However, Hall (1989) concludes that the role of communities is often marginalised:

> ■ . . . In nearly every case study of hallmark events the most important decision of all, whether to host an event or not, is taken outside of the public arena and behind the closed doors of a private office or city hall. Indeed, often government may have no initial say as to whether to host an event or not, as with the winning of the America's Cup by Alan Bond in 1983. Therefore, public participation usually becomes a form of placation in which policy can only be changed in an incremental fashion and then only at the margins. The substantive policy decision, that of hosting the event, still remains. In this situation, public participation within the planning process becomes reactive rather than proactive. Instead of a discussion of the advantages and disadvantages of hosting events, public participation becomes a means to increase the legitimacy of government and developers' decisions regarding the means by which events should be held. ■

This makes it all the more important for governments to be accountable, through the political process, for the allocation of resources to events. Hall (1992) maintains that political analysis is an important tool in regaining community control over hallmark events, and ensuring that the objectives of these events focus on maximising returns to the community.

PHYSICAL AND ENVIRONMENTAL IMPACTS

An event is an excellent way to showcase the unique characteristics of the host environment. Hall (1989) points out that selling the image of a hallmark event includes marketing the intrinsic properties of the destination, and quotes the use of images of Perth's beaches, the Swan River and historic Fremantle in advertisements for the America's Cup, and the emphasis on the creation of an aesthetically pleasing environment in the promotion of Sydney's Darling Harbour.

However, host environments may be extremely delicate and great care should be taken to protect them. A major event may require an environmental impact assessment before council permission is granted for it to go ahead. Even if a formal study is not required, the event manager should carefully consider the likely impact of the event on the environment. This impact will be fairly contained if the event is to be held in a suitable purpose-built venue, for example, a stadium, sportsground, showground or entertainment centre. The impact may be much greater if the event is to be held in a public space not ordinarily reserved for events, such as a park, town square or street. Aspects such as crowd movement and control, noise levels, access and parking will be important considerations. Other major issues may include wear and tear on the natural and physical environment, heritage issues and disruption of the local community.

Good communication and consultation with local authorities will often resolve some of these issues. In addition, careful management logistics may be required to modify impacts. In Sydney, the Manly Jazz Festival worked for several years to progressively reduce the traffic impact of visitors to the festival by developing a system of fringe parking and shuttle buses to the event area. Many food and wine events have reduced their impact on the environment by using biodegradable containers and utensils instead of plastic, and selling wine-tasting souvenir glasses which patrons can take home after the event. Many event managers are discovering that such measures make good financial as well as environmental sense.

When staging large events, the provision of infrastructure is often a costly budget component, but this expenditure usually results in an improved environment and facilities for the host community, and provides a strong incentive for it to act as host. Brisbane profited from the transformation of the Expo 88 site into the Southbank leisure and entertainment precinct, and Sydney's available public space was enhanced when the 1988 Bicentennial celebrations caused derelict railway goods yards to be redeveloped, creating the Darling Harbour leisure precinct. Similarly, the Australian Formula One Grand Prix has given Melbourne a first-class motorsport venue, although some people argue that this has been at the cost of the public leisure amenity of Albert Park.

■ The Sydney Olympic Games *and the environment*

The Sydney Olympic Games will provide Sydney with sporting facilities to take it well into the twenty-first century, as well as major infrastructure improvements in accommodation, transport and communications. However, the preparation of the site and the building of the Olympic Village raise major environmental issues which are magnified by the scale and profile of the project. The Sydney Olympic Games' environmental guidelines are based on principles adopted at the United Nations Earth Summit. They are expressed in ecologically sustainable development policies which include commitments to energy conservation; water conservation; waste avoidance and minimisation; air, water and soil quality; and the protection of significant natural and cultural environments.

In the planning and construction of Olympic facilities and the running of the Games, these guidelines commit Sydney to initiatives including:
• Conduct of environmental and social impact studies
• Minimisation of adverse impacts on Olympic sites and nearby residents
• Protection of the natural environment and threatened ecosystems
• Enforcement of Environmental Guidelines on suppliers and contractors
• Concentration of venues in compact zones

- Placement of all venues and the majority of training venues within 30 minutes travel from the Olympic Village
- Use of energy efficient design and materials
- Maximum use of renewable sources of energy
- Water conservation and recycling
- Best practice in waste reduction and avoidance
- Use where practicable of non-toxic substances
- Use of recyclable packaging and non-disposable cutlery and crockery at food outlets where possible
- Use of recycling bins at all Games venues
- Information transferred electronically where possible to conserve paper, supplemented by paper recycling procedures
- Public transport being the only means of access by spectators to events at Olympic sites.

The extent to which these high ideals survive the pressures of time and cost will be revealed as the Games unfold through the construction and staging phases.

POLITICAL IMPACTS

Politics and politicians are an important part of the equation that is contemporary events management. Ever since the Roman Emperors discovered the power of the Circus to deflect criticism and shore up popularity, shrewd politicians have had an eye for events which will keep the populace happy and themselves in power. No less an authority than Count Niccolo Machiavelli, adviser to the Medicis in the sixteenth century, had this to say on the subject:

> ■ A prince must also show himself a lover of merit, give preferment to the able and honour those who excel in every art... Besides this, he ought, at convenient seasons of the year, to keep the people occupied with festivals and shows; and as every city is divided into guilds or into classes, he ought to pay attention to all these groups, mingle with them from time to time, and give them an example of his humanity and munificence, always upholding, however, the majesty of his dignity, which must never be allowed to fail in anything whatever. ■

The Royal House of Windsor took this advice to heart, providing some of the most popular events of the century with the Queen's Coronation and the fairytale-like wedding of Charles and Diana. Australian Prime Minister Robert Menzies made good use of the public affection for the British royal family, with royal tours to Australia providing a boost to the popularity of his government. Successive Australian politicians have continued to use the spotlight offered by different events to build their personal profiles and gain political advantage. South Australian Premier Don Dunstan used the Adelaide Festival to create an image of Adelaide as the 'Athens of the South', and of himself as a visionary and enlightened leader. Sallyanne Atkinson used

Brisbane's Expo 88 and successive Olympic bids to boost her mayoral profile. New South Wales Premier Neville Wran and colleague Laurie Brereton used the building of Darling Harbour to create an image of New South Wales as a go-ahead State, but critics at the time accused them of creating a monument to themselves. Prime Minister Bob Hawke bathed in the glory of Alan Bond's America's Cup victory. And continuing in the grand tradition, Victorian Premier Jeff Kennett used a succession of events including the Australian Formula One Grand Prix, rugby's Bledisloe Cup and the Presidents Cup golf tournament to create an image of himself as a winner — and his rival, New South Wales Premier Bob Carr, as the loser — in the race for events.

Arnold et al. (1989) leave no doubt about the role of events in the political process.

■ Governments in power will continue to use hallmark events to punctuate the ends of their periods in office, to arouse nationalism, enthusiasm and finally, votes. They are cheaper than wars or the preparation for them. In this regard, hallmark events do not hide political realities, they are the political reality. ■

Governments around the world have realised the ability of events to raise the profile of politicians and the cities and States that they govern. Events attract visitors, and thus create economic benefits and jobs. This potent mixture has prompted governments to become major players in bidding for, hosting and staging major events. Brisbane built up a strong reputation with events such as the Commonwealth Games, Expo 88, the Lions Convention and the World Masters Games. Sharry (1997) describes how, with the coming of Super League, Brisbane grasped the opportunity to host the Super League Grand Final. Brisbane City Council commissioned a study by Griffith University that assessed the economic impact of the event to be worth over $7 million, leading it to decide that a serious bid should be made to host the Grand Final. The bid was first developed by staff of the ANZ Stadium, and refined through discussions with executives of Super League and the Brisbane Broncos. A week of activities was planned for the lead-up to the match. These included a ball, a street parade, a city festival, a golf event, family activities at Southbank, an awards ceremony, breakfasts, and a civic reception. Plans were made to enlarge the capacity of the stadium with temporary seating, and an impressive multimedia presentation was commissioned. Brisbane's efforts were rewarded by hosting the Super League Grand Final, which set new benchmarks for the enhancement and packaging of major sporting events.

This increasing involvement of governments in events has politicised the events landscape, as recognised by Hall (1989).

■ Politics are paramount in hallmark events. It is either naïve or dupli[citous] to pretend otherwise. Events alter the time frame in which planning occurs and they become opportunities to do something new and better than before. In this context, events may change or legitimate [sic] political priorities in the short term and political ideologies and socio-cultural reality in the longer term. Hallmark events represent the tournaments of old, fulfilling psychological and political needs through the winning of hosting over other locations and the winning of events themselves. Following a hallmark event some places will never be the same again, physically, economically, socially and, perhaps most importantly of all, politically. ■

It is important to acknowledge that events have values beyond just tangible and economic benefits. Humans are social animals, and celebrations play a key role in the wellbeing of the social structure. Events can engender social cohesion, confidence and pride. Perhaps this is the key reason why governments should value and support events.

TOURISM AND ECONOMIC IMPACTS

Governments are increasingly turning to tourism as a growth industry capable of delivering economic benefits and job creation. Events in turn are seen as catalysts for attracting visitors, and increasing their average spend and length of stay. They are also seen as image-makers, creating profile for destinations, positioning them in the market and providing a competitive marketing advantage. This has led to the creation of a new field, known as event tourism, which Getz (1997) defines as:

■ 1. The systematic planning, development and marketing of events as tourist attractions, catalysts for other developments, image builders, and animators of attractions and destination areas; event tourism strategies should also cover the management of news and negative events.
2. A market segment consisting of those people who travel to attend events, or who can be motivated to attend events while away from home. ■

Government tourism bodies often consciously use events to position their destinations in the market. Key objectives of the Tourism New South Wales Events Strategy (1996) are to:
• Position Sydney and New South Wales as the events capital of Australia and reinforce the brand of Sydney and New South Wales as defined by Tourism New South Wales in its marketing strategies.
• Develop and promote existing and new international calibre events for Sydney, which position it as a cultural capital of Asia and the Pacific.
• Capitalise on the opportunity provided by the Sydney Olympic Games to brand New South Wales as a unique lifestyle destination — a centre for sport, fitness and healthy lifestyle.
• Identify and develop events in regional New South Wales that express the cultural strengths of the State and serve as flagships for the promotion of regional tourism.
If events are to be effective in positioning their destinations in the market, they must strive for authenticity and the expression of the unique characteristics of their communities. Visitors want to do what local residents

do, and experience the things that they enjoy about the destination. The New South Wales Tourism Masterplan (1995) argues that 'Those destinations that preserve, enhance and celebrate the things that set them apart and give them a meaning of their own, will produce a more rewarding visitor experience and a higher yield for the host community.'

Conversely, destinations that produce events solely for tourists, without meaning for their own communities, run the danger of the results being inauthentic and shallow. Exploitative or badly managed events with inadequate planning or facilities can damage the reputation of a destination.

Events *and seasonality*

A strong advantage of event tourism is that it can attract visitors in the low season, when airline and accommodation providers often have surplus capacity. Additional economic benefit is derived when visitors use what would otherwise be under-utilised tourism infrastructure. Getz (1997) describes the way that events can overcome seasonality by capitalising 'on whatever natural appeal the off-season presents, such as winter as opposed to summer sports, seasonal food and produce, and scenery or wildlife viewed in different places and under changing conditions'. He also notes that 'in many destinations the residents prefer the off-season for their own celebrations, and these provide more authentic events for visitors'.

Many Australian destinations have developed events to enliven off-season periods. Some examples are the summer program at Thredbo in the New South Wales snowfields, which has used special interest music festivals to attract guests in the off-season summer months; and the Sydney Festival, which has transformed the traditionally quiet midsummer period in the city into a highlight of the events calendar.

Events enhance *the tourism experience*

Events can provide newness, freshness and change, which sustain local interest in a destination and enhance its appeal to visitors. Tourist attractions and theme parks incorporate events as a key element in their marketing programs. Movie World on the Gold Coast, Australia's Wonderland in western Sydney and the Crown Casino in Melbourne all use extensive event programs to increase market profile and attract repeat visits. Getz (1997) notes the use of events by a wide variety of tourism attractions to animate and interpret their products.

> ■ Resorts, museums, historic districts, heritage sites, archaeological sites, markets and shopping centres, sports stadia, convention centres, and theme parks all develop programs of special events. Built attractions and facilities everywhere have realized the advantages of 'animation' — the process of programming interpretive features and/or special events that make the place come alive with sensory stimulation and appealing atmosphere. ■

■ Events as catalysts *for development*

An event can enhance the quality of life of a neighbourhood, by adding to its sense of place and residential amenity. Companies like Citywest Development Corporation, in charge of the redevelopment of Sydney's Pyrmont peninsula, are now designing events strategies which use events as image-builders for the community. Likewise, Sanctuary Cove in Queensland used the Ultimate Event concert with Frank Sinatra to promote itself as the ultimate luxury real estate development in Australia.

Large events act as catalysts for urban renewal, and for the creation of new or expanded tourism infrastructure. The Melbourne Olympic Games in 1956 provided major facilities that contributed to the city's reputation as a sporting centre for several decades. Other examples are the provision of facilities at the port of Fremantle in Western Australia for the America's Cup defence in 1986–87, the Expo 88 site in Brisbane and the Homebush Bay site for the Sydney Olympic Games, all of which gained infrastructure development through hosting large-scale events. Hotel and facilities development, better communications and improved road and public transport networks are some of the legacies left by these events.

■ Economic *benefits*

The strong growth of the festival and special event sector in Australia is part of a general economic trend away from an industrial product base to a more service-based economy. The expenditure of visitors, spread over travel, accommodation, restaurants, shopping and other tourism-related services, is just one way that a host community can benefit from an event. Events can also provide a boost to other areas of the economy. The construction industry — witness the construction boom resulting from the Sydney Olympic Games — is often stimulated by the need for new or improved facilities to stage a major event. Employment is temporarily boosted by the expenditure involved in staging an event. Thus whole mini-economies surround and work off the events industry.

The expenditure generated by events also circulates in the wider economy. For example, the meal consumed by the event visitor results in further business for the companies that supply and transport food produce. This indirect or induced expenditure is known as the multiplier effect, and while there is considerable disagreement on the calculation of multipliers, it is generally agreed that event expenditure does have a flow-on effect on the economy. This generalised benefit to the wider economy provides the impetus for governments to become involved in bidding for and staging events.

Table 2.2 summarises the economic benefits of a number of recent events in Australia. The results are not strictly comparable, as the methodologies for evaluating events vary widely. However, the table does demonstrate the considerable tourism and economic benefits which flow from major events.

■ Table 2.2
Comparative
table of
economic
benefits of
events

EVENT	TOTAL ATTENDANCE ('000s)	TOTAL VISITORS INTERSTATE and OVERSEAS ('000s)	TOTAL EXPENDITURE INTERSTATE and OVERSEAS VISITORS ($M)	IMPACT ON GROSS STATE PRODUCT (GSP) ($M)
World Cup of Athletics, Canberra 1985	46	10	7.8	18.8
Australian Formula One Grand Prix, Adelaide 1992	260	19	14.4	37.4
Sydney Gay and Lesbian Mardi Gras, 1993	550	5	7.5	12.0
World Masters Games, Brisbane 1994	23*	18	27.5	50.6
World Police and Fire Games, Melbourne 1995	7*	9	11.5	21.7
Adelaide Festival, 1996	42	6	7.8	13.0–15.5

* Figure stated is number of participants in event and does not count accompanying persons.

Events have the potential to provide niche development opportunities for city and State governments. As outlined in the preface and the case study in chapter 12, Tamworth has developed a year round strand of economic activity based on its positioning as the country music capital of Australia. In another example, Uekrongtham (1995) demonstrates that theatre can have a major impact on tourism and the economy with the 1992 Broadway theatre season worth US$2.3 billion to the economy of New York City, and the 1990–91 West End theatre season worth £114 million to the city of London. He quotes Tourism Victoria research which concludes that in two and a half years the Phantom of the Opera attracted 550 000 visitors worth at least A$300 million to Melbourne. Auckland in New Zealand is maximising the economic benefits of staging the America's Cup defence in 2000 by integrating its marine industry components and stakeholders through MAREX (Marine Export Group), placing its marine industry at the centre of a range of exciting developments (Davies 1996). Sydney is using the staging of the Olympic Games to position itself as a centre of excellence for sport and healthy lifestyle (Tourism New South Wales 1995). Sydney's hosting of the Paralympic Games is also opening up a niche market opportunity in sport for the disabled.

■ Cost–benefit *analysis*

Money spent on events represents an opportunity cost of resources that may have been devoted to other needs in the community. This has caused governments to look at the cost–benefit analysis of events, and has given rise to a specialised branch of economic study. Burns and Mules (1989) reported on a survey of the economic impacts of the 1985 Australian For-mula One Grand Prix in Adelaide. They estimated the tangible or measur-able benefit–cost ratio at an upper bound of $23.630:7.520 million, and a lower bound of $24.806:6.571 million, or to put it more simply, from 3.1:1 to 3.8:1. After adjustment for a $5 million Federal Government grant to the event, they concluded that the benefit–cost ratio of money spent on the event was better than just about any other use of the money for the higher bound, and was beaten only by expenditure on communications, commu-nity services or public administration for the lower bound.

Extensive surveys of residents and business houses were carried out to assess the social, less tangible costs and benefits associated with running the event. Positive or 'psychic' benefits included a week-long carnival of fringe entertain-ments, the feeling that 'the whole world is watching' and the general air of excitement created by the media. Negative impacts included traffic congestion, noise, road accidents, vandalism, loss of amenity and possibly loss of business to those business houses near the circuit. Where possible, financial values were attributed to these social benefits and costs (see table 2.3). Social costs were measured at $9.66 to $12.26 million, and social benefits in excess of $28 million.

■ Table 2.3
Social benefits and costs of the Australian Formula One Grand Prix in Adelaide

SOCIAL COSTS		SOCIAL BENEFITS
Traffic congestion (time lost)	$6.2m	Psychic income $28m+
Property damage	$0.26m	• general excitement
Increased vehicle thefts and		• good opinions of oneself
thefts from vehicles	n.a.	• extra shopping access
Noise	n.a.	• opportunity to have guests
Accidents	$3.2–5.8m	• home hosting opportunities
		• pleasure in 'experiencing' the event

The researchers concluded that social costs did not appear to be signifi-cant in relation to the overall surplus of tangible benefits, and that all things considered, the Grand Prix was a successful hallmark event that produced significant social benefits for the State.

■ **Monitoring** *long term impacts*

Impacts that are calculated during the actual time frame of an event tell only part of the story. In order to form a full picture of the impact of an event, it is necessary to look at the long-term effects on the host community and its economy.

A study by Selwood and Jones (1991), four years after the America's Cup defence in Fremantle in 1987, gives some indication of the aftershock of this event. They point out that Fremantle's profile as a destination was greatly enhanced by the attention it received: in 1989 Fremantle was visited by 83 per cent of international visitors to Western Australia and 13 per cent of all inter-national visitors to Australia (a higher proportion than in the year before the event) and was ranked as the State's leading tourist attraction. The city was left with a legacy of infrastructure and quality tourism developments that were either initiated or expedited by the event. The America's Cup had also placed Fremantle on the map of world sailing, making it a staging post for the Whitbread Round the World Race, and attracting the world's leading sailors to Perth on a regular basis for events such as the Australia Cup. The Francis Ford Coppola movie *Wind* was filmed in Fremantle, featuring five of the yachts that participated in the defence, along with another feature film *The Great Pretender*.

On a wider level, the Western Australian EventsCorp, the first of its kind in Australia, grew out of the America's Cup office with the encouragement of the Western Australian Development Commission. This shows how organisations set up to stage an event can subsequently evolve to have a broad and continuing role in attracting visitors to a destination. With a brief to attract or initiate hallmark events for the State, it has already staged the 1991 and 1998 World Swimming Championships and the Golden Oldies Rugby Festival.

The study found that the America's Cup defence had accelerated development and hastened gentrification of Fremantle, but that this process had inevitably caused some social dislocation, and increased pressure on low-income earners. The influx of a range of new groups with different values into Fremantle created some tension. For example, for the period of the Cup defence, the licensing hours of waterfront pubs were extended to match international standards. This encouraged a flourishing of late night drinking and entertainment venues, which remained when the hours went back to normal. This created problems of disturbance and vandalism for local residents. The study concluded that the America's Cup defence had increased the levels of employment and economic activity in the tourist and heritage industries in Fremantle, and significantly improved the infrastructure of the city for the benefit of residents and visitors. However, the loss of the defence in 1987 had probably protected Fremantle from further development pressures fuelled by international capital, and allowed instead the steady long-term development of Fremantle's tourist industry.

SUMMARY

All events produce impacts, both positive and negative, which it is the task of the event manager to assess and balance.

Social and cultural impacts may involve a shared experience, and may give rise to local pride, validation or the widening of cultural horizons. However, social problems arising from events may result in social dislocation if not properly managed. Events are an excellent opportunity to showcase the physical characteristics of a destination, but event environments may be very delicate, and care should be taken to safeguard and protect them. Many events involve longer-term issues affecting the built environment and the legacy of improved facilities. Increasingly, environmental considerations are paramount, as shown by the comprehensive environmental guidelines which have been developed for the Sydney Olympic Games, in conjunction with Greenpeace, to manage their environmental impact.

Political impacts have long been recognised by governments, and often include increased profile and benefits to the host community. However, it is important that events fulfil the wider community agenda. Governments are attracted to events because of the economic benefits, job creation and tourism which they can provide. Events act as catalysts for attracting tourists and extending their length of stay. They also increase the profile of a destination, and can be designed to attract visitors during the low-season when tourism facilities are under-utilised. Large events also serve as catalysts for urban renewal, and for the creation of new tourism infrastructure. Events bring economic benefits to their communities, but governments need to weigh these benefits against costs when deciding how to allocate resources.

Questions

1 Describe some examples of events whose needs have been perceived as being in conflict with those of their host communities. As the event manager, how would you resolve these conflicting needs?

2 Describe an event with which you are familiar and which has been characterised by social problems or bad crowd behaviour. As the event manager, what would you have done to manage the situation and improve the outcome of the event? In your answer, discuss both the planning of the event and possible on-the-spot responses.

3 Select a major event that has been held in your region, and identify as many environmental impacts as you can. Evaluate whether the overall environmental impact on the host community was positive or negative, and recommend steps which could be taken to improve the balance.

4 Describe an event that you believe was not sufficiently responsive to community attitudes and values. What steps could be taken in the community to improve the situation?

5 Identify an event in your region which has a significant tourism component, and examine the event in terms of its ability to:
(a) increase tourist visits and length of stay
(b) improve the profile of the destination
(c) create economic benefits for the region.

6 Select an event in which you have been involved as a participant or close observer, and identify as many impacts of the event as you can, both positive and negative. Did the positive impacts outweigh the negative?
(a) What measures did the organisers have in place to maximise positive impacts and minimise negative impacts?
(b) As the event manager, what other steps could you have taken to balance the impacts and improve the outcome of the event?

CASE STUDY

The Australian
Motorcycle Grand Prix

Picturesque Phillip Island has hosted three international Motorcycle Grand Prix events, most recently in October 1997. Best known for its Fairy Penguin Parade and seal colonies, the island also has a strong tradition of motor racing dating back to the 1960s. It provides one of the most spectacular backdrops for motor racing events in the world, with rolling green hills and rugged cliff faces plunging to the surf-swept rocks that face the Bass Strait.

Organising a large international event consisting of approximately 100 000 spectators, on a small island with a population of only 6500 residents, presents many challenges which require a great deal of planning and coordination to overcome. This planning occurs at State and local levels and involves tourism and event organisers, motorcycle associations, police, traffic, emergency and health services.

For this event, the 'tyranny of distance' is a major difficulty. Phillip Island is 120 kilometres south-east of Melbourne, approximately one and a half hours' drive. By road, the island is only accessible by a narrow two-lane bridge connecting it to the mainland, and it has very limited sea and air access. In addition, the island's patchwork of roads — sometimes congested through normal use during holiday periods — are ill-suited to the massive volumes of spectators commuting to and from the event. The event itself, which runs over a four-day period climaxing on the last day in the internationally televised 500cc race, attracts thousands of tourists who come either for the duration of the Grand Prix or to witness daily events. To efficiently move and accommodate these spectators requires a detailed and integrated traffic management plan and the establishment of temporary campsites for an additional 15 000 campers. A notable aspect of this planning has been the establishment of the Grand Prix Rally which allows many thousands of motorcycle enthusiasts to ride to the island in a convoy, complete with police escort!

Building positive relations between the police and the 'bikie' fraternity has also been an integral part of the event, given the poor history of similar events in other Australian States. A violence prevention plan has been developed, featuring close liaison with motorcycle associations, a community policing style, and the encouragement of 'bikie stewards' to allow for self-policing among the participants at various camping grounds and points of congregation.

To combat crowding at a few central sites on the island, temporary liquor outlets and entertainment were organised at different campsites, which enabled diffusion of participants to a range of smaller more manageable locations.

Another special feature of this event is the adoption of a public health approach, emphasising harm minimisation. Coordinated through the local San Remo Community Health Centre, health authorities have instituted the 'Ride Safe' health promotion campaign featuring the slogan 'Condoms — safest rubber on the island'. The campaign involves volunteers circulating through the crowd and a track-side caravan providing information, education and counselling on health related issues of HIV, hepatitis C, sexually transmitted diseases and drug and alcohol use.

These initiatives and others have ensured the prevention and management of a number of potential problems at the event, and have contributed to high levels of consumer and resident satisfaction with the Australian Motorcycle Grand Prix at Phillip Island.

Neil Mellor
Senior Research Officer
Turning Point Alcohol and Drug Centre
Victoria

Questions

1 If you were the public relations officer for the Australian Motorcycle Grand Prix, how would your public relations plan support the crowd control strategies developed for the event?

2 List the crowd behaviour and social issues discussed in the case study, and the strategies used to address them. What other issues might be involved in an event of this kind, and what strategies would you use to address them?

3 Identify an event that has existing or potential crowd behaviour problems. How might some of the principles developed at Phillip Island apply to this event? State the strategies which you consider to be the most useful, and explain how they would need to be modified to serve the particular conditions at the event.

REFERENCES

Arnold, A., Fischer, A., Hatch, J. & Paix, B. 1989, 'The Grand Prix, road accidents and the philosophy of hallmark events', in *The Planning and Evaluation of Hallmark Events*, eds G. J. Syme, B. J. Shaw, D. M. Fenton & W. S. Mueller, Avesbury, Aldershot.

Burns, J. P. A. & Mules, T. J. 1989, 'An Economic Evaluation of the Adelaide Grand Prix', in *The Planning and Evaluation of Hallmark Events*, eds G. J. Syme, B. J. Shaw, D. M. Fenton & W. S. Mueller, Avesbury, Aldershot.

Davies, John 1996, 'The Buck Stops Where? The Economic Impact of Staging Major Events', paper presented to the Australian Events Conference, Canberra.

Department of Sport, Recreation and Tourism, Research and Development Section 1986, *Economic impact of the World Cup of Athletics held in Canberra in October 1985: Discussion Paper*, Canberra.

Ernst and Young 1994, *World Masters Games Brisbane 1994: Economic Impact and Market Research Study*, Report prepared for the Queensland Events Corporation, Brisbane.

Ernst & Young 1996, *1995 World Police and Fire Games: Economic Impact Assessment*, Melbourne.

Getz, Donald 1997, *Event Management and Event Tourism*, Cognizant Communication Corporation, New York.

Hall, Colin M. 1989, 'Hallmark events and the planning process', in *The Planning and Evaluation of Hallmark Events*, eds G. J. Syme, B. J. Shaw, D. M. Fenton & W. S. Mueller, Avebury, Aldershot.

Hall, Colin M. 1992, *Hallmark Tourist Events — Impacts Management and Planning*, Belhaven Press, London.

Machiavelli, Niccolo 1962 (1514), *The Prince*, trans. L. Ricci, Mentor Books, New York.

Market Equity SA Pty Ltd 1996, *1996 Adelaide Festival: An Economic Impact Study*, Report prepared for the South Australian Tourism Commission, Department for the Arts and Cultural Development and the Australia Council, Adelaide.

Marsh, Ian & Greenfield, John 1993, *Sydney Gay and Lesbian Mardi Gras: An Evaluation of its Economic Impact*, Sydney Gay and Lesbian Mardi Gras Ltd, Sydney.

Price Waterhouse, Economic Studies and Strategies Unit 1993, *1992 Formula One Grand Prix: Economic Evaluation*, Canberra.

Selwood, John H. & Jones, Roy 1991, 'The America's Cup in Retrospect — the Aftershock in Fremantle', in *Leisure and Tourism: Social and Environmental Change*, eds A. J. Veal, P. Jonson & G. Cushman, Centre for Leisure and Tourism Studies, University of Technology, Sydney.

Sharry, Stephen 1997, 'A Super Win', *Australian Leisure Management*, vol. 1, no. 3, pp. 30–32.

Soutar, Geoffrey N. & McLeod, Paul 1989, 'The impact of the America's Cup on Fremantle residents: some empirical evidence', in *The Planning and Evaluation of Hallmark Events*, eds G. J. Syme, B. J. Shaw, D. M. Fenton & W. S. Mueller, Avesbury, Aldershot.

Sydney Organising Committee for the Olympic Games, *Sydney 2000 — Environmental Guidelines*, http://www.sydney.olympic.org/env/index.htm

Tourism New South Wales 1996, *Events Strategy*, Sydney.

Tourism New South Wales 1995, *New South Wales Tourism Masterplan to 2010*, Sydney.

Uekrongthan, Ekachai (1995). *The Impact of Theatre on Economy and Tourism*, prepared for Cameron Mackintosh Pty Ltd.

FURTHER READING

Giddings, Chris (1997). *Measuring the Impact of Festivals — Guidelines for Conducting an Economic Impact Study*, National Centre for Culture and Recreation Studies, Australian Bureau of Statistics.

CHAPTER 3

Conceptualising
the event

LEARNING OBJECTIVES

After studying this chapter, you should be able to:

- identify the range of stakeholders in an event

- describe and balance the overlapping and conflicting needs of stakeholders

- describe the role of government, corporate and community sectors in events

- discuss trends and issues in Australian society that affect events

- understand the role of sponsorship in events

- develop partnerships with sponsors and the media

- identify the unique elements and resources of an event

- understand the process of developing an event concept.

As discussed in the previous chapters, events have become professionalised, and are increasingly attracting the support of governments and the corporate sector. One aspect of this growth is that events are now required to serve a multitude of agendas. It is no longer sufficient for an event to meet just the needs of its audience. It must also embrace a plethora of other requirements including government objectives and regulations, media requirements, sponsors' needs and community expectations. The successful event manager must be able to identify the range of stakeholders in an event and manage their individual needs, which will sometimes overlap and conflict. As with event impacts, the event will be judged by its success in balancing the competing needs, expectations and interests of a diverse range of stakeholders.

Mal Hemmerling (1997), architect of the Australian Formula One Grand Prix in Adelaide and former chief executive of SOCOG, describes the task as follows:

> ■ So when asked the question 'what makes an event successful', there are now numerous shareholders that are key components of modern major events that are looking at a whole range of different measures of success. What may have been a simple measure for the event organiser of the past, which involved the bottom line, market share, and successful staging of the event are now only basic criteria as the measures by other investors are more aligned with increased tourism, economic activity, tax revenues, promotional success, sustained economic growth, television reach, audience profiles, customer focus, brand image, hospitality, new business opportunities and investment to name but a few. ■

■ **Figure 3.1**
The relationship of stakeholders to events

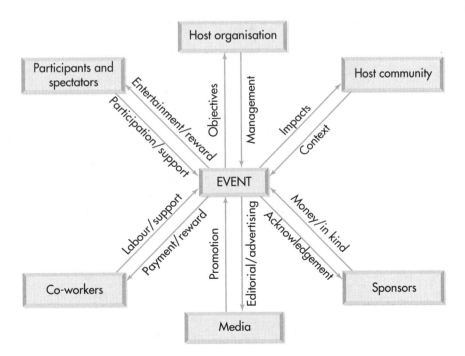

Events have become so much a part of our cultural milieu that they can be generated by almost any part of the government, corporate and community sectors.

Governments create events for a range of reasons, including the social, cultural, tourism and economic benefits generated by events. Some government departments have an events brief as part of their delivery of services, for example, State events corporations, ministries of Arts, Sport and Recreation and ministries of Racing. Other departments generate events as a means to achieve related objectives — Tourism to increase and extend tourist visits, Ethnic Affairs to preserve cultures and encourage tolerance and diversity, and Economic Development to assist industry and generate jobs. Many other departments are involved in one-off events to promote specific goods and services such as health promotions, Seniors Week, and Heritage Week. Such events may celebrate special days such as Australia Day, Anzac Day or World Environment Day. They are often characterised by free entry and wide accessibility, and form part of the public culture.

The corporate sector is involved in events at a number of levels. Companies and corporations may sponsor events in order to promote their goods and services in the marketplace. They may partner government departments in the presentation of events that serve common or multiple agendas. Companies may also create their own events in order to launch new products, increase sales or enhance corporate image. These events, although they may still offer free entry, can be targeted at specific market segments rather than at the general public.

■ **Table 3.1**
Event typology

EVENT GENERATORS	TYPES OF EVENTS
GOVERNMENT SECTOR	
Central government	Civic celebrations and commemorations e.g. Australia Day, Centenary of Federation
Event corporations	Major events — focus on sporting and cultural events
Public space authorities	Public entertainment, leisure and recreation events
Tourism	Festivals, special interest and lifestyle events, destinational promotions
Convention bureaus	Meetings, incentives, conventions, exhibitions
Arts	Arts festivals, cultural events, touring programs, themed art exhibitions
Ethnic affairs	Ethnic and multicultural events
Sport and recreation	Sporting events, hosting of State, national and international events
Gaming and racing	Race meetings and carnivals

Table 3.1
(*continued*)

EVENT GENERATORS	TYPES OF EVENTS
Economic development	Focus on events with industry development and job creation benefits
Local government	Community events, local festivals and fairs
CORPORATE SECTOR Companies and corporations	Promotions, product launches and image building sponsorships
Industry associations	Industry promotions, trade fairs, conferences
Entrepreneurs	Ticketed sporting events, concerts and exhibitions
Media	Media promotions e.g. concerts, fun runs, appeals
COMMUNITY SECTOR Clubs and societies	Special interest groups
Charities	Charity events and fundraisers

Within the corporate sector there are also entrepreneurs whose business is the staging or selling of events. These include sports or concert promoters who present ticketed events for profit, and conference organisers or industry associations who mount conferences or exhibitions for the trade or public, for example, wine shows, equipment exhibitions or medical conferences. Media organisations often become partners in events organised by other groups, but also stage events for their own promotional purposes or to create program content. Examples are radio stations promoting their identity through concerts, newspapers promoting fun runs, or television networks presenting Christmas carol programs live to air.

Still other events emanate from the community sector, serving a wide variety of needs and interests. These may include service club fundraisers, car club gatherings, local art and craft shows — the spectrum is as wide as the field of human interest and endeavour. All of these sources combine to create the wonderful tapestry of events that fill our leisure time and enrich our lives.

THE HOST COMMUNITY

To understand the role of the host community in events planning it is useful to examine some trends and issues in the Australian community as it approaches the new millennium. It is a time of rapid change — in the community, workplace, and social structure and in the view which Australians have of themselves and their place in the world. While this can lead to insecurity, and to a nostalgia for earlier, simpler times of full employment and old fashioned family values, it also offers the exhilaration of new challenges and new directions, as evidenced by the debate on Australia's relationship with Asia, and the thrust toward a republic. Savage (1997) maintains that a major effect of multiculturalism has been a shift to a more pluralist society with a multiplicity of elements, and away from the more homogenous culture of the 1940s, 1950s and 1960s:

■ There is the belief that this 'old' Australian culture has died and there is now no singular thing which is Australian culture. It is notable that many of the nostalgic icons of Australianess (e.g. Aeroplane Jelly, Vegemite, FJ Holden) come from this period rather than more recent periods. ■

Hamill (1997) also notes this mood of uncertainty, and points to a survey of two hundred Australian boys and girls aged between 12 and 17, which was designed to identify their role models and heroes. The survey asked 'If you could be anybody in the world, who would you like to be?'. Surprisingly, for most Australian boys the first choice was over 6 foot tall and black — Michael Jordan — followed by My Father. For girls, despite the many votes for Elle Macpherson and the late Princess Diana, the clear winner was My Mother. Hamill relates this swing toward the values of the family to the phenomenon of cocooning, or creating a safe haven in the home from the threats and uncertainties of the outside world:

■ The impulse is to turn inwards when it gets too tough outside. It could be the recession, it could be AIDS, it could be crime, or it could be something as simple as rude waiters and road rage. ■

Hamill sees this phenomenon expressed in other key trends such as home improvement, health food and dieting. A further trend which could impact on events and their management is the desire for fantasy adventure, where people seek safe travel experiences as an emotional release to compensate for the physical retreat into their cocoons. Short breaks built around events which provide challenging experiences in a controlled environment may well become a future trend.

■ The mood *of the millennium*

So what will be the mood of the Australian community at the dawn of the new millennium? There is some cause for optimism. The events climate will be dominated by three milestone events — the new millennium itself, which will see Sydney and Australia as a focus of global celebrations; the Sydney Olympic Games; and the Centenary of Federation celebrations in 2001, which may serve as an antidote to the inevitable post-Olympic hangover. Hamill (1997) sees the Olympics as having the potential to unite the nation:

■ I believe that once the gun fires at 8.00 a.m. on the very first Olympic event, which is the women's Triathlon, once we realise that 2.5 billion viewers from around the world are watching us... something great will be released all over this country. It is then that we will realise it is not just Sydney's Games, it is Australia's Games. The Olympics can showcase us like nothing ever before and probably nothing ever again. ■

However, Golds (1996) sounds a note of caution:

■ As we approach the midnight of the 20th century, which happens to coincide with our hosting of the Olympic Games, I fear we will be forced to come to premature, packaged conclusions about our identity for the sake of CNN... let's hope that we, as a culture, resist coming to the sorts of hasty conclusions about ourselves that one often comes to when one knows that somebody else is watching. Let's hope we have the courage to see ourselves through our own eyes. ■

■ **Working with** *the host community*

It is important to recognise the impact of the event on the host community, and for it to own and participate in the event. The host community may include residents, traders, lobby groups and public authorities such as council, transport, police, fire and ambulance brigades. The event manager should aim to identify and involve community leaders and to consult them in the planning of the event.

Councils may have certain requirements, such as parade and catering permits. Often police and councils will combine on such matters as street closures, special access and parking arrangements.

If the event is large enough to impact significantly beyond the boundaries of the venue, a public authorities' briefing may identify innovative ways to minimise the impact and manage the situation. For example, the Australia Day fireworks spectacular at Sydney's Darling Harbour regularly attracts 300 000 spectators, most of whom used to depart immediately after the end of the fireworks, causing an hour-long traffic jam on the surrounding freeways. By stepping down the entertainment in stages, working with point duty police and implementing one-way traffic in some areas, the delay was reduced to less than half that time.

Host communities have past experience of different events, and event managers can draw on this knowledge to ensure an event's success. In Sydney, public authorities have consciously used major occasions such as Australia Day and New Year's Eve as practice runs for the Olympics, with event organisers, public transport and public authorities working together to trial operations and refine solutions.

In addition to formal contact with authorities, the event manager should be aware of the all-important local rumour mill that can often make or break the host community's attitude to the event. In the early 1970s, the Aquarius Festival was staged by the Australian Union of Students at Nimbin in northern New South Wales. Part of the philosophy of the festival was to avoid all paid advertising, on the grounds that advertising would create a consumer mentality with people expecting the festival to be done for them. 'You are the program — the festival is what you make it' was the message to participants. The belief was that word of the festival would spread 'on the lips of the counter culture' — that a good idea would have the power to sell itself.

Twenty thousand people from all over Australia, as well as from some odd corners of the globe, eventually made the journey to Nimbin. But there were some fascinating rumours and counter rumours spread by its supporters and detractors along the way. At times the rumours promised a spectacular festival, and then just as suddenly they would reverse, giving the impression that the festival would be a disaster. Tracking, containing and managing these rumours became a core task in organising the festival, and provided a good object lesson in the best publicity of all — word of mouth.

Fifteen years after the Aquarius Festival, Stephen Hall, who was Director of Special Events for New South Wales' massive celebrations of Australia's Bicentenary, was asked how the events program was going. He replied that the Sydney public had become so satiated with events that normal publicity had become completely ineffective, and that only one thing mattered — word of mouth.

SPONSORS

Recent decades have seen enormous increases in sponsorship, and a corresponding change in how events are perceived by sponsors. There has been a shift by many large companies from seeing sponsorship as primarily a public relations tool generating community goodwill, to regarding it as an important part of the marketing mix. Successful major events are now perceived as desirable properties, capable of increasing brand awareness and driving sales. They also provide important opportunities for relationship building through hosting partners and clients. Corporations invest large amounts in event sponsorship, and devote additional resources to supporting their sponsorships in order to achieve corporate and sales goals.

Sweaney (1997) defines commercial sponsorship as 'a high profile form of collaborative marketing between organisations which usually involves an investment in an event, facility, individual, team or competition, in return for access to an exploitable commercial potential.'

In order to attract sponsorships, event managers must offer tangible benefits to sponsors, and effective programs to deliver them. Large corporations such as Coca-cola and Telstra receive hundreds of sponsorship applications each week, and only those events which have a close fit with corporate objectives and a demonstrable ability to deliver benefits will be considered.

Sponsors as *partners in events*

It is important for event managers to identify exactly what sponsors want from an event, and what the event can deliver for them. Their needs may be different from those of the host organisation or the event manager. Attendance numbers at the event, for example, may not be as important to them as the media coverage that it generates. It may be important for their chief executive to officiate, or to gain access to public officials in a relaxed atmosphere. They may be seeking mechanisms to drive sales, or want to strengthen client relationships through hosting activities. The event manager should take the opportunity to go beyond the formal sponsorship agreement, and to treat the sponsors as partners in the event. Some of the best ideas for events can arise from such partnerships. Common agendas may be identified which support the sponsorship and deliver additional benefits to the event.

Toyota was a major sponsor of the Grand Australian Sumo Tournament held in Sydney and Melbourne in June 1997. Toyota supported its sponsorship with a Sumo Sale national advertising campaign in television and print media, which contributed to the Sumo visit being seen as a major cultural event celebrating the centenary of Australia/Japan relations. The sponsorship helped to promote sales for Toyota, as well as increasing the profile of the event. Likewise in 1992, State Bank supported its sponsorship of Sydney's Sesquicentenary celebrations with a campaign through its branches, and an enormous birthday cake in its colours, which was cut and distributed at Darling Harbour. The sponsorship identified State Bank with the celebrations, and provided the event with an additional promotional outlet through the bank's customers.

MEDIA

The expansion of the media, and the proliferation of delivery systems such as cable and satellite television and the Internet, have created a hunger for media product as never before. The global networking of media organisations, and the instant electronic transmission of media images and data, have made the global village a media reality. When television was introduced to Australia in time to cover the Melbourne Olympic Games in 1956, the world still relied largely on the physical transfer of film footage to disseminate the images of the Games interstate and overseas. Australia's Bicentennial celebrations in 1988 featured an Australia-wide multi-directional television link-up which enabled Australians to experience the celebrations simultaneously from a diverse range of locations and perspectives, seeing themselves as a nation through the media as never before. The opening ceremony of the Winter Olympic Games in Nagano in 1998 featured a thousand member world choir singing together from five different locations on five continents, including the forecourt of the Sydney Opera House. Global television networks will follow New Year's Eve of the new millennium around the world, making the world seem smaller and more immediate. When the 2000 Olympics begin, a simultaneous global audience estimated at two and a half billion people will be able to watch the event tailored to their own national perspectives, with a variety of cameras covering every possible angle. Events such as the funeral of Diana, Princess of Wales, have become media experiences shared by millions as they are beamed instantly to a global audience. In Britain alone, the Princess's death attracted record media coverage.

This revolution in the media has in turn revolutionised events. Events now have a virtual existence in the media at least as powerful, sometimes more so, than in reality. The live audience for a sports event or concert may be dwarfed by the television audience. Indeed, the event may be created primarily for the consumption of the television audience. Events have much to gain from this development, including media sponsorships and the payment of media rights. Their value to commercial sponsors is greatly increased by their media coverage and profile. However, the media often directly affect the way events are conceptualised and presented, as in the case of One Day Cricket or Super League, and can have a profound effect on the relationship of the event with its live audience. So far sports events have been the main winners (and losers!) from this increased media attention. The range of sports covered by television has increased dramatically and some sports, such as basketball, have been able to rise from relative obscurity in Australia to assume a high media profile, largely because of their suitability for television production and programming.

The available media technology influences the way that live spectators experience an event. Sweaney (1997) reported on the Seven Network's plans to construct a state-of-the-art digital broadcasting centre adjacent to the planned Melbourne Docklands Stadium, which will be the new home for Seven in Melbourne. The wiring of the stadium allows for digital television and will enable every spectator to have a unique seat with personalised communication services. Increasingly, spectators' viewing capabilities are technologically enhanced to parallel those of people watching at home.

Media interest in events is likely to continue to grow as their ability to provide community credibility and to attract commercial sponsors is realised. Parades, spectacles, concerts and major public celebrations are areas of potential interest to the media, where the need to make good television is likely to influence the direction and marketing of events. The role of the media can vary from that of media sponsors to becoming full partners — or even producers — of the event.

Whatever the role of the media, it is important for the event manager to consider the needs of different media groups, and to consult them as important stakeholders in the event. Once the media are treated as potential partners, they have much to offer the event. The good media representative, like the event manager, is in search of the good idea or unusual angle. Together they might just dream up the unique approach that increases the profile of the event and provides value in turn to the media organisation. The print media might agree to publish the event program as editorial or as a special insert, or might run a series of lead-in stories, competitions or special promotions in tandem with sponsors. Radio or television stations might provide an outside broadcast, or might involve their on-air presenters as comperes or special participants in the event. This integration of the event with the media provides greater reach and exposure to the event, and in turn gives the media organisation a branded association with the event.

CO-WORKERS

The event team that is assembled to implement the event represents another of the key stakeholders. For any event to be truly effective, the vision and philosophy of the event must be shared by all of the team, from key managers, talent and publicist, right through to the stage manager, crew, gatekeepers and cleaners. No matter how big or small, the event team is the face of the event, and each is a contributor to its success or failure.

Most people have experienced events which went well overall, but were marred by some annoying detail. There are different ways of addressing such problems, but team selection and management are always crucial. The Disney organisation has a system where the roles of performer, cleaner, security etc. are merged in the concept of a team looking after the space. The roles tend to ride with the needs of the moment — when the parade comes through, it's all hands on deck! The daily bulletin issued to all staff members reminds them that customers may only ever visit Disneyland once, and their impressions will depend forever on what they experience that day. This is a very positive event philosophy.

PARTICIPANTS AND SPECTATORS

Last but not least are the 'punters' on the day — the participants and spectators for whom the event is intended and who ultimately vote with their feet for the success or failure of the event. Good market research will help to identify the potential audience. Their needs and expectations will be covered in detail later in chapter 6, the chapter on marketing. An important element of meeting these needs is touching the emotions: a skilled event manager strives to make events meaningful, magical and memorable. Hemmerling (1997) describes the criteria by which spectators judge an event:

■ Their main focus is on the content, location, substance and operation of the event itself. For them the ease with which they can see the event activities, the program content, their access to food and drinks, amenities, access and egress etc., are the keys to their enjoyment. Simple factors such as whether or not their team won or lost, or whether they had a good experience at the event will sometimes influence their success measures. Secondary issues, such as mixing with the stars of the show, social opportunities, corporate hospitality and capacity to move up the seating chain from general admission to premium seating are all part of the evaluation of spectator success. ■

DEVELOPING THE EVENT CONCEPT

Once the stakeholders in the event have been identified and their needs established, the event manager is in a position to focus the event and develop an event concept to satisfy these needs.

Certain parameters may already be defined. The time, venue and participants in the event may already be set, as is often the case with a major sporting fixture or championship. If not, choosing the time and location of the event are two vital considerations.

If the event is outdoors, getting the timing right will be crucial, as will be matching the needs of the event to the venue. If the audience is to be comfortable, midwinter may not be ideal. If the event is held in midsummer, the timing may need to avoid the heat of the day. The choice of venue must represent the best compromise between audience comfort, accessibility, cost and the needs of the event.

An important part of developing the event will be identifying unique elements and resources which can make the event special, and contribute to its imagery and branding. Australia Day at Darling Harbour in 1993 had to be special, as an important International Olympic Committee delegation was scheduled to attend. It was the largest single delegation to visit Sydney, and its purpose was to conduct a final inspection of the city before the vote to decide the host city for the 2000 Olympics was held. The organisers identified Sydney Tower as having the potential to be transformed by pyrotechnics into a giant Olympic Torch. The idea was workshopped and incorporated into the event, creating a memorable image, which made the cover of *Time* magazine and played a part in convincing the delegation that Sydney was capable of staging a major celebration if awarded the Olympic Games.

■ Brainstorming

Once the parameters of the event have been set, it is desirable to brainstorm the concept of the event, letting the imagination soar and consulting as many stakeholders as possible. A good way to do this is to meet with them individually at first, establishing relationships and allowing each stakeholder to become comfortable with its role in the event. In these discussions ideas will arise, but the process should be acknowledged as exploratory, not yet seeking to reach fixed conclusions.

Once the diverse stakeholders are brought to the meeting table, the ideas will start to flow. This is a time to ignore restraints of practicality — of cost, scale or viability. That time will come. The task is to create and to dream, and no idea should be dismissed as too wild to consider. The goal is to discover the right idea, the one that resounds so that everyone recognises it and is inspired by the challenge and the potential that it offers. This is where the skills of an event director come to the fore — the ability to draw out ideas, to synthesise content and eventually to engineer compromise. No matter how good an idea or how strong its support, eventually it must serve the objectives of the event, and be deliverable within the available resources. With some good fortune, this idea may be identified in a single meeting, but most often the process will take several meetings and weeks or months of patience and hard work. But the results will be worthwhile if a strong vision for the event emerges, one that is shared and supported by all stakeholders, and which inspires confidence and commitment. This process is at the very heart of creative event planning, and when it works well it is one of the joys of being in the business.

■ The synergy *of ideas*

Most good events emerge from a synergistic group process. Such a process was illustrated in 1993, when the New South Wales Australia Day Council brought together a group of people to devise a program of celebrations for the Sydney Olympic bid announcement.

The brief had some unusual features. The announcement of the successful bid to stage the 2000 Olympic Games was to be made by IOC President, Juan Antonio Samaranch, in Monte Carlo at 4.20 a.m. Sydney time.

The event organisers faced a challenging dilemma. If Sydney was successful, it created an opportunity for a memorable celebration, and for images of the winning city to be beamed around the world by the media. If Sydney lost, its inhabitants were unlikely to be impressed by being woken up before dawn.

With a collective brains trust of some of Sydney's top event directors and media strategists, they set about the challenge of answering the brief. The selection of a venue presented a difficult choice. As Homebush Bay had been selected as the Olympic site, it made sense to reveal it to the world. On the other hand, the Sydney Opera House is undoubtedly the symbol of Sydney, instantly recognised around the world.

In the end, as is often the case with difficult choices, it was decided to include both. A party would be staged for the site workers and school children at Homebush Bay, and an official reception and public celebration would be held several kilometres away on the west side of Circular Quay, with the Opera House in the background. If Sydney was successful, the two parties would be connected by a series of pyrotechnic rockets which would be fired up into the air at intervals along the harbour foreshore. Thus the approach of A and B (win or lose) scenarios started to emerge. Media strategists began work on the images that would feature in the television transmission that was planned for the winning city. A live cross of one minute provided a unique window of opportunity to showcase Sydney to the world. The organisers favoured the image of fireworks exploding over the Opera House, but how to dress the Opera House in celebratory mode?

The answer came from one of those marvellous synergistic processes, with one person building on the idea of another until the solution was reached. It started with the idea of laser image projections beamed on the Opera House shells. The obvious content was the ribbon device that was the logo for the bid. Finally the idea emerged: why not place the ribbon on the outline of the shells, which were the original inspiration for the logo? It was one of those ideas which everyone instantly recognised as the right idea, but for which no single individual could totally claim credit.

Good ideas have a habit of winning support, and the concept was rapidly adopted by a cooperative Opera House management and the lighting sponsor Philips, who had the technical expertise and commitment to carry it through. When Samaranch uttered the words, 'And the winner is... Sydney!', they were ready with the switch, to reveal the idea to the world.

With the increased involvement of governments and the corporate sector, events are required to serve a multitude of agendas. The successful event manager must be able to identify and manage a diverse range of stakeholder expectations. Major stakeholders are the host organisation staging a particular event, and the host community, including the various public authorities whose support will be needed. Both sponsors and media are important partners, and can make important contributions to an event in support and resources beyond their formal sponsorship and media coverage. The vision and philosophy of the event should be shared by co-workers in the event team, and the contribution of each should be recognised and treated as important. Ultimately it is the spectators and participants who decide the success or failure of an event, and it is crucial to engage their emotions.

Once the objectives of the event and the unique resources available to it have been identified, the next priority is to brainstorm ideas with stakeholders so that a shared vision for the event can be shaped and communicated. No event is created by one person, and success will depend on a collective team effort.

Questions

1 Who are the most important stakeholders in an event, and why?

2 Give examples of different events staged by government, corporate and community groups in your region and discuss their reasons for putting on these events.

3 Focusing on an event that you have experienced first-hand, list the benefits that the event could offer a sponsor or partner.

4 Using the same event example that you discussed in the last question, identify suitable media partners and outline how you would approach them to participate in the event.

5 What are the means by which an event creates an emotional relationship with its participants and spectators?

6 What events can you think of that demonstrate a unique vision or idea? What techniques have been used to express that vision or idea, and why do you consider them to be unique?

7 Imagine you are planning an event in the area where you live. What are its unique characteristics, and how might these be expressed in the event?

8 Name a major event that you have attended or in which you have been involved, and identify the prime stakeholders and their objectives.

The Heysen Festival
at Hahndorf

The inaugural Heysen Festival at Hahndorf in South Australia was held over ten days in October 1997, to coincide with the anniversary of the birth of legendary artist Sir Hans Heysen. It spearheaded a new era in cultural tourism and special event development and marketing among the traders and community of Hahndorf.

Hahndorf is a unique German village situated in the picturesque Adelaide Hills, just twenty minutes from the heart of Adelaide. This historic precinct has over a hundred shops, including ten galleries, diverse attractions, coffee shops, award-winning restaurants, and speciality and souvenir stores. The magnificent Main Street is lined by trees and features superb historic buildings. For many visitors to Hahndorf simply walking along Main Street is entertainment enough.

Participating traders reported that the inaugural Heysen Festival focused visitors' attention on their particular premises and product, and attracted a more discerning visitor, with an eye for quality and a greater spending capacity. This result was achieved through a range of creative strategies that used existing town features, businesses and organisations to present an exciting integrated event.

The Heysen Festival involved some thirty-eight artists, both local and from other parts of the State, working and exhibiting in thirty-eight businesses for the ten days of the festival. Venues included the post office, butcher's shop, pizza bar and newsagent, and the emphasis was on exposing the arts to the general public.

The activity was packaged and promoted as the Artist's Trail, and visitors were given a brochure containing a map and details about each trader and artist. Special flags created by community groups were displayed outside the participating premises, including the logo of the Artist's Trail. As well as marking each location, the flags added to the colourful atmosphere of the street.

Hahndorf is also the site of The Cedars, the historic house, garden and studio of Sir Hans Heysen, and of the famous Hahndorf Academy, which is a regional visual and performing arts centre.

The Cedars is open daily to the public, and for the birthday celebrations it was the focus of special exhibitions featuring works by Heysen at Hahndorf. Soirees were conducted in the grand dining room of the house, complete with wine, coffee and Lady Heysen cake, made especially from a recipe handwritten in German by Lady Heysen, the artist's wife. The garden and studios were alive with music and poetry during the celebrations.

The Hahndorf Academy also operates quality craft working studios, and is the home of the German Migration Museum. For the inaugural festival, the Hahndorf Academy Foundation introduced a unique Heysen Art Prize Competition and Exhibition for Traditional Australian Landscape. The organisers are working toward this being a significant national art award in the future.

A further group of artists took part in an on-site art competition, each painting a work depicting a historic building on Main Street. The artists had to complete the work on site between 10.00 a.m. on the opening Saturday and 4.00 p.m. on the following Friday. On the last Saturday and Sunday the works went on public display where they were judged. At some of the sites street theatre and/or music were combined, creating a wonderful interaction between the working artist, performers and the public.

Much of Hans Heysen's work focused on Hahndorf and Main Street, and a special Heysen Interpretive Walk was devised. The route led visitors on a historic journey, featuring eight locations in Main Street, where works by Heysen were displayed. Visitors had the opportunity to see the town through his eyes. Arts South Australia (through its minister) has offered support for the establishment of a permanent Interpretive Walk at Hahndorf, with the installation expected to be completed in time for the 1998 Festival.

The festival was an initiative of the Tourism/Special Events Section of the District Council of Mount Barker (the principal sponsor) and a partnership between the council, Hahndorf Traders, Hahndorf community, Hahndorf Academy Foundation, *The Artists' Voice*, the Heysen family, Dance Excentrix and the South Australian Country Arts Trust.

Artistic product and activities contribute much to the social and cultural fabric of community lifestyle in Hahndorf and the Adelaide Hills, with much untapped potential for economic benefit to the wider community, particularly through initiatives such as the Heysen Festival at Hahndorf.

Barry W. Wilkins, OAM, has been a festivals administrator, adviser and producer for over 25 years and is presently Manager, Tourism and Special Events for the District Council of Mount Barker, South Australia

Questions

1 Identify as many stakeholders in the Heysen Festival at Hahndorf as you can, and list the likely benefits to each stakeholder.

2 What potential negative impacts might result from the staging of the festival in Hahndorf, and how would you address these in the event plan?

3 From the event description in the case study, what do you think was the likely process of conceptualising the event?

4 Can you think of locations in your region where a similar event model might be applied? List the potential stakeholders, and describe the steps you would take in conceptualising the event.

REFERENCES

Golds, Rosey 1996, 'Waltz out Matilda for 2000', *Sydney Morning Herald*, 15 March, p. 11.

Hamill, Alex 1997, 'The mood of the Australian consumer as we move toward the new millennium', paper delivered to The Big Event New South Wales Tourism Conference, Wollongong, NSW.

Hemmerling, Mal 1997, 'What makes an event a success for a host city, sponsors and others?', paper presented to The Big Event New South Wales Tourism Conference, Wollongong, NSW.

Savage, Gillian 1997, 'Our Culture?', *Australian Leisure Management*, vol. 1, no. 5, pp. 54–55.

Sweaney, Karen 1997, 'Sponsorship Trends', and 'Developing the Docklands', *Australian Leisure Management*, vol. 1, no. 3, pp. 18–19, and vol. 1, no. 5, p. 16, respectively.

PART 2

EVENT MARKETING

AND MANAGEMENT

4

The planning *function*

LEARNING OBJECTIVES

After studying this chapter, you should be able to:

- understand the importance of planning to ensure the success of an event

- construct an appropriate vision and mission for an event

- construct objectives for an event which are specific, measurable, achievable, relevant and time-specific

- use various techniques for selecting the most suitable strategies to achieve the objectives of a festival or event

- construct an appropriate organisational structure for an event which will facilitate the achievement of its objectives

- prepare position descriptions for personnel involved in an event.

In its simplest form, the planning process begins by assessing the current position of an organisation, then determining a future desired position and the methods needed to achieve it. In other words, the planning process is concerned with ends and the means to achieve those ends.

Good strategic planning is crucial to the success and survival of an organisation. The link between an organisation's formal planning processes and its subsequent performance is well documented. For example, Robbins et al. (1997) demonstrated that a formal planning process produces superior financial outcomes. They found that the quality of the planning — and its subsequent implementation — is the most important factor in an organisation's effectiveness. Moreover, they concluded that ineffective organisational plans were in most cases attributable to environmental changes, rather than the planning process itself.

Successful planning ensures that an organisation remains competitive. It has been demonstrated (Flavel & Williams 1996) that entities that think about the future, construct meaningful plans and then implement them prosper in good times and survive the bad, and U.S. research (Thune & House, cited in Stoner et al., 1985) has shown that organisations which engage in formal planning consistently outperform, in all financial criteria, those which do not.

In event management, proper planning is also essential. Catherwood and Van Kirk (1992), from the accounting firm Ernst and Young, are consultants to major events such as the Olympics. They state:

> ■ ... planning is a process that must continuously occur... until the end of the event. It is crucial to have as a foundation for this ongoing planning a vision, a statement, or concept that can be easily articulated and understood. ■

Without planning, it is possible that the finished product will disappoint not only the intended audience but the organising bodies themselves.

■ Planning *for events*

An event plan needs to be both comprehensive and flexible. For an event manager the plan is an important guide, which must be able to accommodate the wide variety of conditions — meteorological, cultural, economic, political, competitive and demographic — which may change and impact on an event.

Critics of the planning process claim that planning is a time-consuming bureaucratic exercise whose benefits are doubtful, and that planning reduces flexibility, which can be the key to the success of a festival or event. But without a plan, members of an event team have little idea of their objectives, and no means to measure their success in achieving them. An effective plan does not reduce flexibility; on the contrary, it provides a clear picture of the current operating environment, allowing a speedy response if that environment changes.

Good event planning is a complex process, involving many important steps, as shown in figure 4.1. Each of these steps are examined in detail in the course of this chapter.

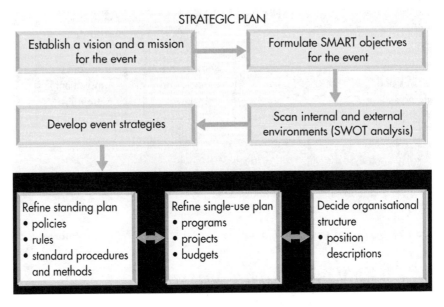

The planning process is usually broken down into two key processes: strategic and operational planning, as shown in table 4.1. In essence, strategic plans focus on setting long-term objectives and deciding on the strategies — the means and schemes — which will achieve them. Operational plans describe the specific steps needed to implement these strategies, and establish quantifiable revenue and expenditure budgets. Strategic plans are usually single-use plans, while operational plans are usually standing plans, which can be activated each time a recurring event is staged. In the planning of a festival or special event, both types of planning are used.

■ **Table 4.1**
Types of plans

BREADTH	TIME FRAME	SPECIFICITY	FREQUENCY OF USE
Strategic	Long-term	Directional	Single-use
Operational	Short-term	Specific	Standing

(**Source:** *Robbins et al. 1997*)

ꝲTRATEGIC PLANS

A model of the strategic planning process is shown in figure 4.2 (on the following page). Such a model provides a coherent framework for event managers to follow, and assists in clarifying such key questions as: what is to be done, by whom, how, and by when. It also helps in identifying the expected outcomes of the event.

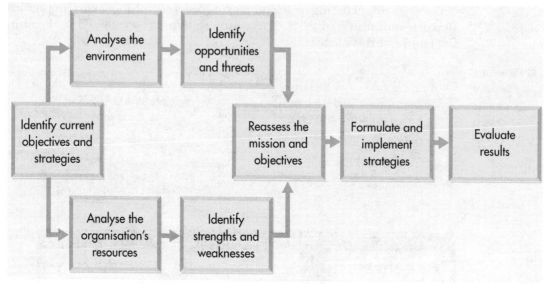

■ **Figure 4.2**   *The strategic planning process*   (**Source:** *Robbins & Stagg 1997*)

■ Vision *and mission*

Every event should have a vision and a mission. The vision can be separate from the mission or the two expressed as one, but usually the vision describes the long-term goals of the event. The mission describes in broadest terms the task that the event organisation has set for itself, stating the reason for staging the event, its stakeholders and its key objectives. Each event has a unique mission, which differentiates it from all other events.

How does this mission evolve? All festivals and special events occur because one person or a group of people believe that holding an event will fulfil some need in a community, region, organisation or company. These needs vary, but they are central to vision and mission development.

For ease of reference, the mission is generally expressed in a concise mission statement of only a few lines. An effective mission statement should answer the following questions:

• Who are our participants (customers)?
• Which participant needs are we satisfying?
• What are the organisers trying to achieve?

Once the mission is defined, it can be used to focus the event's organisers upon the task at hand, leading to the formulation of clear event objectives and strategies. It is also an important means to provide all who are involved in the event (either in a paid or volunteer capacity) with a clear understanding of the event and their role in it.

A coherent mission statement can be an invaluable tool for establishing a common direction in a team, and promoting unity among its members.

Figure 4.3 is an example of a mission statement from a volunteer organisation, the Sydney Women's Festival. In this document, the word 'motivation' is used to describe the mission. The statement effectively sets out the vision and mission of the festival, answering the questions discussed previously. It identifies the event's customers (women from diverse backgrounds), the needs it aims to satisfy (to forge a greater sense of power, identity and community) and the outcome which the organisers are trying to achieve (to celebrate and enjoy the diversity of women's experience in a carnival atmosphere).

Slogan
'Women Create Your Future'

Vision Statement
To create a nexus which celebrates and recognises the diversity of women's lives, explores and creates new opportunities for women, increases communication between groups and individuals, and is accessible and gives meaning to the whole community.

Motivation
The primary motivation is to bring together women from diverse backgrounds, to share skills and experience, to celebrate and enjoy; in the carnival atmosphere of the Sydney Women's Festival. This is a unique opportunity to cross over and interact between women's groups and forge a greater sense of women's power, identity and community.

■ Objectives

Once the mission has been decided, the event planner must establish the event's objectives. Well conceived objectives are a core element in the planning process, and are distinguished by several key features. These can be summed up in the acronym SMART:

Specific: carefully focused on the mission of the event

Measurable: expressed in a concise and quantifiable form so that they can be assessed after the event

Achievable: the objectives can be realised given the human, financial and physical resources available to the event organisation

Relevant: applicable to the current environment in which the event organisation operates

Time-specific: to be achieved by a designated time.

Depending on the mission of the event, objectives can vary greatly. For example, an event might aim to:

- reach a purely financial target (e.g. raise $50 000 for charity X)
- engage community participation (e.g. attract 50 000 people to the event's activities)
- raise awareness (e.g. after the event, 65 per cent of the population of Perth will know that whooping cough is a preventable disease in children)
- enhance product quality (e.g. the event will attract ten practitioners with international reputations to display their expertise)
- recover costs or make a profit (e.g. to produce a surplus of revenue over expenditure of $X)

- ensure participant satisfaction (e.g. 95 per cent of participants sampled will express a satisfied or better rating of the event)
- achieve growth in event dimensions, including public participation (e.g. the event will consist of 25 activities, 20 per cent more than the previous year and attract 20 per cent more participants)
- increase efficiency (with no increase in financial resources, the event will consist of ten more activities than the previous year's event)
- increase market share (this event will attract more people than any other event of its type in Australia this year).

As with all objectives, the crucial element is that they adhere to the SMART principle. Otherwise they are merely immeasurable vague hopes and desires, without benchmarks for success. Without such benchmarks, event managers cannot determine whether they have been successful in achieving their desired future ends and, just as importantly, identify those objectives that were not achieved. This is always an important part of the process of planning and delivering an event, since it allows event managers to analyse areas where planning was unsuccessful, and decide ways to improve performance for future events.

Objectives for an event such as the Sydney Women's Festival would be based on its mission, and could include:
- to produce 30 different activities for women in the world of business, politics, finance, health, community, and the arts
- to create a festival environment which will attract 5000 women and their partners to celebrate women's affairs
- to generate sufficient revenue from sponsorship, fundraising and admittance fees to cover all costs.

All of these objectives are time-specific to the activities of the festival for that particular year.

■ Strength, Weaknesses, Opportunities and Threats (SWOT) *analysis or environmental scanning*

After the event's objectives are decided, the next step in the strategic planning process is to analyse external and internal environments (or surroundings). This is called performing a strengths, weaknesses, opportunities and threats (SWOT) analysis, or, as it is sometimes called, environmental scanning.

The external environment consists of all the outside factors which surround the event and which can impact on its success. The internal environment consists of the resources available to the event organisation — including physical, financial and human resources.

The external environment is usually assessed first, and consists of many factors. The main factors include:
- **Economic:** The economic climate affects the volume and value of goods and services produced in a region. Economic features such as unemployment, inflation, interest rates, tariff protection and levels of wages and salaries can

impact on the demand for a particular event. For example, in an area of high unemployment, an event featuring conspicuous consumption of material goods would be inappropriate. Alternatively, events which celebrate different stages of the economic cycle can be very successful. For example, harvest festivals, which originated in medieval Europe to celebrate a successful farming season, are still popular events in rural areas.

- **Social:** The social life of a particular community results from interaction between the people who live there. Various institutions play a role in society, such as churches, charities, sporting groups, social groups, occupational groups, business organisations and artistic bodies. The people of a region may come together under the aegis of a community group such as Rotary or Apex to celebrate unique features of that area.
- **Cultural:** Culture can be defined as an historically derived design for living, shared by a discrete group of people. It encompasses such things as food, dress, architecture, language, shared beliefs, myths and values. It also includes artistic endeavours, recreation and leisure activities, and popular culture such as cinema, pop music and dance. Any planned event must address its target audience carefully: for example, planners of youth events must be aware that the youth culture of each generation is very different from its predecessor, and create activities accordingly.
- **Political/legal:** The deliberations of all levels of government become laws or regulations which affect the way people live in a society. For example, laws regulating the consumption of food and alcoholic beverages have changed radically in Australia since the 1950s, making outdoor food and wine festivals possible.
- **Technological:** Changes in equipment and machines have revolutionised the way people undertake tasks. A contemporary example of this is the use of the Internet to promote festivals and special events. Entering the word 'festival' into an Internet search engine will produce links to a multitude of events in all parts of the globe.
- **Demographic:** The composition of society in terms of age, gender, education and occupation changes over time. A striking example is the entry of the baby boom generation (people born between 1945 and 1960) into middle age. The generation that gave the world rock'n'roll, blue jeans and relaxed sexual mores is, and will continue to be, a large market for event managers, and will always have very different needs to the preceding and succeeding generations.
- **Meteorological:** The expected weather patterns of a particular area are a basic environmental consideration. This environment must be closely monitored when planning outdoor events!
- **Competitive:** The activities of organisations who operate in the same market are always a reference point for event managers.

A thorough scanning of the full range of factors that make up the external environment will reveal the event's target market(s), its range of activities, and opportunities for promotion, sponsorship and fundraising. Similarly, threats to the successful operation of the event can also be identified. Over a period of time, environmental factors can change, sometimes dramatically, necessitating adjustments to an event's objectives or design.

For example, the ethnic composition of many regional areas of Australia and New Zealand has undergone marked change, and the resultant shifts in the social and cultural environments of those areas have affected the demand for festivals celebrating particular cultures. In another example, a predicted reduction in government funding of cultural events is patently a threat to an event organisation dependent on such funding for much of its revenue.

When the analysis of the external environment is complete, the next step is to undertake an internal analysis of the event organisation's physical, financial, informational and human resources to establish its strengths and weaknesses.

Strengths can be such things as management or creative expertise; ownership or access to appropriate physical plant such as stages, sound systems and transportation; access to appropriate technology such as ticketing systems and information processing; access to financial resources; reputation and brand names; possession of a large volunteer base; existing cordial relationships with government and contacts with potential sponsors. Weaknesses could be the opposite of these or the event organisation's competitive position. For example, if two events catering for similar markets were held around the same time, one would probably be in a weaker competitive position than the other. In another example, meteorological conditions can be a strength for an event occurring in Townsville in Australia's tropical north in July, or a weakness if the event is planned for cyclone-prone February.

STRATEGY SELECTION

The scanning process gathers crucial information that will be used by the event manager in selecting strategies to achieve the event's mission and objectives. Strategies must utilise strengths, minimise weaknesses, avoid threats and take advantage of any opportunities which have been identified. A SWOT analysis is a wasted effort if the material which is gathered by the analytic process is not used in strategy formulation.

Several generic strategies which can be adopted by festival and event managers are summarised below.

■ Growth *strategy*

Late twentieth century human endeavour appears to be characterised by an obsession with size. In events, this is expressed in a desire to be bigger than last year; than other events; than other communities' events. Bigger is often thought to be better, particularly by ambitious event managers. Growth can be expressed as more revenues, more event components, more participants or consumers, or a bigger share of the event market. It is worth pointing out that bigger is not necessarily better, as some event managers have discovered. An example of this is the Sydney Festival (a cultural festival which takes place in Sydney each January). It adopted a growth strategy by absorbing other events taking place in Sydney in January and calling them umbrella events. Some critics asserted that by doing this the festival lost focus. A subsequent festival director responded by concentrating the festival on Sydney Harbour's foreshores, decreasing the number of event components but increasing their quality.

It is important to recognise that an event does not necessarily have to grow in size for its participants to feel that it is better than its predecessors — this can be achieved by dedicating attention to quality activities, careful positioning and improved planning. However, a growth strategy may be appropriate if historical data suggest there is a growing demand for the type of event planned, or if a financial imperative necessitates increasing revenues. The annual Woodford Folk Festival substantially increased attendance by incorporating contemporary rock acts into the event's line-up in an attempt to appeal to a market segment with a strong propensity to attend musical events. Increased revenues enabled the festival to repay much of its debt.

■ Consolidation or *stability strategy*

In certain circumstances it may be appropriate to adopt a consolidation strategy — that is, maintaining attendance at a given level by limiting ticket sales. This strategy is effective because supply is fixed while demand grows: eventually ticket prices can be increased, allowing the quality of inputs into the event to be improved. Tickets to performances at the Port Fairy Folk Festival are sold well in advance, allowing its managers to ensure high quality outcomes at no risk of financial deficit.

■ Retrenchment *strategy*

An environmental scan may suggest that an appropriate strategy would be to reduce the scale of the event but add value to the existing components. This strategy can be applicable when the operating environment of an event changes. Retrenchment can seem a defeatist or negative strategy, particularly to longstanding members of an event committee, but it can be a necessary response to an unfavourable economic environment or in cases where the socio-cultural environment has substantially changed. For example, the management of a community festival may decide to delete those festival elements that were poorly patronised and focus only on those that have proven to be popular with its target market.

■ Combination *strategy*

As the name suggests, a combination strategy includes elements from more than one of these generic strategies. An event manager could decide to cut back or even delete some aspects of an event which no longer appeal to the target market for the event, while concurrently increasing the role of other aspects.

▇ Strategy evaluation *and selection*

Most management writers such as Stoner et al. (1985) and Robbins et al. (1997) believe that strategic alternatives can be evaluated by using four main criteria:
1. Strategies and their component parts should be consistent. That is, strategies selected should complement each other.
2. Strategies should focus on the elements that the environmental scan has identified as important, and disregard other elements.
3. Strategies should deal with problems with which the event organisation's resources can cope.
4. Strategies should be capable of achieving the event's objectives.

It is important to stress that the strategies chosen must be congruent with the findings of the SWOT analysis.

▇PERATIONAL PLANS

Once the strategic direction of the event has been agreed, and the strategic plan designed, the implementation of the plan can commence. This process can be carried out by means of a series of operational plans. The connections between each aspect of the planning process are shown in figure 4.4.

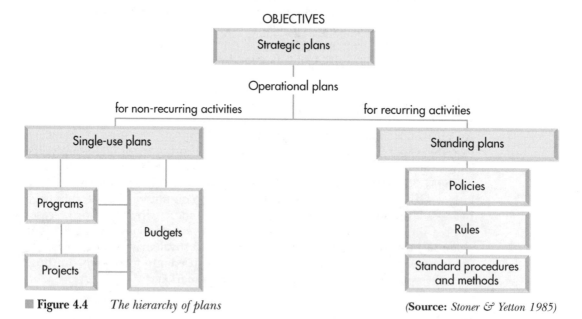

▇ **Figure 4.4**   *The hierarchy of plans*   (**Source:** *Stoner & Yetton 1985*)

Strategic plans describe the general thrust of how the festival or event is to achieve its agreed objectives (which of course are expressed in a way which is SMART: specific, measurable, achievable, relevant and time-specific). From these strategies are formed the operational plans needed to implement them. These consist of single-use plans and standing plans.

Single-use *plans*

Single-use plans are designed to achieve a particular objective. Most one-off festivals and events are developed from them. For example, the Sydney Women's Festival would have been based on a single-use plan for its 1996 festival, as it was the first of its type. In subsequent years, the festival would differ to a large or small degree, and each event would need its own single-use plan. The plans for most festivals are summarised in their programs which can be made up of several projects. Therefore a program can — depending on the size of the festival — cover a wide range of activities or projects.

Now the planning process must formulate the specific actions which will be needed to deliver the event's program, in accordance with the stated strategic thrust. This involves deciding various aspects, such as: the person or event department responsible for carrying out the plan; the allocation of financial, physical, human and communication resources; and a timeframe for each action. The person responsible for the program may then delegate responsibility for the different projects which make up the program to their subordinates.

Delegation can be a powerful method to engage the commitment of members of the event team, and highlights the important concept of staff responsibility or empowerment in event management. Many studies, including those of Robbins and Mukerji (1994) and Heskett et al. (1997) have shown that people who are given an opportunity to contribute their ideas, suggestions and creativity to the planning process are much more likely to take 'ownership' of their program or project than those who are merely expected to carry out a process decided by others. Staff who feel ownership of a program or project are more committed to achieving its desired outcomes, as they have been empowered by participating in the decision-making and planning process.

Events such as the Sydney Women's Festival are usually made up of several programs, each with a set of objectives. Each program, consisting of several projects, is 'owned' by a member of the event management team. Possible programs for this type of event include a cultural program to deliver music, drama and fine art projects; a feminist program presenting speakers, guest celebrities and writing on feminist topics; a culinary program with food stalls, wine tents, guest speakers and producing a festival cookbook; and a women in industry program introducing pioneering women speakers, business recruitment and seminars.

Each of these programs would use a budget as a technique for planning and control (see chapter 8). The budget is simply a statement of the resources approved to carry out the program in a temporal and quantified format, and also specifies the anticipated revenues from the program.

A budget is made up of two components, expenditure and revenue. The expenditure budget lists projected expenditure on the different resources needed to achieve the program's objectives and the accounting period in which the expenditure is to take place. It would include such cost factors as human (labour and entertainers' fees), physical (logistics and staging, i.e. cost of equipment, supplies and consumables) communications, energy, marketing and financial (insurance, interest etc.). The revenue budget lists the projected earnings of each element or project of the program from applicable revenue sources. These include box office, sponsorship, government grants, merchandising and the sale of goods and services. For commercial events, the revenue budget also includes any funds allocated from the marketing budget of the company for whom the event is produced.

This budgeting process is an integral aspect of planning. Frequently, it is the means by which alternative courses of action can be quantified and considered, allowing the most efficient to be chosen. The key to this process is that it be guided at all times by the event's objectives and the agreed strategies for achieving them. An inexperienced event manager sometimes can disregard this principle during the budget planning process, thereby negating the purpose of strategic planning.

The budget planning process is also the link between planning and controlling an event's activities as illustrated by figure 4.5.

The information contained in the budget acts as the control mechanism for event managers because it allows them to compare actual and budgeted expenditure and revenue. If there is a discrepancy between the two they can either:
1. change activities in an appropriate way so actual and budgeted results are congruent;
2. change the budget plan because circumstances have changed.

■ **Figure 4.5**
The connection between planning and controlling

(**Source:** *Stoner & Yetton 1985*)

■ Standing *plans*

Most festivals are not one-off events, but occur at regular intervals — yearly, biennially or, in the case of some major sporting events, every four years. In this case a single set of decisions can outline policies, standard procedures and rules. This is where standing plans are helpful.

Standing plans, as shown in figure 4.4, are made up of policies, rules, and standard procedures and methods. Robbins et al. (1997) define policies as guides that establish parameters for decision making. By contrast, rules are explicit statements that tell managers what they can or cannot do. Standard procedures and methods are defined as a series of interrelated sequential steps that can be used to respond to common or anticipated occurrences.

Each event will develop these three elements to produce its own particular standing plan. An event such as the Sydney Women's Festival, for example, might develop a policy that all board members and executive staff must be women, or that the board must approve all capital expenditure in excess of $5000. Possible rules might include one that states that no volunteer can be asked to work more than eight hours per day, and any program manager who chooses to ignore this rule would need to be able to justify this decision. A standard procedure might be that any unused tickets be refunded at once, no questions asked, with a smile. The advantage of this trio of standing plans is that managers at all levels of the event organisation need not spend time considering issues which arise on a regular basis, as the plan ensures that they will be dealt with in a consistent and coherent manner.

ORGANISATIONAL STRUCTURE

During the planning process, the organisational structure of the organisation must also be decided. In the same way that a house takes its shape from its structural framework, an event organisation's strategies and objectives are the product of its structure.

The majority of event organisations — with the exception of those responsible for major sporting events such as the Olympics — have a small number of staff. Therefore their organisational structures usually display what Robbins et al. (1997) describe as a low level of complexity. They are characterised by a low degree of differentiation of work between different positions within the organisation, minimal geographic dispersion of the organisation and minimal vertical levels of decision-making within the organisation. For such small organisations, three types of organisational structure are common:
- simple structures
- functional structures
- network structures.

Large organisations make use of further organisational modes such as:
- task forces
- committees.

Simple *structures*

As the name suggests, a simple structure has a low level of complexity. As figure 4.6 (on the following page) shows, all decision making is centralised with the manager, who has total control over all the activities of the staff. This is the most common structure in small business (and event organisations) as it is flexible, adaptable to changing circumstances, easy to understand, and has clear accountability — the manager is accountable for all the activities of the event. Because of this flexibility, staff are expected to be multiskilled and perform various functions. This can mean individual jobs are more satisfying, and produce high staff morale. However, because of a lack of specialisation, staff may not achieve a high level of expertise in any one area.

This structure has its disadvantages. For example, once the organisation grows beyond a certain size decision making can become very slow — or even non-existent — as a single executive has to carry out all the management functions. Also, if the manager has an autocratic style, staff can become demoralised when their expertise is not fully utilised. There is an inherent risk in concentrating all expertise and information about the management of an event in one person — obviously, sickness at an inappropriate time could. prove disastrous for the event.

■ **Figure 4.6**
*A simple
structure*

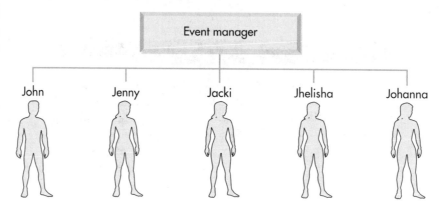

■ **Functional** *structures*

As the name suggests, a functional structure departmentalises employees by their function, that is, by their intended output. Figure 4.7 shows a functional organisation for an outdoor musical festival. Employees can achieve efficiencies (that is, produce more output with the same inputs) by specialising in particular tasks, rather than attempting all tasks involved in producing an event.

The advantages of a functional structure can be summarised as follows:
• staff become expert in their particular specialisation
• duplication of equipment and expertise is avoided
• staff feel comfortable working with fellow specialists in their department
• the organisation can become more effective (able to achieve its objectives) and more efficient (producing more with less).

■ **Figure 4.7**
*A functional
structure*

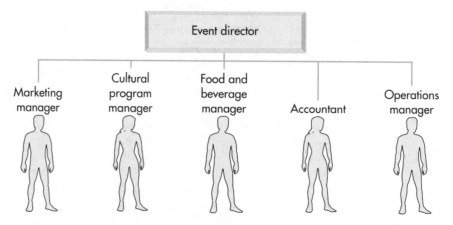

Like most constructs, a functional structure can have some disadvantages. These can be summarised as follows:
- functional managers can lose sight of the organisation's objectives in pursuit of their functional tasks
- there is a potential for conflict between functions which can inhibit the overall success of the event
- staff have little understanding of the role and outputs of other functions, and this can cause animosity and a lack of cooperation
- there is a heavy reliance on the event director to coordinate all of the functional activities to ensure event objectives are met
- functional managers may find it difficult to move up to an event director's position as they lack 'the big picture', that is, a broad perspective of an event's activities and outcomes.

Of course, many techniques can be used to overcome some of these disadvantages. Multiskilling strategies can be used to rotate staff through different functional departments and regular meetings between all functional departmental heads will ensure clear communication is maintained. Staff can be kept fully informed of the event's objectives, strategies, tactics and budget by means of regular staff meetings or newsletters, and these methods can also be used to make staff aware of the revenue and expenditure budget position. All these activities are essential elements of the leadership function of the event manager, and will be discussed in chapter 5.

■ **Network** *structures*

Robbins et al. (1997) define the network structure as a 'small centralised organisation that relies on other organisations to perform its basic business functions on a contract basis', as figure 4.8 (on the following page) shows. It is a fairly new way of thinking about organisational structure, which made its appearance in management theory during the late nineties.

Most festival or event organisations (with the exception of mega sporting events, and ongoing commercial events) are by definition of a limited duration, and are inactive for much of the time between events. This makes it impractical to maintain a large organisational structure of the functional type, unless it is chiefly composed of unpaid volunteers. The network structure can be appropriate for an event organisation because of several key advantages:
- it can be more efficient than other structures, which means lower costs and greater output
- it enables specialist firms with current expertise and experience to be contracted on a needs basis, with no 'down time'
- budgeting can be much more exact as most costs are contracted and therefore known beforehand
- it is flexible and dynamic as the core management group is made up of only a few people or one individual, and can quickly make decisions and change strategies and tactics if the environment changes

- when the event directorate and the contractors are linked by an effective computer network, communications can be rapid, resulting in swift reaction to any problems which arise.

The disadvantages of this type of structure include:
- quality control may be difficult to achieve as the work is performed by contractors
- reliability of supply of goods and services is not assured, as contractors may have other regular clients who are given priority
- deficiencies in contractor performance can result in expensive and lengthy legal proceedings
- coordinating employees who work for various other companies can be difficult.

Nevertheless, the concept of the network structure is supported by contemporary management thinking on downsizing, sticking to core activities and outsourcing, and can be very effective for certain kinds of events.

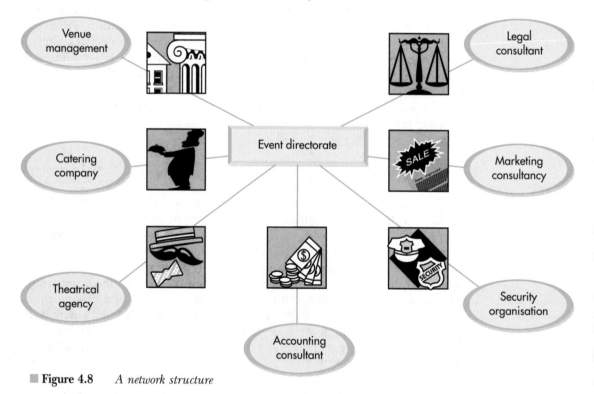

■ **Figure 4.8** *A network structure*

■ Task forces *and committees*

Large organisations, such as local government authorities (LGAs), sometimes decide to produce a one-off event by assembling a task force. This temporary structure is composed of staff with appropriate skills from various departments within the organisation, and disbands once the event has been held, its members returning to full-time duty in their functional department. Once assembled, a task force forms the management group for the event. It performs the planning function described in this chapter and utilises both internal and external resources to achieve the event's objectives as it sees fit.

A committee has a similar structure to a task force, and can be defined as a permanent task force. If a local government authority, for example, decided to produce an annual Australia Day event, an appropriate structure would be a standing committee made up of representatives from all departments within the LGA with a function to fulfil to meet the event's objectives. In this way experience and expertise would be built up over time, allowing the formation of a corporate memory.

Each organisational structure has its advantages when used appropriately. Table 4.2 shows the advantages of each structural design, and its likely application in event management organisation. In all cases, the selection of a structure must be based on the available resources, the strategies which have been developed to achieve the event objectives and the operating environment.

■ Table 4.2
Organisation structure options

STRUCTURAL DESIGN	ADVANTAGES	WHEN AND WHERE WILL THIS DESIGN BE APPLIED?
Simple	Flexibility, economy, speed	In small event organisations, in simple and dynamic environments
Functional	Efficiency by task specialisation	In large event organisations which produce a single service
Network	Flexibility, economy, speed	When many reliable suppliers are available
Task force	Flexibility	In large organisations which need to produce a one-off event
Committee	Flexibility	In large organisations responsible for annual events which need expertise that crosses functional lines

(**Source:** *Adapted from Robbins et al. 1997*)

THE POSITION DESCRIPTION

The next step in the planning and organising process is to decide the structure of each job. It is important to specify the area of responsibility for each position within the organisational structure, and establish reporting relationships between positions. In large organisations, this is usually documented in a format known as a position (or job) description.

Position descriptions are helpful to managers in recruiting, selecting, inducting and training new employees. As Clarke (1991) states, 'almost every well-managed business maintains some formal job descriptions of the content of particular jobs'. Gerstein and Reisman (1987) report that inadequate position descriptions are a cause of poor employee selection. Mitchell et al. (1988) argue that position descriptions show staff how their various roles contribute to the successful achievement of organisational goals.

It may not be necessary for position descriptions to be formal written documents in small event organisations where a verbal briefing can be sufficient. However, the benefits of written job descriptions to an organisation are many and include:

- preparing job descriptions can help the event director to clarify what role an organisation's human resources will play in achieving its objectives
- a written job description is a record which can be used to avoid misunderstandings between staff and the executive about the roles and responsibilities of various positions
- the process of matching each job to a specific set of outcomes can avoid duplication across positions, and reduce ambiguity, overlap and inefficiencies
- these documents assist in the formal appraisal of personnel involved in the event.

The content of a position description is not fixed but depends on the context. However, the following elements are usually found in part or total in a job description (Clark 1991):

- **Function:** States in a broad way what an employee has to accomplish.
- **Responsibilities:** Lists the tasks the job incumbent needs to accomplish.
- **Authority:** Lists the authority the incumbent has to spend money, hire and fire, use resources.
- **Relationships:** Specifies the position to which the incumbent reports, those which report to the incumbent, and any people in other organisations with which the incumbent has contact.
- **Accountability:** Describes the basis on which the incumbent will be judged.
- **Specification:** Lists the personal qualities required for a person to perform in the position.

It is usual for a position description to be supported by an organisational chart which shows the structure and reporting relationships within the organisation as a whole.

There are many different ways of accomplishing the task of choosing an organisational structure and developing position responsibilities. The process can be formally pursued, resulting in written organisational charts and position descriptions. However, organisations that are small, under the total control of one person, and not reliant on government grants may choose to conduct the process informally, relying on oral communication to disseminate the plan. Whatever method is chosen, it must be done with the particular needs of the organisation in mind.

Planning is the basis for all successful events. To be successful, an event manager must gain a clear understanding of why the event exists (its mission), what it is trying to do for whom (its objectives), and decide the strategies needed to achieve these objectives. These must be set out and quantified in a detailed operating plan and its associated budget. It is also necessary to prescribe policies, procedures and rules for the event to ensure consistency of action among the various participants in its production.

The most common barrier to effective planning is the failure of managers to establish measurable objectives (i.e. SMART objectives). If the outcomes of an event are not measurable, then there is no way that management or team success can be judged. A comprehensive plan not only provides a blueprint for the execution of an event, but provides a basis for analysing the actual event outcomes against planned outcomes, enabling an event management organisation to deliver better events in the future.

Questions

1 Prepare a mission statement for each of the following events:
(a) The Sydney Gay and Lesbian Mardi Gras
(b) A rural town's cultural festival
(c) The Australian University Games
(d) A special event of your choice.

2 Select one of the above events and complete the following event planning process:
(a) Prepare a set of objectives and a SWOT analysis for the event.
(b) Demonstrate how each of your objectives satisfies the SMART principle.
(c) List the strategies suggested by your SWOT analysis.
(d) Formulate an operational plan for the event on the basis of the strategies you outlined in part (c).
(e) What type of organisational structure will best suit the planned event?
(f) Draw a plan of the organisational structure that you selected in part (e).
(g) Write a brief position description for each of the positions on your plan.

3 Imagine you are the director of the Woodford Folk Festival in Queensland.
(a) What environmental factors would you need to consider in organising the festival? Classify these as external or internal.
(b) List the main aspects that you consider necessary to a standing plan for this event. How are these different to the aspects you would include in a single-use plan?
(c) Construct an organisational chart for the festival.
(d) Write a position description for your job as festival director.

Sydney Theatre Company
Foundation Fundraising Party

MISSION AND OBJECTIVE FOR THE EVENT

The first Sydney Theatre Company (STC) fundraising party a (K)night of Medieval Mayhem, was held in 1995 in a disused tram shed in Glebe. Eleven hundred guests attended what turned out to be a landmark event for STC. So successful was the fundraising, that the decision was taken to make it an annual party. The STC Foundation was then established with the purpose of raising money specifically for the company and its research and development program.

Subsequent parties have enjoyed similar success with attendances increasing to 1200 guests for A Fabulous Night At The Trocadero in 1996, held in a container terminal at Darling Harbour with the HMAS Sydney and crew participating; I'll Take Manhattan in 1997 sold out in three weeks with 1300 guests and a waiting list of over 100. The 1998 party, The Last Romanov White Ball (followed inevitably by the red revolution) expected 1400 guests. For each of these events, up to thirty corporate tables has been sold.

The producers aim to take the guests out of the everyday and into a theatrical interpretation of another time and place. The format of the night consists of drinks preceding a three-course dinner. Three major production numbers featuring choreographed song and dance surround the central fundraising activity of the night, the auction. The latter part of the evening is either live or club music depending on the party's theme. Shows are spectacular, with large numbers of performers (for Trocadero there were over 500) and many surprise elements. All STC Foundation events have been hailed as parties of the year with Trocadero named by the *Sydney Morning Herald* as one of the best parties of the decade.

REASON FOR FUNDRAISING

Research and development ensure the future of any theatre company. Without the ability to experiment and develop new projects, theatres are restricted to staging existing works or those developed by companies that are more affluent. Before the establishment of the STC Foundation, all research and development were funded by box office receipts. This resulted in the company's director having either to program a subscription series of safe choices to guarantee sufficient revenue, or limit research and development to an affordable minimum. Without guaranteed funding, development of long-term projects was not possible.

ORGANISATION

As an established theatre company, STC is in a unique position in event management, having considerable resources in personnel skilled in every area of production, plus substantial staging materials, props and wardrobe. It also has the advantage of being able to broker deals with suppliers based on an ongoing connection with the Company.

However, the party must be scheduled into STC's busy year to ensure staff availability and avoid clashes with main stage productions. So that STC's resources are not overloaded, freelance personnel are brought in to manage key areas. The final party production team is structured as follows:

Producers: STC
Director: STC
Technical director: STC
Box office and marketing: STC
Production manager: freelance
Design and choreography: freelance
Stage management: freelance
Sound, lighting, staging and catering: contract
Public relations: freelance
Security: contract

All other crew and staff are drawn from the STC on either a paid or volunteer basis.

There are two producers for STC events: Wayne Harrison, who directs the show, and Camilla Rountree, who manages the other organisational aspects and coordinates the entertainment and sponsorship.

PLANNING THE TIME LINE

February:
- The theme for the party is chosen by the producers and presented to the Foundation for a date to be chosen.
- Once the theme is adopted, creating the image for the party commences. This image must convey the mood of the event as well as lending itself to an invitation, poster and program. It is therefore an important marketing tool.
- The producers engage the designer and choreographer and find a suitable venue. Once these three elements are in place, the entertainment can be planned.

April:
The main organisation of the event begins.
- A meeting of the creative team is called, involving the choreographer, the designer and the producers. The director outlines his or her ideas and the first of many discussions takes place. Over the following months the content of the show will change several times within the overall concept. This may be due to availability of artists, complications with staging, budget constraints or the advent of that most wonderful of things, 'a great idea'.
- A budget is drawn up, taking into account all projected costs at commercial rates, plus a contingency. As there is never sufficient money, sponsorships and deals are always necessary.
- The designer is given a broad outline of what will be needed to stage the event: the nature of the show; the number of guests; the number of corporate tables; whether a buffet or sit down dinner is planned and any other specific requirements. The designer then draws up a floor plan to scale. This is the blueprint for the night and is used by every department. It will show seating arrangements, placement of performance areas and their dimensions, entrances, exits, catering and bar areas, and facilities such as toilets, taps, fire equipment and lighting grids. Without this plan, the party cannot progress to the next stage.

May:
- Work has commenced on sponsorships.
- Caterers have been contracted and briefed.
- Hiring companies have been given the dates.
- Details of the party are placed in EXSTCE, the STC magazine that is sent to the subscriber base of 20 000. This promotes advance bookings so the STC Box Office is briefed.

June:
- Regular planning meetings commence, involving the creative team and the technical director. By this stage the producers are sourcing and booking artists for the show.

July:
- All the printed material for the party has now been approved and is sent to the printers.
- Advertisements are placed in STC subscription series programs.

August:
- Invitations are posted.
- The box office appoints an extra person to be responsible for processing bookings for the party.
- The publicists commence the job of creating media awareness of the party by sending out press releases.

September:
- The production manager joins the team. From this point on he or she takes over the detail of staging, lighting, sound and catering needs. The production manager works closely with the STC technical director and the producers to coordinate work being carried out in-house with that being done by external contractors. Regular trips to the location are required to make sure every department is familiar with the venue.
- The designer finalises details for staging and building of props, table lighting and the dressing of the room.

October:
- The costume designer joins the team. Where original costumes are required, fabrics are bought and made up in the STC workrooms. Other clothes are sourced from various hiring and theatre companies. Costumes for waiters and ushers are organised. Artists are called in for fittings.
- A catering coordinator ensures that all glassware, cutlery and crockery are suitable, that the quantities are correct and that everything is delivered on time, collected after the event and returned to its source.
- Music tracks are prepared by a musical director. If a live band or orchestra is performing for a production number, music charts will have to be prepared for the musicians.
- The production manager prepares a preliminary running order for the show. This schedules every aspect of the night from the arrival of the guests to the last dance track. Sometimes at this point problems arise with timing and logistics and the running order has to change.

Three weeks prior:
- Seating is finalised and tickets are posted to guests.
- All artists' contracts are finalised.
- A production assistant commences. It is the production assistant's job to send out delivery details for everything required for the event, to coordinate artists and prepare cell sheets for rehearsals and wardrobe checks.

Two weeks prior:
- Rehearsals commence.
- Program for the night is finalised and printed.

PRODUCTION WEEK

Monday:
- The riggers commence. Once they have finished, construction of the staging starts. Depending on the scale, this can take a day or more. Lighting and sound usually take about two days. Security guard at night.

Thursday:
- The room is ready for a rough rehearsal.
- Plotting of the sound and lighting begins.
- Wardrobe is set up at the venue and fittings for extras held.
- Cold rooms arrive and are switched on ready for food and beverage delivery.

Friday:
- Tables and chairs are set up.
- All catering requirements are delivered.
- Generators and 'porta-loos' are delivered as needed.
- Rehearsals take place with sound and lighting checks.

Saturday:
- Tables are set.
- Dressing of the venue is completed.
- The caterers begin the on-site preparation of the food.
- Rehearsals all day, so lunch is provided for the cast and crew.

On the night:
- Everyone on standby from one hour before the guests arrive.
- Last minute checks take place, and then it us up to the professionalism of everyone involved to make sure the night runs smoothly.

Sunday:
- Clean up begins as soon as the last guest leaves.
- Staging, lighting and sound equipment is struck.
- Catering equipment is packed ready for collection.
- Tablecloths bundled. Tables and chairs stacked.
- Props and wardrobe packed.

Monday:
Everything is collected and the venue cleaned.

OUTCOMES

The STC Foundation parties have been particularly successful both artistically and as fundraisers, bringing in over $200 000 per event.

SUMMARY

To run a successful event there are five golden rules:

1. Plan well in advance.
2. Once you have chosen your theme stick to it, but remain flexible enough to allow ideas to develop.
3. Employ people who are expert in their fields.
4. Learn what elements to prioritise; some things are more difficult to organise than you think.
5. For a fundraiser, remember your objective and be constantly on the alert for ways of doing things inexpensively but with style.

If you have a clear vision of what you want to achieve, are working with skilled people and have enough time, you can overcome many difficulties, even budget overruns. Budgets usually blow out in the last few days when problems that have not been foreseen must be solved with money. With careful planning and enough time, most problems can be avoided. The last ingredient is always luck; added to a professional approach to event planning, things are usually right on the night.

The Sydney Theatre Company Foundation Party is produced by Wayne Harrison and Camilla Rountree.

Sydney Theatre Company
By Camilla Rountree, Producer, Foundation Events and Wayne Harrison,
Executive Producer, Sydney Theatre Company

Questions

1 Write a mission statement for the STC Foundation events.

2 Describe two key objectives for the 1998 event. In what ways do these correspond to the SMART principle?

3 Describe the strategies that the STC Foundation party uses to achieve its objectives.

4 Construct an organisational chart for the event.
   (a) What type of organisational structure does it demonstrate?
   (b) Suggest reasons why this structure would suit the requirements of this event.

5 Write a position description for Camilla Rountree's position in the event organisation.

6 Construct a policy document for the event that lists appropriate policies and procedures for producing the event.

7 Would you classify the process described in the case study as a single-use plan or a standing plan? Explain your answer.

REFERENCES

Catherwood, D. & Van Kirk, R. 1992, *Special Event Management*, John Wiley & Sons, New York.

Clark, R. 1991, *Australian Human Resource Management*, McGraw-Hill, Sydney.

Flavel & Williams 1996, *Strategic Management*, Prentice Hall, Sydney.

Gerstein, M. & Reisman, H. 1987, 'Strategic Selection', *Art of Managing Human Resources*, ed. E. Schiem, Oxford University Press, New York.

Heskett, J., Sasser, W. & Schelesinger, L. 1997, *The Service Profit Chain*, The Free Press, New York.

Mitchell, T., Dowling, P., Kabanoff, B. & Larson, J. 1988, *People in Organisations*, McGraw-Hill, Sydney

Robbins, S., Bergman, R. & Stagg, I. 1997, *Management*, Prentice Hall, Sydney.

Robbins, S. & Mukerji, D. 1994, *Managing Organisations*, Prentice Hall, Sydney.

Stoner, J., Collins, R. & Yetton, P. 1985, *Management in Australia*, Prentice Hall, Sydney.

FURTHER READING

McGuire, M. 1997, 'Events and travelling exhibitions', *Making It Happen*, ed. R. Rentschaler, Centre for Professional Development, Melbourne.

5

Leadership and
human resources

LEARNING OBJECTIVES

After studying this chapter, you should be able to:

- outline procedures for recruiting and selecting staff and volunteers for an event

- implement effective induction and training programs for staff and volunteers

- understand what motivates people to perform effectively and efficiently

- understand how effective team building of volunteers is carried out

- implement procedures to ensure compliance with statutory provisions on payment of wages, occupational health and safety, and employee and volunteer records.

WHAT IS LEADERSHIP?

One definition of management, by the pioneering management writer Mary Parker Follett, is 'the art of getting things done through the efforts of others'. This means that the 'others' (staff and volunteers) must first be carefully chosen according to specific criteria; must receive appropriate training; be given direction on what they are to achieve, and how their efforts contribute to the festival or special event as a whole; be given appropriate rewards; be appropriately motivated to achieve the goals set for them; and be treated in accordance with legislation regulating employees and volunteers.

All these actions contribute to the leadership role of festival and event managers. In particular, this chapter deals extensively with leadership in relation to volunteers, because for many festivals they constitute the great bulk of the work force. However, volunteers are not just unpaid labour but people with needs, who probably present a greater leadership challenge than paid employees, since the rewards they seek are intangible, and intrinsic to the job itself; they do not seek the extrinsic reward of a salary.

Human resource issues and leadership are often overlooked in the management of small businesses such as festival and event organisations. Effective management of human resources is vital to the success of an organisation whose purpose is to produce a customer-focused festival. It can be overlooked or assumed to be simply common sense, to the detriment of the event's outcomes. People who are selected without thought, who are poorly trained and have little idea of their function and how it contributes to the event's outcomes are not able to satisfy the expectations of the event's customers by delivering customer service of consistent quality. This chapter outlines procedures and policies that enable event managers to undertake this function effectively.

HUMAN RESOURCE REQUIREMENTS

The number and type of human resources required for a particular event is determined through the strategic planning process. That is, the number and type of human resources required depends on the strategies adopted to achieve an event's objectives. For example, if an event's strategy is to focus on quality customer service, the number of people required will be greater than if other strategies, requiring less intensive human resources, are adopted.

Once the strategic and operational plans are agreed on, it is then possible to determine the number and types of human resources required to produce the event successfully. Getz (1997, p. 186) suggests that this procedure can be done using the three step method of:

1. Breaking down the program into separate tasks. For example the things that people must do to produce the event can be broken down into preparing the site, setting up fencing, erecting tents, toilets, stages and signs, cleaning up and disposing of waste and returning equipment to owners.

2. Determining how many people are needed to complete the different tasks. For example, do all the tasks have to be done in order, by the same crew, or all at once, and do they have to be done by a larger crew?
3. Making a list of the numbers of people, the supervisors and the skills needed to form the best possible crew.

The most difficult task in this process is step 2, particularly if the festival or event is new, or the event manager has no experience in a particular type of event. Human resource management writers, such as Clark (1992), propose the use of work study models to make human resource forecasts, though he warns it has short-term applicability only. However, as special events are by definition short term, this model can be effectively applied to human resource forecasting for events. They are generally very simple, as the following example of a musical festival shows.

Number of participants expected	25 000
Number of arrivals in peak hour period	10 000
Number through one gate per hour	2 000
Number of gates required	5
Number of turnstile operators required	5

Clark (1992) claims that the most common method of human resources planning used in Australian business (and, it can be assumed, also used by festival and special event managers) is managerial judgement. That is, each of the events' department heads calculates how many and what type of human resources he or she requires in order to meet their objectives. In order to forecast human resource needs, they take into account demand forecasts, the site of the event, previous instances of similar events, and strategies adopted by the event. As Clark (1992, p. 56) points out 'there has been little attempt to develop a theoretical framework for this type of planning', probably because it is intuitive and easy to comprehend.

After establishing how many staff and volunteers are required and what their level of skills must be, the next step is to recruit and select appropriate personnel.

■ Recruitment *and selection*

In chapter 4 it was pointed out that a position or job description is helpful to managers when recruiting and selecting new employees. The process of completing a position description can clarify what personal qualities, such as education, training, experience, stamina, social skills, strength and vitality, are required for each job type. The job specification lists the education, training and experience an incumbent needs to do the job successfully. The recruitment of paid employees and volunteers is a process illustrated by figure 5.1.

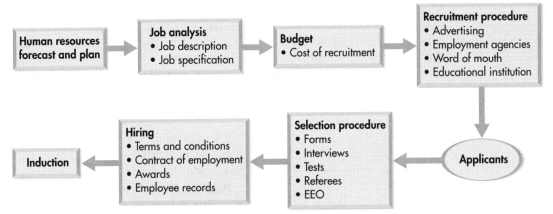

■ **Figure 5.1** *The recruitment of paid and voluntary employees* **(Source:** *adapted from Clark 1992)*

Some of the important factors to be considered when recruiting and selecting staff are discussed below.

- *Budget.* Depending on the size of the event, a budget (that is, an agreed amount of the festival's funds) can be allocated for recruitment costs. These budgeted funds can be used for payment of employment agencies or, alternatively, for advertising and other recruitment costs, such as travel expenses of non-local applicants and search fees for executive placement firms. The act of setting a budget acts as a control mechanism that ensures recruitment costs are realistic and that they are maintained.
- *Recruitment procedures.* It may be appropriate, depending on the types of positions which need filling, to use private or public sector employment agencies. However, because of the perceived attractiveness of working on special events, it is usually cheaper to recruit by means of advertisements in appropriate newspapers or trade journals. Nevertheless, it must be recognised that the time spent by a manager on this time-consuming process is also a cost.

■ **Figure 5.2**
An example of a job advertisement for an events manager

EVENTS MANAGER, Clerk. Grade 7/8, Sydney Botanic Gardens. Pos. no. R8G 9716. Total remuneration package valued to $51,005 p.a. (salary $43,328 – $47,960). Responsible for managing community and commercial use of Gardens' lands, including special events and venue hire. **Essential:** Demonstrated extensive experience in events management or related industry. Excellent oral and written communication skills. Demonstrated customer service, negotiation, team and interpersonal skills. Well-developed administrative, planning, staff and financial management skills. Ability to manage competing demands for land use. Computer skills in word processing, spreadsheets and venue booking systems. Current driver's license. Ability to implement EEO, OH & S policies and practices. **Desirable:** Database skills. An understanding of the role of a botanic garden. Tertiary qualifications in events management or a related field. Membership of ISES. Inquiries: Andrew Mitchell (02) 9231 8119

- *Voluntary staff.* Volunteers are gathered from a wide variety of sources. One source of volunteers, which is sometimes forgotten, is the major sponsor. As part of the sponsorship agreement, the sponsor may provide the event with temporary workers who have a wide range of skills, including managerial, financial planning and marketing skills. Universities and colleges of further education can also be a source of volunteers, particularly those universities and colleges offering courses in festival and special event management. Other sources worth investigating are service clubs, such as Apex and Rotary, who can provide food and beverage facilities (from which they raise funds for their activities); community and special interest groups who have some affinity with the mission of the event; and people who have worked on previous events. According to Bradner (1995), other sources from which volunteers can be recruited are:
  - retired and senior volunteer programs for people over 55
  - religious groups
  - community service programs
  - alumni groups
  - senior centres and retirement homes, and
  - professional organisations (accountants, lawyers).

  Obviously, the type of event affects the type of volunteer. It would be unrealistic to request senior citizen centres to supply volunteers for a rock festival.
- *Selection.* Application forms can be used to ensure all applicants have supplied equivalent biographical and historical data. However, this is not generally necessary for small organisations if the advertisement is written in such a way that the qualities being sought are clearly spelt out and the applicants are advised to address these in their letter of application. From this, unsuitable applicants can be culled and those thought suitable can be invited to attend an interview.

  The use of targeted selection techniques is claimed by Clark (1992, p. 249) to reduce common selection mistakes. This system is made up of six components:
  1. Use of past behaviour to predict future behaviour. That is, the manner in which a person completed a task in the past is the best predictor of the way that person will complete a task in the future.
  2. Identify the critical job requirements from the job description and person specification.
  3. Use effective interviewing techniques by asking appropriate questions, which can elicit responses that identify an applicant's ability in the critical job requirement.
  4. Use several interviewers, who, in post-interview discussions, can present behavioural evidence to support their ratings of an applicant's suitability for the position.
  5. If appropriate, supplement interview information with observations from behavioural simulations. For example, if the position is for a sponsorship manager, applicants can be asked to present a sponsorship proposal to a potential sponsor.

6. Systematically incorporate procedures which ensure that Equal Employment Opportunity (EEO) legislation is adhered to and that no applicants can claim they have suffered discrimination.

Since management can be defined as the art of achieving corporate objectives through the efforts of others, some of the most important decisions event managers make are those on staff selection. As the best predictor of future behaviour is past behaviour, the use of previous employers as referees can clarify whether an applicant is able to perform a task effectively. However, to avoid embarrassing the applicant, he or she must consent to contacting the referee.

Not all volunteers may be suitable for the various tasks involved in producing an event. It is therefore reasonable to screen volunteers for suitability, usually by interview. Bradner (1997, p. 72) suggests the use of a form to help structure the interview in a way that aids effective recruitment. An example of such a form is shown in figure 5.3.

Figure 5.3
Example of an interviewer's check list

Interviewer's check list

Name of volunteer: .... Date: ....

Position sought: ....

Background relevant to position: ....

Reasons for applicant becoming involved in event: ....

....

Does applicant understand requirements for position (e.g. training, time

involved, criminal record check, etc.)? ....

Amount of time applicant is available to work on event: ....

Perceived strengths for position: ....

Perceived weaknesses for position: ....

Special needs: ....

Accept ☐ Yes ☐ No

Applicant notified .... [Date/time]

- *Hiring.* Because most events are, by definition, of a short-term nature, most paid staff will be employed on a contractual basis for a specific period of time. The contract (which can be a legal document, a letter of appointment or merely a verbal agreement) says that the employee agrees to perform certain activities in return for an agreed salary and other emoluments, and lays out the rights and obligations of the employer and employee. Unsuccessful applicants should be informed as soon as possible.

■ Induction

To engender and maintain paid staff's and volunteers' enthusiasm for their role in the event and for its successful outcome, it is important that staff — particularly volunteers — are given an induction or orientation period. The first step is to discuss the job description with the new staff member. To avoid misunderstandings and later recriminations, it is important that paid employees and volunteers understand clearly what is expected of them. A simple way to accomplish this is for volunteers to sign a position description. Bradner (1997, p. 75) suggests that the information shown in figure 5.4 fulfil this function.

■ **Figure 5.4**
Example of a job description and contract for a volunteer

Volunteer job description and contract
Job title: ....
Supervisor: .... Location: ....
Objective (Why is this job necessary? What will it accomplish?): ....
Responsibilities (What specifically will the volunteer do?): ....
Qualifications (What special skills, education, or age group is necessary to do this job?): ....
Training provided: ....
Benefits (parking, transportation, uniforms, food and beverage, expenses): ....
Trial period (probation, if required): ....
References required (yes or no): ....
Any other information: ....
Date: ....
Signature of volunteer (Signatures to be added at time of mutual agreement.) ....
Signature of supervisor: ....

This process ensures the volunteer is aware of what is required and what benefits he or she is to receive. The event manager knows what tasks the volunteer is capable of and willing to perform. This then becomes the basis of a mutually rewarding experience.

If not handled well, it can be a disturbing experience to become part of a new and unfamiliar organisation. An induction period can replace such an experience with a commitment to making an event successful. Getz (1997, p. 189) suggests the following activities be part of an effective induction program:

- Provide basic information about the event (mission, objectives, stakeholders, budget, locations, product details).
- Conduct tours of venues, suppliers, offices and any other contacts the staff may need.
- Make introductions to other staff and volunteers.
- Provide instruction about organisational culture, history and working arrangements.
- Give an introduction to the training program.

A well-planned and organised induction period welcomes staff and volunteers to the event organisation and engenders a sense of belonging to and enthusiasm for the event and its mission. Bradner (1995) suggests that an induction kit be given to each new employee or volunteer containing such things as:

- an annual report
- a message from the chairperson welcoming staff and volunteers
- a clear name badge
- a staff list
- a uniform, whether it be a T-shirt or something more formal, made from a quality fabric
- a list of sponsors
- a list of stakeholders
- any other appropriate items.

It is important that the induction reflect the tone of the event. For example, the atmosphere at an induction for volunteers for a contemporary music festival may be loud and lively whereas a flower carnival's may be dignified, elegant and sedate. Refreshments are served and presentations should be made by enthusiastic and knowledgable staffers during this induction ceremony.

The outcome of the induction process should be a group of volunteers who are committed to the event, enthusiastic and knowledgeable about their role in it and aware of what part their job plays in the totality of the event.

■ Training

All staff and volunteers need training of some type if they are to make an effective contribution to the event. This can range from informal, on-the-job training carried out by a co-worker to a formal program using an extensive range of training techniques. For staff (particularly volunteers), this training process reinforces the idea that their services are important and they are making a significant contribution to the event. It also enables them to grow personally, to gain new skills and to increase their confidence.

The type and extent of the training required can be identified from the gaps that exist between current performance and desired performance. Identification of these gaps comes from:

- performance appraisals of existing staff (in which staff identify the training they require to be effective)
- analysis of job requirements (the skills identified in the job description)
- survey of personnel (the skills that staff say they need).

Because of the infrequent nature and short duration of events, training of event volunteers usually takes place on the job under the direction of the event manager or a supervisor. For this to be effective it should be structured to include:

- defined learning objectives. These outline what the trainee should be able to do at the end of the training.
- appropriate curriculum. The content of the training should be appropriate to the learning objectives.
- appropriate instructional strategies. These can take the form of discussion groups, lectures, lectures/discussions, case studies, role-playing, demonstrations or on-the-job training.
- well-conducted training. The trainer is not an expert handing down instructions from on high but a facilitator who can identify, explain and model the skills, observe trainees' attempts and correct their errors.
- evaluation. This is to assess whether the trainees have acquired the appropriate skills.

Hughes et al. (1992) developed a simple model of learning for use by casual teachers in the TAFE system. This model, which can be used quite effectively by supervisors and trainers of event volunteers and staff, emphasises the importance of reflection by the trainee and feedback from the trainer in achieving desired training objectives. Appropriate methods for training event personnel are:

- guided discussions; that is, asking the group questions which draw on their existing knowledge and then building on that base
- case studies of previous or similar events
- discussion groups to talk about the task involved in order to arrive at a course of action
- role-plays of situations in which personnel may find themselves
- exercises which apply the information received (adapted from Lulewicz, (1997).

This process of learning is modelled in figure 5.5.

As can be seen from figure 5.5, essential elements of the training process are reflection and feedback. That is, trainees think deeply about the connections between what they already know about the topic and the new information they receive; they relate new knowledge to experience, and use theory to extend experience. Feedback from the trainer, supervisor or peers, or through their own reflection, enables trainees to adjust their actions until the task can be correctly completed. It is unlikely that anyone has learnt a new skill without this process of reflection and feedback.

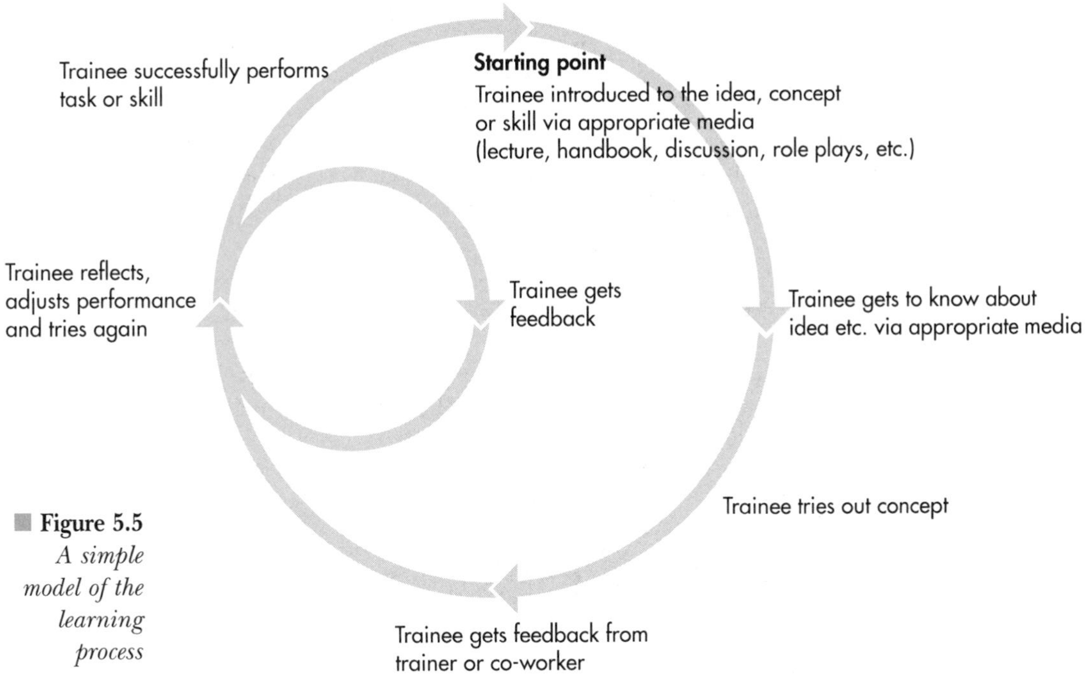

Figure 5.5
A simple model of the learning process

The diagram shows a circular learning process with the following stages:

Starting point
Trainee introduced to the idea, concept or skill via appropriate media (lecture, handbook, discussion, role plays, etc.)

Trainee gets to know about idea etc. via appropriate media

Trainee tries out concept

Trainee gets feedback from trainer or co-worker

Trainee gets feedback

Trainee reflects, adjusts performance and tries again

Trainee successfully performs task or skill

MOTIVATING STAFF AND VOLUNTEERS

Motivation is what commits people to a course of action, enthuses and energises them and enables them to achieve goals, whether the goals are their own or their organisation's. The ability to motivate other staff members is a fundamental component of the event manager's repertoire of skills. Without appropriate motivation, paid employees and volunteers can lack enthusiasm for achieving the event's corporate goals or for delivering quality customer service or can show a lack of concern for the welfare of their co-workers or event participants.

At first glance, it may be thought that pure altruism (an unselfish devotion to the welfare of others) is an important motive for volunteering to assist in events. Although this idea is supported by Flashman and Quick (1985), the great bulk of work done on motivation stresses that although people may assert they are acting for altruistic reasons, they are actually motivated by a combination of external and internal factors, most of which have little to do with altruism. As Moore (1985, p. 1) points out, 'volunteers clearly expect to obtain some type of reward for their participation and performance'. The parameters of that reward are discussed in this section.

Much work has been done over the years, by researchers from a variety of disciplines, on what motivates people, particularly in the workplace. The theories proposed by these researchers provide a solid basis for understanding motivation. Theories relevant to the motivation of volunteers are used in this section as a framework to help readers understand why people are motivated to do something and how this process can be facilitated. The theories of motivation most relevant to festival and special event workers (both paid and unpaid) are content theories and process theories. Each is discussed along with its relevance to festival and special event workers.

■ Content *theories*

Content theories concentrate on what things initially motivate people to act in a certain way or, as Peach and Murrell (1997, p. 223) point out, 'the needs individuals are attempting to satisfy through their actions'. This is shown diagramatically in figure 5.6.

■ **Figure 5.6**
Basis of content theories of motivation

Content theories say that a person has a need — a feeling of deprivation — which then drives the person towards an action that can satisfy that need. Abraham Maslow's (1954) hierarchy of needs, shown in figure 5.7, popularised the idea that needs are the basis of motivation.

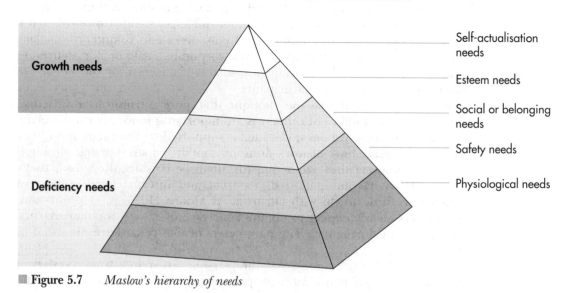

■ **Figure 5.7**   *Maslow's hierarchy of needs*

In essence, Maslow's theory proposes that lower order needs must be satisfied before people are motivated to satisfy the next higher need. That is, people who are trying to satisfy physiological needs of hunger and thirst have no interest in satisfying the need for safety until their physiological needs are satisfied. The first three needs are perceived as deficiencies; they must be satisfied in order to fulfil a lack of something. In contrast, satisfaction of the two higher needs is necessary for an individual to emotionally and psychologically grow.

Although little empirical evidence exists to support Maslow's theory, it can give insights into the reasons why people volunteer. People who feel a need for social interaction, making new friends, or belonging to an organisation with perceived prestige are satisfying social needs. Those who have satisfied the first three needs may be motivated by the need for gaining the esteem of friends and family by performing a particular task, which is prestigious in some way. Finally, people may volunteer in order to undertake a task that they believe will help them achieve their potential as a person and thereby be self-fulfilled.

Another researcher who influenced thinking on motivation is Herzberg (1982), who proposed the concept of motivators and hygiene factors. He suggests that what he refers to as hygiene factors do not in themselves motivate people but demotivate if they are perceived to be inadequate in any way. Motivating factors are things such as achievement and recognition. The Herzberg theory is represented diagrammatically in figure 5.8.

■ **Figure 5.8**
*Herzberg's
Theory of
Hygiene*

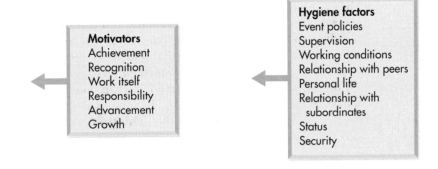

(**Source:** *adapted from Robbins & Mukerji 1994*)

This theory suggests that event managers can motivate staff and volunteers by instituting processes of recognising achievement, empowering staff so they can take responsibility for the outcomes of their part of the event, and giving opportunities for them to grow in skills, experience and expertise. At the same time, certain hygiene factors can act as demotivators: the attitudes of supervisors; working conditions such as meal and coffee breaks and hours of work; the status of one job compared with another (e.g. stage crews having higher status than crowd control staff); policies such as the type of uniforms given to volunteers — these can all be demotivators. Fixing these things will not motivate people but it will prevent them being demotivated. Although Herzberg's work has its contemporary critics, it does supply a useful framework for thinking about how to structure the workplace to maximise motivation.

However, as Peach and Murrell (1997) put it, while content theories that focus on need fulfilment are important in understanding what motivates people, it is sometimes difficult to know which need is dominant in a person, as different people are motivated by different needs. Content theory alone does not adequately describe what motivates work performance.

■ Process *theories*

Process theories concentrate on how motivation actually works — what its effects are. Adams's (1965) equity theory and Vroom's (1964) expectancy theory best represent this concept. Equity theory can be represented by the equation:

$$\frac{\text{My rewards (outcomes)}}{\text{My contributions (inputs)}} = \frac{\text{Your rewards (outcomes)}}{\text{Your contributions (outcomes)}}.$$

Two important characteristics of equity theory, which must be carefully thought about by event managers, are firstly, that over-rewarding some has the same demotivating effect as under-rewarding others; and secondly, that feelings of inequity are based on perceptions that may or may not equate with the event manager's perception of reality and can vary between individuals.

Equity can be defined in this context as the ratio between a person's effort and skills and their rewards (such as recognition, prestige, tasks allocated) compared with the rewards others receive for similar inputs. If inequity is perceived, the aggrieved person may try to make colleagues change their behaviour, either by increasing or decreasing input, depending on the perceived inequity. This process is modelled in figure 5.9.

■ **Figure 5.9**
*Responses to
perceived
equity or
inequity*

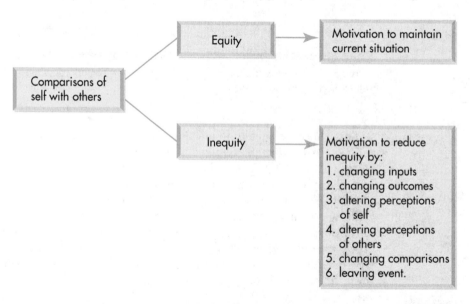

The question of perceived inequity is somewhat problematic for event managers, as it is difficult to know staff's perceptions of how they are being treated. The best way, of course, is to maintain constant and open communication lines between managers and their personnel. By this process event managers can pick up perceptions of inequity and take action to change these perceptions.

Expectancy theory (a kind of process theory) proposes that the motivation to act in a particular way comes from a belief that by doing something a particular outcome will result (expectancy); that this outcome will then result in a reward (instrumentality); and finally, that the rewards for accomplishing this outcome are sufficient to justify the effort of doing it (valence).

The application of expectancy theory to the situation of a volunteer working on a community cultural festival might be as follows.

- A volunteer has an expectancy that by working on the event, there will be enhanced involvement in cultural activities by the community in which he or she lives.
- The volunteer's role in the festival will contribute to (or be *instrumental* in) the goal of enhancing community cultural life.
- The volunteer's improved self-esteem, prestige and recognition, plus the enhancement of community life, are sufficiently worthwhile to justify the effort involved in being a volunteer.
- *Valence* is the sum of the internal rewards (self-actualisation or self-esteem) and external rewards (social interaction, prestige, recognition, increased status within the community).

A crucial point is whether volunteers actually believe or expect that by working on the community arts festival, cultural opportunities will be enhanced. If they do, their efforts will be greater than if they did not expect that to happen. Next, if volunteers believe that their efforts will be instrumental in that goal being achieved, they will be motivated to produce their best efforts in helping to achieve that goal. Finally, the reward for achieving this goal must be greater than competing rewards from other activities such as spending time with family, sport and involvement in other organisations. It is from this theoretical framework that Peach and Murrell (1995, pp. 238–9) derive their reward and recognition techniques, which are shown as table 5.1 (page 96).

An appropriate system of recognition of effort and extrinsic rewards for performance should be part of any event's human resources management plan. By conscientiously endeavouring to

- get to know staff and volunteers
- maintaining dialogue between management and staff
- developing an understanding of what motivates each individual and
- monitoring changes in the external and internal environments of the event

an event manager can ensure that reward and recognition procedures are appropriate and act as motivators for staff and volunteers.

REWARD SYSTEMS THAT WORK	RECOGNITION TECHNIQUES THAT WORK
• Rewards that integrate the needs of the individual and the organisation in a win–win understanding • Rewards based on deep appreciation of the individual as a unique person • Rewards based on job content, not conditions — rewards intrinsic to the job work best. • Assignment of tasks that can be performed effectively, leading to intrinsic need satisfaction • Consistent reward policies that build a sense of trust that effort will receive the proper reward • Rewards that can be shared by teams so that winning is a collective and collaborative experience	• Carefully constructed systems that are built on the motives and needs of volunteers — individualised need recognition for each person • Recognition integrated into task performance, where clear performance objectives are established • Corporate growth and development objectives also become opportunities for recognition. • Longevity and special contributions recognised frequently, not just every ten years • Recognition grounded deeply on the core values of the organisation; what is recognised helps as a role model.

TECHNIQUES FOR EFFECTIVE VOLUNTEER TEAM-BUILDING

Volunteers are individuals with different motivations to satisfy different needs, different demographics, and different skills and education. To be effective, they have to be melded into a team that is committed to achieving an objective. In order for this to happen, effective team-building techniques should be used.

Battle (1988, p. 98) believes that to be successful, leaders must be able to mould their people into a team. Battle advocates that the seven steps for effective team building are to:
• establish a common objective
• train the team
• provide the team with constant communication
• be enthusiastic at all times
• execute the agreed plan
• recognise, reward and motivate the team
• evaluate progress of the plan regularly.

These steps have been expanded by Nancy Macduff (1997, pp. 208–10), an internationally recognised authority on volunteer programs, into a fourteen-element formula for effective volunteer teams. These are shown below, with adaptations to suit an event environment.

1. *Teams are a manageable size.* Most effective teams have between 2 and 25 people, with the majority having fewer than 10. If the event uses a large number of volunteers, break them up into smaller teams of around 10.

2. People are appropriately selected to serve on a team. Care and attention should be paid to selecting people with the right combination of skills, personality, communication styles and ability to perform, thereby improving the chances of the team being successful. For example, the crowd control team at an event would have similar personal characteristics and personalities.

3. *Team leaders are trained.* Leaders who find it difficult to delegate and want to do everything themselves make poor leaders. Try to ensure team leaders have training in supervision skills.

4. *Teams are trained to execute their tasks.* It is unrealistic to expect teams to perform effectively without appropriate training. The training should include the team's role in the event and how that role contributes to the overall success of the event.

5. *Volunteers and staff are supported by the event organisation.* Teams must feel that the administration is there to support their endeavours, not to hinder them.

6. *Teams have objectives.* The purpose of the team is spelt out in a measurable objective. Having a plan to achieve those objectives helps build trust.

7. *Volunteers and staff trust and support one another.* People trust each other when they share positive experiences. As each team is aware of the event's objectives and how their role helps to achieve those objectives, they trust their co-workers and support their efforts.

8. *Communication between volunteers and the event organisation is both vertical and horizontal.* Communication, which means sending 'meanings' and understandings between people, is a process involving an active and continuous use of active listening, the use of feedback to clarify meaning, the reading of body language, and the use of symbols that communicate meaning. Communication travels in all directions — up and down the reporting line and between teams and work groups. Working together is facilitated by good communication.

9. *The organisational structure promotes communication between volunteers and staff.* The organisation's structure, policies and operating programs permit and encourage all members of the organisation to communicate with their co-workers, their managers and members of other departments. This helps build an atmosphere of cooperation and harmony in the pursuit of common objectives.

10. *Volunteers and staff have real responsibility.* A currently fashionable management concept is 'empowerment'. This means giving staff authority to make decisions about their work and its outcomes. For example, a group of volunteers has the somewhat mundane task of making sandwiches. If they are empowered with the authority to decide what sandwiches to make, how to make them, and where to sell them, their enthusiasm for the task will probably be enhanced and there will be a corresponding improvement in outcomes.

11. *Volunteers and staff have fun while accomplishing tasks.* Events are fun things! People working in them expect to have fun as well. Event managers should strive to engender an atmosphere of humour, fun and affection between co-workers within the culture of the organisation. Such things as ceremonies to acknowledge exemplary contributions to the event, wrap-up parties, and bump-in celebrations can facilitate this.

12. *There is recognition for the contributions of volunteers and staff.* Formal and informal appreciation of the work of volunteers should be expressed by paid staff, and the work of the paid staff is publicly recognised and appreciated by volunteers. This mutual appreciation should be consistent, public and visible.

13. *Volunteers and staff celebrate their success.* Spontaneous celebrations with food, drink, friendship and frivolity should be encouraged by management of the event to recognise the achievement of objectives. The event manager should allocate a budgeted amount for these occasions.

14. *The entire organisation promotes and encourages the wellbeing of volunteer teams.* Everyone in the organisation sees himself or herself as part of a partnership and actively promotes such relationships.

Once teams are in place and operating effectively, the event manager should monitor the performance and productivity of the teams by observing their activities and maintaining appropriate communication with team leaders and members.

If deficiencies are noticed during the monitoring procedure, appropriate action can be taken in terms of training, team structure or refinement of operating procedures. These actions should occur in a climate of mutual trust.

STATUTORY REQUIREMENTS FOR STAFF AND VOLUNTEERS

All Australian States and Territories have legislation usually known as the *Occupational Health and Safety Act,* which is designed to reduce the likelihood and severity of illness and injury at work. Volunteers, being unpaid, are not covered by this legislation. However, the common law provision of public liability gives volunteers a similar right to recover damages from an event organiser if they are injured or fall sick because of their activities at the event.

According to Workplace Change NSW (n.d.) this legislation 'places a general duty of care on employers (i.e. event organisers) to:
• provide and maintain safe systems of work
• make arrangements for ensuring the safe use, handling and storage of materials
• provide necessary information, instruction, training and supervision.'

The Act also obligates event staff to take reasonable care for the health and safety of persons participating in an event, and for those who may be affected by their acts at work. They must also cooperate with any requirement imposed in the interests of health, safety and welfare by the employer (the event manager, in this case) or any other person authorised under the Act.

Workplace Change NSW (n.d.) recommends the instigation of a risk management approach to occupational health and safety. Because many events involve large numbers of people gathered together in a sometimes unfamiliar environment, it would seem sensible to utilise this approach, not only for staff members' health and safety but also for participants at the event. A risk management approach entails three elements:

1. Identify hazards by keeping records of accidents and injuries, conducting safety inspections of the event site, and noting all machinery and substances that could be potentially hazardous. Examples in an outdoor event are heating, cooking and cooling substances, earth-moving equipment and electrical equipment for stages and generators.
2. Assess the risks by deciding how likely it is that a hazardous event will occur and what the consequences are likely to be.
3. Control the risks by firstly trying to eliminate them. If this is not possible, the risk should be minimised by appropriate controls and procedures.

Part of the 'wrap-up' procedures of an event should be a review of the risk management plan and, at the same time, a refinement of the procedures.

■ **Labour** *legislation*

Labour legislation regulates employers' dealings with their employees in terms of pay and conditions. This legislation generally sets out minimum rates of pay, and conditions such as annual leave and working hours. Of course, there is nothing to stop an event manager from paying more than the awarded minimum, as the labour market is not controlled, except by minimum conditions. These awards can vary between each State and Territory of Australia and obviously from country to country. To ensure compliance with appropriate legislation, event managers who employ paid labour should consult the Department of Industrial Relations in their State, who undoubtedly can supply a handbook with details of current labour legislation.

Many paid employees of events are employed as casual workers. To compensate for the irregular nature of their work, these employees are paid loadings above the normal full-time hourly rate. It is the responsibility of the event manager to ensure these employees are paid appropriately.

A recent change in the industrial scene in Australia and New Zealand is the introduction of enterprise agreements. Like an award, this agreement sets out for employees their minimum conditions of employment, which are specific to a particular employer rather than an industry.

If large numbers of employees are used in an event, an enterprise agreement can engender an atmosphere of trust and of working together to achieve a commonly sought objective.

Records of paid employees must also be kept. These should include:

- name
- employment classification
- whether full time or part time
- whether permanent, temporary or casual
- whether an apprentice or trainee
- date when first employed
- date when terminated
- remuneration and hours worked
- leave records
- superannuation contributions.

Although it is not a legal requirement, it is also sound practice to keep records of volunteers. These should include:

- name and address
- role in event
- performance appraisal
- willingness to volunteer again
- skills and expertise
- access to special equipment.

This information facilitates human resource planning for future events.

SUMMARY

The management of human resources is an essential aspect of the event manager's job. Without a motivated, trained, enthusiastic and willing work force, no event can achieve its desired outcomes. Adherence to the principles and practices of human resource leadership will assist in achieving a longstanding event and desired outcomes.

Questions

1 You are general manager of a blues festival. You have calculated that 100 volunteers will be needed for serving food and beverages, ticket sales, gate control and security. Identify sources from which you could recruit these volunteers, write a volunteer job description and contract for these four tasks and construct an interviewers' check list for these positions.

2 Prepare an induction program and a training program for the volunteers you have recruited.

3 How would you motivate the volunteers to provide a high standard of quality customer service to the patrons of the festival?

4 In what ways would you empower the volunteers?

Volunteers rescue
Antarctic heritage

This case study describes an event staged to publicise a large Australian company — Australian Associated Press (AAP). Like many corporate events, this event occurred to gain, amongst other outcomes, positive publicity for a large corporation. The case study is concerned with recruitment, induction, training, motivation and deployment of volunteers in an unusual context.

Nine men and two women lived in tiny red pyramid tents on the Antarctic ice for six weeks while they worked to save Mawson's Huts — Australia's most significant Antarctic heritage asset — at Cape Denison over the summer of 1997–98. They slept two to a tent in winds of up to 190 kilometres per hour and shared a communal space that was only 3.5 metres square — this was their kitchen, living room and dining room. Christmas dinner, when all were present at the same time, was eaten standing up.

All 11 members of the AAP Mawson's Huts Foundation expedition were volunteers (most of them unpaid) from four States of Australia and from all walks of life. Including the journey to Antarctica and back, plus a couple of weeks of preparation and debriefing, the project called for a commitment of almost three months over December, January and February. The volunteers emerged from the exercise a very closely knit team and firmer friends than when they had begun, with rarely a cross word spoken between them. This was no mean achievement given the conditions under which they had to work and live, and the fact that they were constantly shadowed by two people filming a documentary on the project, which would be screened on the Nine Network in 1998.

David Killick was the AAP journalist with the team. He wrote a daily diary, and noted on day 68 as their ship, the *Akademik Sholakskiy*, neared port:

> ■ We were up early this morning for our last get-together as a team. Afterwards we shake hands and have our group photo taken. It's all but over. Rod Givney (the team doctor) and I retire to our cabin and start packing our masses of gear. It's been almost 10 weeks now that we've slept elbow to elbow in tiny tents and ship cabins and never once has he offered a word of complaint about any of my noxious personal habits. An amazing performance. I will miss Rod, who has been great company and a voice of reason throughout the trip.
>
> What an experience we have had this summer. Even before the memories are shuffled and dimmed and distorted by time, I know this has been a trip I shall remember for the rest of my days — and as much for the people as for the place. Not one fight, never a voice raised in anger. Thirteen people flung into one of the worst places on earth and coming out friends. ■

The harmony and stability of the group was due in no small part to careful team selection. Its members were chosen from well over 100 applicants. Each was highly skilled in his or her own area of expertise but with the ability to help in other areas too. Most had been to Antarctica at least once before, some of them several times. All were aged in their 40s to early 50s, except David Killick, who was 29. (By contrast, Mawson at 29 was the senior member of his expedition, with most of its members aged in their early 20s.) Several team members already knew each other. All were subjected to the extensive interviews and medicals at the Australian Antarctic Division usual for senior officers chosen to staff Australia's Antarctic bases over a winter or summer season. They took part in a week-long bonding and team building exercise at Cradle Mountain and in Hobart three months before departure.

Their task was daunting. Cape Denison is 3000 km south of Hobart and 1200 km from Australia's nearest Antarctic station. A ship had to be hired, at a cost of $750 000, to transport the team and its equipment to the site and return in six weeks — weather permitting — to pick them up.

AAP — the national news, information and telecommunications group — established the AAP Mawson's Huts Foundation in 1996 to raise funds for the restoration of the fragile baltic pine huts built by the Australasian Antarctic Expedition (AAE) of 1911–14 led by Sir Douglas Mawson. Mawson called Cape Denison the 'home of the blizzard' and it is now recognised as the windiest place on earth, where the katabatic winds, funnelled down the high plateaus from the South Pole, have been recorded at up to 300 kph. Eighty-six years exposure to such harsh conditions had left the huts on the knife edge of survival.

The AAP expedition experienced average wind speeds of 70 kph, with days of relative calm interspersed with blizzards lasting three or four days at a stretch. In fact, the only real advantage they had over Mawson's men was modern satellite communications and the knowledge they would be there for six weeks rather than two years. That they were able to successfully complete all their objectives was a tribute to the organisation of the expedition and its team spirit. To take advantage of the periods of good weather and 24-hour daylight, the carpenters in particular worked long into the night or dashed off to work at midnight. When the wind suddenly stopped howling round their tent, they said, it woke them up.

The team's tasks included recladding the roof of the workshop section of the main hut with baltic pine planks to match the original timber used, replacing cedar beams that provided the internal support structure, and repairing or replacing the skylights to limit the ingress of snow and ice. Mainly through the use of a chainsaw, 41 cubic metres (over 30 tonnes) of ice and snow were removed from the main hut.

The team also repaired and stabilised the three smaller huts used for scientific experimentation, and re-erected the large memorial cross placed by Mawson in remembrance of the two men who lost their lives during his explorations and carried out valuable archaeological work. By the end of their stay, they had also completed a small, self-contained base camp, out of sight of the Mawson heritage site — the first such facility Australia has had in this part of the Antarctic since Mawson's time.

The team comprised:

- expedition leader Alan Grant, 50, of Brisbane, a company director, landscape architect and land surveyor, who was station leader at Mawson base over the 1993 winter and summer seasons
- conservation team leader Geoff Ashley, 43, of Sydney, an architect and built-heritage specialist with particular expertise in the conservation of historic sites
- archaeologist Dr Estelle Lazer, 42, of Sydney University, who had spent two summers in Antarctica and who was a member of the last expedition to have worked on the huts in 1984–85
- medical officer Dr Rod Givney of Adelaide, who was medical officer at Casey station for a year in 1989–90
- artist and photographer Alasdair McGregor, 43, of Sydney, who is also a qualified architect and who had previously visited Antarctica and Heard and Macquarie islands
- camp manager and chef Joan Russell, 51, who had been station leader at Macquarie Island and at Casey station, and is director of personnel with the South Australia Police
- carpenters David Gillott of North Tamborine, Queensland, with two seasons in Antarctica behind him, Paul Delaney, 48, of Mylor, South Australia, who had completed four tours of duty at the Australian bases, and Ted Bugg, 42, of Sheffield, Tasmania, a Parks and Wildlife ranger at Cradle Mountain
- communications officer Allen Rooke, 46, of Wooli, NSW, the Antarctic veteran of the party had spent six winters and nine summers on the polar continent, and
- journalist and qualified chef David Killick of AAP Sydney, whose most rugged outdoor experience was bushwalking in the Blue Mountains.

Only Alan Grant, who was required to be seconded to the Antarctic Division, Geoff Ashley and David Killick were paid for their work. The others gave freely of their time and labour, drawn by a passion for Antarctica, the heritage significance or romance of the project, or the sheer adventure. Most described it as a once-in-a-lifetime opportunity and none would hesitate to do it again.

The project had the strong backing of the Antarctic Division, the Australian Heritage Commission and the Federal Government, which contributed $250 000 towards its costs. Senator Ian Mcdonald, parliamentary secretary responsible for the Antarctic, publicly congratulated the team, saying 'Mawson's huts are the main symbol of Australia's long and rich history of operations in Antarctica. The team has completed an extremely valuable and successful program to help ensure their survival.

'These modern day heroes have proudly served Australia's national interest under the most challenging weather conditions known to man', he said, adding that the project was an excellent example of what could be achieved through the partnership of government and the private sector.

Les Murphy
Public Affairs Manager, AAP
and a Director of the AAP Mawson's Huts Foundation

Questions

1 Why is this an 'event'? How is it different from and similar to other events that you know of?

2 Who is the audience for this event?

3 What is the 'vision' of this event?

4 What are its objectives?

5 What motivated the volunteers?

6 Who are the event's stakeholders?

7 What would be the most appropriate selection criteria for the volunteers?

8 How could the induction process be improved?

9 What stakeholders' needs were satisfied by this event?

REFERENCES

Adams, J. Stacy 1965, 'Inequity in social exchange', in *Advances in Experimental Social Psychology*, ed. L. Berkowitz, Academic Press, New York.

Battle, R. 1988, *The Volunteer Handbook*, Volunteer Concepts, Austin, Texas.

Bradner, J. 1997, 'Recruitment, orientation, retention' in *The Volunteer Management Handbook*, ed. T. Connors, John Wiley & Sons, New York.

Clark, R. 1992, *Australian Human Resources Management*, McGraw Hill, Sydney.

Flashman R. & Quick, S. 1985, 'Altruism is not dead: a specific analysis of volunteer motivation' in *Motivating Volunteers*, ed. L. Moore, Vancouver Volunteer Centre, Vancouver.

Getz, D. 1997, *Event Management and Event Tourism*, Cognizant Communication, New York.

Goldblatt. J. 1997, *Special Events: Best Practices in Modern Event Management*, Van Nostrand Reinhold, New York.

Herzberg, F. 1982, *The Managerial Choice: To Be Efficient or To Be Human*, Olympus, Salt Lake City, Utah.

Hughes, C., Toohey, S. & Hatherly, S. 1992, 'Developing learning centred trainers and tutors', *Studies in Continuing Education*, vol. 14, no. 1.

Lulewicz, S. 1995, 'Training and development of volunteers' in *The Volunteer Management Handbook*, ed. T. Connors, John Wiley & Sons, New York.

Maslow, A. 1954, *Motivation and Personality*, Harper & Row, New York.

Moore, L. 1985, *Motivating Volunteers*, Vancouver Volunteer Centre, Vancouver.

Peach, E. & Murrell, K. 1995, 'Reward and recognition systems for volunteers' in *The Volunteer Management Handbook*, ed. T. Connors, John Wiley & Sons, New York.

Robbins, S. & Mukerji, D. 1994, *Managing Organisations*, Prentice Hall, Sydney.

Vroom, V. 1964, *Work and Motivation*, John Wiley & Sons, New York.

Workplace Change NSW (no date) *Small Business Employer's Handbook*, New South Wales Department of Industrial Relations, Sydney.

6

The marketing
of events

LEARNING OBJECTIVES

After studying this chapter, you should be able to:

■ describe how the marketing concept can be applied to festivals and special events

■ understand needs and motivations of festival and event customers

■ conduct a market segmentation analysis to establish appropriate target markets for an event

■ forecast probable demand for an event

■ construct a marketing plan for an event which contains appropriate pricing, promotion, place and product strategies.

The father of modern marketing and the originator of the marketing concept of the four Ps (product, price, place, promotion), E. Jerome McCarthy, defines the marketing concept as 'the idea that an organisation should aim all its efforts at satisfying its customers — at a profit' (McCarthy & Perreault 1987, p. 7). The entire focus of an organisation should be on satisfying the wants and needs of an identified group of people with some homogeneous characteristic — the target market. This is in contrast to a popular view of marketing that assumes it is concerned only with selling or advertising. Marketing does not encompass only these activities, but much more. In 1960, Theodore Levitt, the Harvard University marketing authority, said 'Marketing... views the entire business process as consisting of a tightly integrated effort to discover, create, arouse, and satisfy customer needs' (Levitt 1980, p. 16). This chapter describes the marketing process.

Following is a definition of marketing in the context of events:

> ■ Marketing is that function of event management that can keep in touch with the event's participants and visitors (consumers), read their needs and motivations, develop products that meet these needs, and build a communication program which expresses the event's purpose and objectives (Hall 1997, p. 136). ■

To illustrate these concepts, the following list shows the marketing activities that an event manager undertakes to produce a successful festival or special event:

- analyses the needs of the target market to establish appropriate event components, or 'products'
- establishes what other competitive events could satisfy similar needs to ensure their event has a unique selling proposition
- predicts how many people will attend the event
- predicts at what times people will come to the event
- estimates what price they will be willing to pay to attend
- decides on the type and quantity of promotional activities telling the target market about the event
- decides on how tickets to the event can reach the target market
- establishes the degree of success of the marketing activities.

All of these activities, essential for a successful event, are part of the marketing function. This chapter explores how the event manager carries out these functions to achieve the objectives set out in the event strategic plan discussed in chapter 4.

■ The need *for marketing*

Some critics of the marketing concept argue that some cultural festivals and events should not be concerned with the target market's needs, but with innovation, creativity and the dissemination of new art forms. The argument goes that consumers' needs are based on what they know or have experienced and therefore innovative or avant-garde cultural experiences will not be accepted by consumers. Thus, if the marketing concept of focusing on customer needs is used, nothing new will ever be produced. As Dickman states, 'administrators were reluctant to even use the word [marketing], believing that it suggested 'selling out' artistic principles in favour of finding the lowest common denominator' (1997, p. 685).

This attitude, while perhaps understandable, is based on a misunderstanding of marketing principles and techniques and can be self-defeating for the following reasons.

- The use of marketing principles gives event managers a framework for decision making that should result in successful events that still allow for innovation and creativity, but cater for a target market segment that has a need for novelty and the excitement of the new.
- Sponsoring bodies require some certainty that their sponsorship will be received by the target market they are seeking. Sound marketing practices will help convince them that a festival or event is an appropriate medium for them to communicate to their target market.
- All three levels of government financially assist many festivals and events. They usually fund only those events whose management can demonstrate some expertise in marketing planning and management.
- Consumers, particularly those resident in major cities, have an enormous range of leisure activities from which to choose to spend their disposable income. This means that a festival or special event which, by definition, can be categorised as a leisure activity, will attract only those who expect to satisfy one of their perceived needs. Therefore, any festival or event needs to be designed to satisfy identified needs of its target market. Failure to do this usually results in an event that is irrelevant to the needs of its target market and does not meet its objectives.

◼ Consumer *expectations*

The marketing concept is just as applicable to a leisure service such as an event as it is to any other product. In fact, it could be even more so, as a leisure service, like other services, is intangible, variable, perishable and inseparable.

For example, consider a customer attending an outdoor jazz and blues festival. Unlike the purchase of goods, there is nothing tangible the customer can pick up, touch, feel or try before purchase. They merely decide to attend the festival based on expectations that a particular need (for entertainment, social interaction, a novel experience, self-education, or any number of needs) will be met.

Consumer expectations come from a combination of marketing communications from the festival organiser, word of mouth recommendations from friends and family, previous experience with this or similar events, and the brand image of the event. The service the customer receives — being entertained — is inseparable from the consumption of the service. In other words, instead of purchasing a good in a shop and then consuming that good somewhere else, production and consumption of the service are simultaneous or inseparable. Customers do not purchase by chance, but have to make a conscious decision to travel to the event site.

Even when markets are tightly segmented into a group of people with a common characteristic, members of the group may have differing perceptions of the benefits they have received from the event experience. This comes about because people are slightly different in their perceptions and attitudes, and therefore their perception of the service they receive and the people they receive it from may be variable. For example, two close friends may attend the jazz and blues festival. One may perceive all the services provided as terrific, yet the other may not be as enthusiastic, despite having experienced the same service.

If the weather is poor on the day of the festival and attendance affected, unsold tickets for that day can not be stored and sold when the weather improves. In other words, leisure services are extremely perishable.

It is these characteristics of leisure experiences such as festivals and events that makes careful, structured thinking and planning of the marketing function integral to the success of any event.

MARKETING MIX

Getz proposes this definition of marketing for events:

> ■ Marketing events is the process of employing the marketing mix to attain organizational goals through creating value for clients and customers. The organization must adopt a marketing orientation that stresses the building of mutually beneficial relationships and the maintenance of competitive advantages (Getz 1997, p. 250). ■

This definition introduces the concept of the marketing mix which McCarthy and Perreault (1987, p. 5) define as 'the controllable variables which the company puts together to satisfy a target group'. McCarthy and Perreault identified these variables as product, price, promotion and place, and each of these variables is discussed in depth in this chapter. 'Controllable' means that the event manager can manipulate or alter these variables in order to achieve an event's marketing objectives.

Product encompasses all of the elements which make up the festival or event. This includes such things as the entertainment offered, standard of service, food and beverage facilities, opportunities for social interaction, consumer participation in the event, merchandising, staff interaction with customers and the 'brand' image the festival or event enjoys among the target market.

Price means the value consumers place on the event experience and are prepared to pay. This value is determined by the strength of the need the leisure experience satisfies and alternative leisure experiences offered by other events and other leisure service providers. The price of an event experience can be varied according to the type of customer (e.g. pensioner concessions) or the time of consumption (e.g. discounted price for previews).

Place has two meanings in event marketing. As well as signifying the geographical location of the event, it also means the purchase point(s) for tickets to the event. For example, the place for a jazz and blues festival not only means the venue (e.g. Byron Bay Showground), but also the method of distribution of tickets to the event (e.g. are they sold only at the gate, or can they be prepurchased and, if so, where?)

Promotion is, as Middleton (1995) points out, the most visible of the four Ps of the marketing mix. It includes all of the marketing communication techniques of advertising, personal selling, sales promotion, some merchandising (T-shirt sales featuring the event, for example), publicity and public relations, and direct mail. Potential consumers are motivated to purchase the leisure experience offered by the event by the design of these messages.

Some marketing writers have developed variations on the original four Ps. For example, Cowell (1984) proposes a seven-P marketing mix of

- product
- price
- promotion
- place
- people
- physical evidence (layout, furnishing of venue, sound quality)
- process (customer involvement in the leisure service).

However, the last three Ps are just part of the product element of the marketing mix.

Getz goes one P further and proposes an eight-P mix of

- product (the service offered)
- place (the location)
- programming (elements and quality of style)
- people (cast, audience, hosts and guests)
- partnerships (stakeholders in producing the event)
- promotion (marketing communications)
- packaging and distribution of tickets
- price (1997, p. 251).

It is Middleton's view that 'it helps the understanding of a central marketing concept to focus on an unambiguous, easy to understand four Ps' (1995, p. 66). The product consists of elements which vary according to the target market, the venue, and other stakeholders. Splitting product into various elements can cause muddled marketing thinking and action.

Table 6.1 (on the following page) summarises the four Ps of the marketing mix and considers the variable elements of each.

FOUR Ps	ELEMENTS
Product:	
• design characteristics/ packaging	Location, staging, entertainment mix, food and beverage provision, seating, queuing, decoration, theme, lighting
• service component	Number of service staff, degree of training, uniforms, standard of service quality
• branding	Prominence given to name of event and what that name means to consumers
• reputation/positioning	Where event is to be positioned in terms of consumer demand — up-market to mass market
Price:	
• time of consumption	Discounted prices at times of low demand
• promotional price	Concessional prices for certain target markets
Promotion:	
• advertising — television, radio, newspaper, magazine, outdoor	The promotional mix
• sales promotion — merchandising, public relations	
• flyers and brochures	
• personal selling via a sales force	
Place:	
• channels of distribution	Tickets available through an agency such as Ticketek or sold by mail from a mailing list

The term 'promotional mix' refers to the many components that can constitute marketing communications between an event and its potential audience (or consumers). It is these variables that the event manager can manipulate to achieve an event's objectives. However, it must be noted that the product, promotion and the place (if a ticketing agency or direct mail is to be used) require a commitment to upfront expenditure which is committed before any revenue is obtained from ticket sales. It is therefore important that the marketing planning processes are thorough, thoughtful and realistic in their forecast of both revenue and expenditure. Any muddle in the marketing process can have disastrous consequences for the viability and longevity of any event.

Figure 6.1 shows how the marketing mix fits in the context of the event organisation and its environments. Chapter 4 discussed how the strategic planning process went about choosing appropriate strategies that can achieve the event's objectives. Some of those strategies are concerned with marketing and will result from a marketing planning process that is embedded in the strategic planning process.

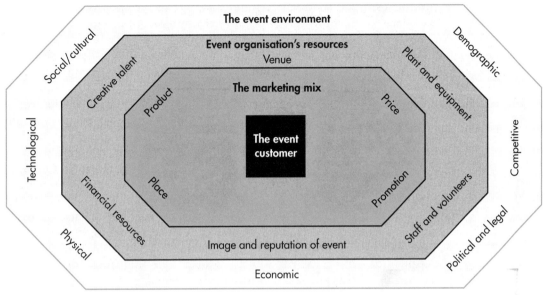

Figure 6.1
How the marketing mix fits in the context of the event organisation

(**Source:** *adapted from Middleton 1995*)

The core of the planning process, as the marketing concept suggests, is the consumer. The event's features should satisfy the needs of a carefully chosen consumer segment. All marketing efforts focus on these needs and how they can be satisfied, either profitably or in a way that achieves the objectives of the event.

The inner ring contains the marketing variables of the four Ps that the event director (or its marketing manager in a large event) can manipulate. A realistic estimate of the revenue and sponsorship that an event or festival can generate, however, will determine the funds that can be spent on product enhancement, promotion and ticket distribution.

■ The marketing *environment*

The marketing efforts of an event do not occur in isolation. They are obviously constrained by the resources of the event organisation. For example, if an event has very few volunteers to assist with all aspects of customer interaction, it would be unrealistic to embark on a process of increasing the quality of customer service. In other words, the marketing effort is constrained by the use of available resources.

All marketing activities are affected by the environments in which they operate. Figure 6.1 shows these to be:

* *social/cultural*: events are a part of a society's culture. Changes in society will lead to changes in the demand for certain events. For example, during the 1950s, May Day parades to celebrate workers' rights were quite large and heavily attended events. Interest waned after many workers' rights were won and the event is now a mere shadow of its former size.

Another example of social change is the greater emphasis many people now place on harm to the physical environment. All events must be seen to be sympathetic to the physical environment or risk a backlash from environmental groups.

- *technological*: the enormous changes wrought by advances in computer and communication technology have caused many advances in the production of events. A computer program now controls fireworks and media broadcasts of events. A computer can program lighting for stage events. Presentations use multimedia; that is, more than one medium to communicate a message, usually audio, video and a slide or Powerpoint presentation.
- *physical*: outdoor events are constrained by weather conditions. Outdoor venues must be left in a perfect condition or risk the wrath of environmental groups.
- *economic*: the economic environment changes according to the economic cycle of a country or region. In times of relative hardship, it may not be appropriate to produce lavish events that some in the community view as conspicuous consumption, whereas during 'boom' times demand for extravagant events could be considerable.
- *political and legal*: most events are constrained by regulations that control such things as noise levels, parking, security, the sale of alcohol, occupational health and safety, and hygienic serving of food.
- *competitive*: events do not take place in a leisure activity void. Consumers have an enormous range of leisure activities from which to choose. Event managers use the four Ps to ensure they can capture a reasonable market share of the leisure dollar.
- *demographic*: this means the characteristics of people, such as their age, gender, occupation, income, personality and interests. All developed countries have an ageing population caused by the boom in births between 1946 and 1960. This large group of people is now ageing (the first are more than fifty years of age) and form a large, usually affluent group of consumers. Another demographic change of consequence for event directors is the increase in double income families, which increases their disposable income and consequently the funds that could be spent on leisure activities. Another recent demographic phenomenon is the increase in the number of educated women, and women who choose careers over families, at least in the early stages of their working life (Loane & Horin 1998), which increases the market for cultural activities that appeal to educated women.

THE EVENT CUSTOMER

The following acronym helps explain the customer decision-making process (Morgan 1996, p. 80):

Problem recognition
Information search
Evaluation of alternatives
Choice of purchase
Evaluation of post-purchase experience.

This process (PIECE) can be applied to the decision to attend a festival or event. The consumer identifies a need that may be satisfied by attending an event or other leisure experience, searches for information about such an experience in different media (entertainment section of newspapers, radio, magazines), then evaluates the alternatives available. The customer then compares the needs the leisure experience can satisfy against a list of attributes. For example, a customer seeks an opportunity to enhance family ties and chooses to attend a community festival that contains elements that all members of the family can enjoy. After experiencing (or 'consuming') the event, the customer evaluates the experience for its capacity to satisfy that need. Table 6.2 shows the implications for event marketers of this process.

■ Table 6.2
The event consumer decision process and the implications for marketing

STAGE IN THE CONSUMER DECISION-MAKING PROCESS	IMPLICATIONS FOR MARKETING STRATEGIES	MARKETING DECISIONS
Recognition of the need	Selection of appropriate target market(s)	Which market — mass or focused?
Search for information	Promotional mix variables	Direct mail, publicity, paid advertising, or other types of advertising?
Evaluation of the alternatives	Event elements design Promotional message	Change the product? Change the promotional mix?
Choice at point-of-sale	Ease of purchase	What are the incentives for sellers?
Evaluation of leisure experience	Service quality	What type of post-event research will be undertaken? How will consumer satisfaction be monitored?

The starting point for this marketing process is the needs of the customer that may be satisfied by attending a festival or event. Little empirical research on needs and motivations for event customers has been published in Australia. However, academic research carried out in North America in recent years gives insights into this issue (Roslow, Nicholls, Laskey 1992; Mohr et al. 1993; Saleh & Ryan 1993; Uysal, Gahan & Martin 1993 and Getz 1991).

Based on their research of customers of a jazz festival and a handcraft festival in Saskatchewan, Canada, Saleh and Ryan (1993) tentatively suggest a sequential decision-making process for festival attendance which supports Morgan's PIECE model. Figure 6.2 (on the following page) illustrates this process. The missing element of evaluation (E) occurs after the leisure experience has occurred.

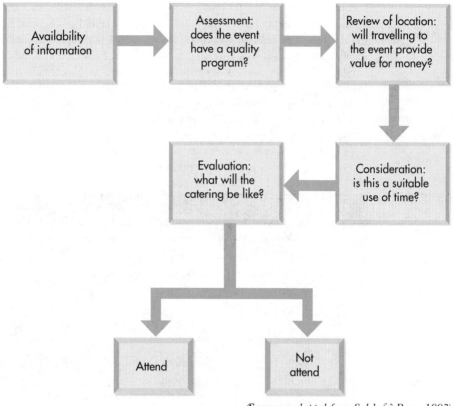

(**Source:** *adapted from Saleh & Ryan 1993*)

A study of customers at a community festival in South Carolina by Uysal, Gahan and Martin (1993) and a study of attendees of a North American hot air balloon festival by Mohr et al. (1993) reported that the five principal motivations (or need satisfiers) for attending festivals are:

• *socialisation*: being with friends, people who are enjoying themselves and people who enjoy the same things

• *family togetherness*: seeking the opportunity so the family can do something together and to bring the family together

• *excitement/thrills*: doing something because it is stimulating and exciting

• *escape:* getting away from the usual demands of life and having a change from daily routine

• *event novelty*: experiencing new and different things and/or attending a festival that is unique.

Although the motivations for visiting both festivals were the same, the order was slightly different. Visitors to the community festival placed 'escape' at the top of their motivations, whereas visitors to the hot air balloon festival considered 'socialisation' the most important motivator. This suggests that visitors to specialised festivals are highly motivated by a desire to socialise with people who share their interests, while visitors to community festivals are more motivated by 'escape' from the ordinariness of day-to-day life.

Getz (1991) adapts Maslow's theory of people having a needs hierarchy. Maslow proposed that needs are satisfied in the following order: physiological, safety, social, self-esteem, self-development. Getz adapted this to propose a three generic needs model. Table 6.3 is an adaptation of Getz's theory.

■ Table 6.3
Needs,
motives and
benefits
offered by
events

NEEDS AND MOTIVES	CORRESPONDING BENEFITS AND OPPORTUNITIES OFFERED BY EVENTS
Physical Physiological needs motivate the need to:	
• eat and drink	eat and drink new, different food and drink
• exercise	participate in sporting activities
• relax	relaxing entertainment
• search for security	recreation in a secure environment
• find sexual gratification	meet people
Social/interpersonal The need for belonging, friendship and love motivate:	
• socialising with family and friends	share a new and different environment
• romance	meet new people
• links to cultural and ethnic roots	renew ties to ethnic and cultural groups
• expressions of community and nationalism	share in the use of appropriate symbols and rituals
• pursuit of recognition for accomplishments	prestige from attending an event
Personal The need for understanding, aesthetic appreciation, growth and self-development motivates:	
• a quest for knowledge	formal/informal learning
• seeking new experiences	unique programs
• creativity	participation in artistic endeavours
• fulfilment of ambitions.	participate in something unique and special.

(**Source:** *adapted from Getz 1991*)

Morgan (1996) identified five other social factors that can influence consumers' leisure behaviour. These can be described in the context of event participation as follows.

• *Family influences*: the desires of children will often influence the leisure behaviour of their parents. The need for family cohesion and the enhancement of familial ties is a strong motivator for many people. This explains the enormous numbers of children accompanied by exhausted parents that can be found at the show bag pavilion of agricultural shows around Australia. Many festivals include entertainment for children for this reason.

- *Reference groups*: groups who influence the behaviour of those with whom they come into close contact (such as peers, family, colleagues and neighbours) are called a *primary reference group*. Those who have less frequent contact are called a *secondary reference group*. Most people tend to seek the approval of members of their reference groups. If it is generally accepted in a particular reference group that attendance at a particular festival is appropriate behaviour, then members of that group are likely to attend. If not, then attendance is very unlikely. Showing examples of a typical reference group (e.g. a nuclear family group) enjoying themselves at a festival can send a message to a target market that may well respond favourably.
- *Opinion formers*: Within any group, some people will be opinion leaders. That is, their opinions on new leisure experiences are sought by the group and generally accepted. These opinion leaders are often media or sporting personalities, which is the reason many of them make a very substantial living endorsing new products and leisure services. The adoption of new leisure services follows a normal distribution curve. Innovators (generally opinion leaders within a group) are the first to try the experience. They are followed by early adopters who are a little more careful about adopting the innovation. However, they still act as opinion leaders for the great majority. Laggards are the last to try something new. Therefore, the promotional messages for any new festival or event should be directed at those who have been identified as opinion formers or innovators.
- *Personality*: Stanton, Miller and Layton define personality as 'an individual's pattern of traits that influence behavioural responses' (1994, p. 138). People can be introverted/extroverted, shy/self-confident, aggressive/retiring, dynamic/sluggish. It is well known that personality affects consumer behaviour. Unfortunately, as personality is difficult to measure in terms of consumer behaviour, it is a marketing tool that is difficult to use. However, festivals that celebrate adventure or sporting prowess would be unlikely to appeal to shy, retiring personalities.
- *Culture*: Australia is an example of a culturally diverse country. Within Australia live diverse groups who have different designs for living. Each of these cultural groups has different buying habits, leisure wants and needs, and attitudes and values. If a particular cultural group is a desired market segment, the four Ps of the marketing mix can be manipulated in order to appeal to that group.

TARGET MARKET SEGMENTATION

Most events do not appeal to everybody. As Hall (1997) observes, the marketing planning activities of event managers must include an understanding of the behaviour of visitors to an event. This includes identifying those market segments that are likely to have their needs satisfied by the event activities or, alternatively, to ensure the event contains those elements which can satisfy an identified target market's needs. The process of identifying appropriate target markets is known as market segmentation. Segmentation can occur by geography, demography or lifestyle (psychography).

Geographic segmentation is concerned with the place of residence of event visitors. A community festival, for example, would probably decide to focus firstly on local residents as the first step in their segmentation exercise. However, if the festival is thought to be of broader interest because of its potential product content, the marketing net could be spread wider. The potential geographic spread could be:
- local residents of the area
- day visitors from outside the immediate area
- intrastate domestic tourists
- interstate domestic tourists
- international inbound tourists
- school excursions.

The chosen geographic segmentation depends on the leisure experience provided by the festival or event. For example, an event such as a capital city agricultural show (e.g. the Royal Easter Show in Sydney) would have a statewide geographic segmentation and probably an interstate market segment for its more specialised event experiences.

Demographic segmentation concerns the measurable characteristics of people, such as age, gender, occupation, income, education and cultural group. A demographic segmentation tool often used by marketers is a socio-economic scale based on occupation (usually the head of the household, in family units). Table 6.4 (on the following page) details the scale in an event context.

Although the data in table 6.4 originated in Britain, they are relevant to all developed countries. Media buyers in advertising agencies first used these classifications, as the system is a very good predictor of reading and viewing habits. For example, in general, As and Bs read broadsheet newspapers, such as the *Sydney Morning Herald* and the *Age* in Melbourne, whereas Cs, Ds, and Es read the tabloid press, such as the *Daily Telegraph* and the *Herald Sun.*

However, these classifications are not always an accurate guide to income. For example, many Cs earn considerable incomes. The essential difference between As, Bs, Cs and the other categories is in the level of education. The higher the level of education, the higher the propensity of a person to participate in cultural activities, including arts and community festivals (Torkildsen 1983). Morgan observes that the age at which individuals terminate their formal education (16 years, 18 years, or after higher education, at 21 years) can indicate their ambition, intelligence and, importantly for event managers, their curiosity about the world in which they live (1996, p. 103). For directors of festivals and events that include cultural elements, their target market is an educated one.

Other demographic variables are gender and age. Women and men occasionally have different needs and some events cater for these different needs. The years in which people are born can affect their outlook on life, their attitudes and values, and their interests. Depending on the event, one or several of these generations can be targeted. Table 6.5 (page 119) shows the different generations born in the twentieth century.

■ Table 6.4 *A classification of socio-ecomoic market segments for events*

GROUP	SOCIO-ECONOMIC GROUP	OCCUPATIONAL EXAMPLES	TYPES OF EVENTS GROUP IS LIKELY TO ATTEND	APPROXIMATE PERCENTAGE OF POPULATION
A	Upper middle class	Higher managerial or administrative, professional: lawyers, doctors, dentists, captains of industry, senior public servants, senior military officers, professors	Cultural events such as fundraisers for the opera, classical music festivals	3
B	Middle class	Intermediate managerial, administrative or professional: university lecturers, head teachers, pharmacists, middle managers, journalists, architects	Cultural events (but purchasing cheaper seats), food and beverage festivals, historical festivals, arts and crafts festivals, community festivals	15
C	Lower middle class	Supervisory, clerical, junior managerial or administrative: clerks, sales representatives, nurses, teachers, shop managers	Most popular cultural events, some sporting events, community festivals	24
D	Skilled working class	Skilled blue collar workers: builders, fitters, waterside workers, police constables, self-employed tradespersons	Motor vehicle festivals, sporting events, community festivals	28
E	Working class	Semiskilled and unskilled workers: builder's labourers, factory workers, cleaners, delivery drivers	Some sporting festivals, ethnic festivals	17
F	Social security	Those at the lowest level of subsistence: pensioners, casual and part-time workers	Very little, except occasionally free community events	13

(**Source:** *adapted from Morgan 1996*)

■ Table 6.5
*The
generations
born in the
twentieth
century*

GENERATION	BORN	AGE IN 2000	FORMATIVE YEARS
World War I	pre 1924	77+	pre-1936
Depression	1924–34	66–76	1936–46
World War II	1935–45	55–65	1947–57
Early boomers	1946–54	46–54	1958–66
Late boomers	1955–64	36–45	1967–76
Generation X	1965–76	24–35	1977–88
Echo boom	1977–94	7–23	1989–2000

(**Source:** *Getz 1997*)

Another method of age segmentation is by life cycle, as shown in figure 6.3. This relies on the proposition that people's leisure habits vary according to their position in the life cycle. For example, full nesters are the target market for events which feature elements for both children and adults, whereas AB empty nesters are the perfect market for a cultural festival featuring quality food and drink and arias from well-loved operas.

■ **Figure 6.3**
*The family
life cycle*

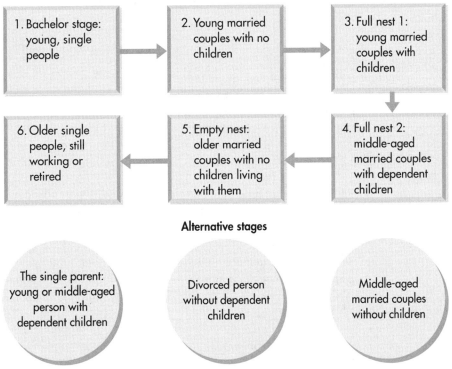

(**Source:** *Stanton, Miller & Layton 1994, p. 97*)

However, care should be taken not to resort to age stereotypes. Many early baby boomers, in or approaching their 50s, are fit, active and interested in all types of culture, popular and contemporary, as well as high culture festivals such as classical music or theatre. It could be argued that the most successful community festivals are those which are inclusive of all age groups, rather than focusing on just one age group.

The Australian Bureau of Statistics (ABS) publishes a great deal of data taken from each census that categorises residential areas according to the demographics of the residents of that area, for example, *Sydney, a Social Atlas: 1996 Census of Population and Housing*. A separate edition is published for every Australian capital city after each census and is a valuable store of demographic information categorised by geographic area (i.e., geodemographic). Cites are broken down into small areas called census collection districts of 200–300 households. The demographic variables of age, ethnicity, education, income, family type, membership of the paid labour force and dwelling type are shown for these districts. Directors of community festivals should find these data very useful for product planning.

Psychographics — segmenting a market according to its lifestyle and values — is another segmentation technique that could be a useful planning tool for event directors. The Roy Morgan Research Centre conducted a study of Australian values and lifestyles, then segmented consumers into these market segments with shared values and attitudes:

- visible achievement
- something better
- socially aware
- young optimists
- a fairer deal
- look at me
- basic needs
- real conservatism
- traditional family life
- conventional family life

(Stanton, Miller & Layton 1994, p. 103).

The names of these groups are somewhat self-explanatory. For example, the socially aware group (seven per cent of all people) see themselves as community-minded and socially responsible. They are 'progressive' in their opinions and are likely to be involved in conservation and environmental matters. They are likely to be found on the committees of community festivals.

However, like personality segmentation, psychographic segmentation of a market has some serious limitations for an event marketeer:

> ■ It is very difficult to accurately measure the size of the lifestyle segments in a quantitative manner. Another problem is that a given lifestyle segment simply might not be accessible... through a firm's [event organisation's] usual distribution system or promotional program (Stanton, Miller & Layton 1994, p. 104). ■

What this type of segmentation can do for an event marketeer is to provide another technique for deep thinking about the characteristics of the target market sought.

To be effective, market segments must be:
- measurable; that is, the characteristics of the segment (socio-economic status, gender age, etc.) must be accessible to the event marketeer
- substantial enough to be worth the effort of targeting
- accessible by normal promotional channels
- actionable by the event organisation in terms of the marketing budget and other resources (Morgan 1996).

𝒫RODUCT PLANNING

The product of an event is a leisure experience which has been carefully produced to satisfy a target market's identified needs. The word 'product' is used, as marketing theory applies to both the production of tangible goods and intangible services. (Chapter 2, 'Conceptualising an event', explores this process.) Figure 6.4 shows this process diagrammatically.

■ **Figure 6.4**
The process of creating an event product

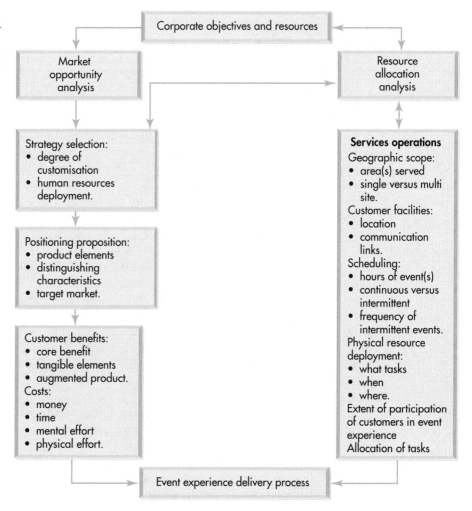

The new concepts introduced in figure 6.4 are customer benefits and costs. The section on pricing further explores the concept of costs (see page 125). Morgan states that a leisure service (or product) contains three elements:

- the core benefit that the customer experiences — an enjoyable leisure experience that satisfies some need(s)
- the tangible benefit that helps deliver the core benefit — the venue, the seating, decoration, etc.
- the augmented product; that is, the additional features that differentiate this event from its competitors — artists, service quality, type of people attracted to the event, parking or transportation facilities, ease of access and exit, etc.

The event planner needs to be aware of all three elements (1996, p. 136).

■ **Product** *development*

This section discusses some product development issues that will help in understanding what constitutes a leisure product, how it evolves and how it can be analysed.

Branding gives an event an easily recognisable identity. One of the best known brands in the world is the five interlocking rings of the Olympics — a special event. Because leisure experiences are intangible, branding is particularly important as it reassures potential consumers that the service will deliver the benefits promised. Clever use of the brand helps the event manager make an intangible phenomenon more tangible for the event consumer.

The *product life cycle* (shown in figure 6.5) illustrates that all events follow a similar pattern of participation as they go through the stages of introduction, growth, maturity and eventual decline. Australian event history is littered with examples of once hugely popular festivals or special events that were once very popular and now no longer exist. For example, the Sydney Waratah and Folkloric festivals and the State Bank Multicultural Carnival no longer exist, yet thousands of people once attended these events. Attendance at Australia Day festivals has waxed and waned as the 'product' has been changed to reflect changing community needs. Only hundreds now attend. To avoid the decline, event managers need to monitor closely public acceptance of the content of their event product to ensure that it is still congruent with the leisure needs of contemporary society.

A simple yet effective tool for effective thinking about product strategies is Ansoff's matrix (1957), shown in figure 6.6. An event that considers its product is appropriate yet is not drawing large numbers may consider a market penetration strategy; that is, using advertising or other forms of promotion to attract more of the same target market. If it is thought that the event leisure experience can reach a different target market(s) without changing the product, a market development strategy can be used. It may be that monitoring consumer satisfaction shows that the current product is not satisfying consumer needs. It would then be necessary to develop new and different products that can. If the event adopted a corporate strategy of growth, it may be appropriate to develop new products for a new market. For example, consumer monitoring might show that the AB section of the population is not attending an event. A product strategy of diversification would result in an event product that would satisfy this target group's needs.

■ Figure 6.5
The product life cycle

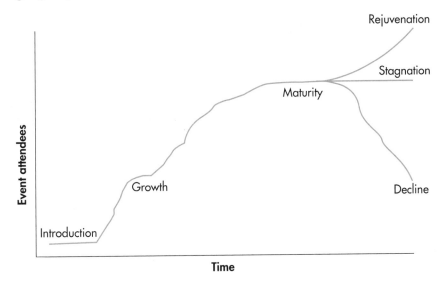

■ Figure 6.6
Ansoff's product/ market matrix

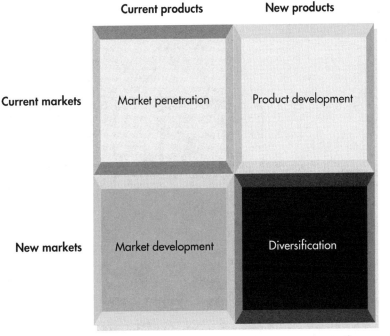

(**Source:** *Ansoff 1957*)

■ Consumer *satisfaction*

Because leisure services are intangible, inseparable and variable, defining service quality is difficult. A definition that examines quality service from the viewpoint of the consumer is 'quality service occurs when the consumers' expectations of the leisure service match their perceptions of the service received'. Quality service is based on perceptions rather than something tangible. Not every customer will be satisfied all the time. However, one of the corporate objectives set out in an event's strategic plan should be a measurement of consumer satisfaction; for example, 95 per cent of event participants will give a satisfied or higher rating of the event. Figure 6.7 shows how consumer dissatisfaction can occur.

■ **Figure 6.7**
Quality: the fit between customer expectations and perceptions

(**Source:** *Morgan 1996, p. 159*)

The consumer's perceptions of the leisure experience are formed from the technical and functional qualities of the experience, as well as any external factors such as wet weather, and personal factors such as an argument with a partner occurring at the event. The consumer's expectations of the event are determined by:

- marketing communications — advertising, publicity, brochures, signs and price which are used to promote the event

- word of mouth recommendations from friends and relatives who describe their experiences of this or similar events
- personal experience of this or similar events.

When the consumer's perceptions match or exceed their expectations, a quality leisure experience has been delivered and the outcome is a satisfied consumer.

Zeithaml, Parasuraman and Berry, (1990) have conducted a lot of research on this topic. They have reduced their original 10 determinants of service quality to a top five:

- assurance — because staff give the appearance of being knowledgeable, helpful and courteous, event consumers are assured of their wellbeing
- empathy — the event staff seem to understand the consumers' needs and deliver caring attention
- responsiveness — the staff are responsive to the needs of the consumer
- reliability — everything happens at the event in the way marketing communications promised
- tangibles — the physical appearance of the event equipment, artists and staff meet expectations.

Concentrating on these aspects of service will result in outcomes that meet corporate service objectives.

PRICING

Festivals and events are leisure activities. Most Australians live in areas that offer many leisure options. This means that price can have a major effect on demand for an event and is an important aspect of an event's marketing mix. Some events charge no entrance fee to consumers, but there are still costs to the consumer of attending, as well as costs for the producer. This section discusses the non-cash costs of price, how price is used in event marketing, the concept of value for consumers, different types of costs, appropriate pricing strategies and issues involved in pricing.

Price has many uses. In a market economy like Australia's, the more highly sought a particular good or service is, the higher the price, so fewer people can purchase it. For an event, price can determine the number of consumers who attend the event. For example, a mass-market event such as an agricultural show must keep its price at a level of affordability to its customers — middle income, middle Australia. On the other hand, an event such as a fund raiser for the Sydney Theatre Company (STC) can ask a much higher price as its target market is much smaller (socio-economic group AB who are subscribers to the STC), but wealthier and therefore willing to pay for a perceived quality experience. However, the high price can represent quality (or 'value for money') to the potential consumer and influence the decision to purchase.

The three foundations of pricing strategies are:

- costs
- competition — the market
- value to the customer.

Value is the sum of all the perceived benefits (gross value) minus the sum of the perceived costs. Therefore, the greater the positive difference between perceived benefits and costs, the greater the net value to the potential consumer. In the STC fund-raiser example, potential consumers compare the perceived benefits — dinner, drinks, entertainment, parking, opportunities to socialise, prestige, novelty of an unusual night out — with the perceived costs — money and non-cash costs. If the STC have adequately communicated these benefits, consumers will perceive that the event offers value and purchase tickets.

Not all costs to the event consumer are cash. Other costs incurred are:

- time — the opportunity cost of the time spent consuming the event experience compared with using that time to enjoy another leisure experience
- the physical efforts required to consume the leisure experience — travel, energy expended
- psychic costs — mental effort to engage in the social interaction required, feeling uncomfortable in certain social settings
- sensory costs — unpleasant climate, uncomfortable seating, unattractive physical environment and unlikeable companions.

Event managers must consider these elements of consumer costs and attempt either to alleviate any difficulties, or to promote them in such a way that they become part of the event. In most events, the people who attend the event become part of the event product. For example, part of the product of the STC fund-raiser is rubbing shoulders with the 'glitterati' who attend. Alternatively, a middle-aged non-drinker will probably not feel comfortable at an event that is largely attended by young men in their twenties who are enjoying a great deal of alcohol.

Types of event costs are:

- fixed — costs that do not vary according to the number of event consumers; for example, venue rent, interest, light, heat and power, volunteer uniforms, artist fees
- variable — costs that vary according to the number of consumers; for example, number of paper plates used at a food festival, catering at a product launch, extra staff required to serve additional customers.

Analysis of costs is the first step in calculating an appropriate price for the event. The next element to consider is the price of competitive leisure experiences. If a similar leisure experience has a price of $x, the choices are to (1) match and charge price $x, (2) adopt a cost leadership strategy and charge $x − 25 per cent, or (3) adopt a differentiation strategy and use a price of $x + 50 per cent and use marketing communications to promote the value of the event.

There are three types of pricing strategies. A revenue-oriented strategy seeks to set a price that will maximise revenue from the target market. The Sydney Theatre Company's fund-raiser is an example of a revenue-oriented pricing strategy. An operations-oriented pricing strategy seeks to balance supply and demand by introducing cheaper prices for times of low demand and higher prices at times of higher demand. Agricultural shows are examples of events that use an operations-oriented pricing strategy. Finally, a target market strategy uses different prices for different target markets.

For example, a three-day music festival could have one price for those who want to participate for all three days (the fanatic market), a day price for the not so keen, and another price to see a headline act.

Figure 6.8 shows the thought processes necessary to construct a coherent pricing strategy. It is also necessary to understand if the event price is elastic or inelastic. If lowering the price can increase demand, the event price is elastic. If the demand for the event will not change, regardless of price reductions, the price is inelastic. These events are usually specialised. Obviously, it would be foolish to attempt to increase revenue by lowering the price of an inelastic event. Figure 6.9 summarises all event pricing issues.

Customer satisfaction about pricing is more than just money. Customer satisfaction also involves convenience, security, credit card acceptance, speed, simplicity and effective use of technology. It is essential that the event manager has a good understanding of the event's fixed and variable costs, competitors' pricing, the value of the leisure experience to the customer and pricing elasticities.

Set pricing objective
(e.g. maximise attendance or maximise revenue)

↓

Select method of determining base price
Cost + pricing
OR
Price based on a balance
between supply and demand
OR
Price set in relation only
to market price

↓

Design appropriate strategies
Price leadership
Price used as a signal of quality
Discounts for selected target markets
Using price to attract new markets

Figure 6.8 *Selecting pricing strategies for events*

How much should be charged?
- What costs must be covered?
- How sensitive are customers to different prices?
- What are leisure competitors' prices?
- What levels of discounts to selected target markets are appropriate?
- Should psychological pricing ($10.95 instead of $11) be used?

What should be the basis of pricing?
- Should each element be billed separately?
- Should one admission fee be charged?
- Should consumers be charged for resources consumed?
- Should a single price for a bundled package be charged?

Who shall collect payment:
- the event organisation or
- a ticketing intermediary?

Where should payment be made:
- at the event,
- at a ticketing organisation, or
- at the customer's home using the Internet or telephone?

When should payment be made:
- when tickets are given out or
- on the day of the event?

How should payment be made:
- cash — exact change,
- credit card,
- EFTPOS, or
- token?

Figure 6.9 *Pricing issues* (**Source:** *adapted from Lovelock et al. 1998*)

Promotion literally means to move forward or to advance. In the marketing context, promotion refers to all of the communication activities that an event director can use to tell the target market about the benefits of the event and consequently advance its sales. These activities are sometimes referred to as the promotional mix or the communications mix of the event. This mix is an integral part of an event's marketing strategy, as figure 6.10 illustrates. The target market, the positioning of the event and its competitive strategy all play a role in deciding the marketing objectives of an event. Decisions about the make-up of the event product, the pricing strategy to be adopted, how tickets to the event are to reach the target market, and by what means prospective customers are to be informed of the event benefits are then made.

Advertising is any form of non-personal promotion paid for by the event organisation. Radio, television, newspapers, magazines, the Internet, billboards or mobile platforms such as buses or taxis can be used for advertising. The mainstream media such as capital city television, newspapers and radio can be very expensive to use. The creative process of producing the messages can also be expensive, especially if it is done by an advertising agency.

Publicity includes all those activities not directly paid for that communicate with the event's target market. An advantage that event directors have is that people generally enjoy reading about sport, the arts and entertainment that an event produces. It is therefore somewhat easier to get publicity. However, the event director must be aware that for a story to be run, it must have some news value (that is, it must be new and of interest to the reader, viewer or listener), be well-written and come from a reliable source. It is therefore important that all such publicity has the imprimatur of the event director.

Sales promotion, sometimes called below-the-line promotion by advertising agencies because they do not receive commission on these activities, are those activities that use incentives or discounts to increase sales.

■ **Figure 6.10**
The relationship between marketing and promotion strategy

(Source: *adapted from Morgan 1997)*

Strategic decisions:
• target markets
• competitive strategy
• positioning

Marketing objectives

The marketing mix:
• product
• price
• promotion
• place

The promotional mix:
• advertising
• publicity
• sales promotion
• direct marketing
• personal selling

The media mix:
• television
• print
• radio
• outdoor posters
• cinema
• direct mail
• Internet
• brochures
• flyers

Examples of sales promotion are family days at an event where families receive a group discount or a free bottle of fizzy drink when they buy a ticket. Sales promotions can generate extra sales in particular target market subsegments.

Direct selling is communicating directly with potential customers in the target market group by the use of a mailing list, the telephone or the Internet. An existing event should have a list of people who have previously attended the event. These data can be gathered quite simply by, for example, conducting a free raffle that requires attendees to supply their name and address. Other events may also sell their mailing lists.

As Getz (1997, p. 305) points out, the role of the promotional mix is to:

- create or increase awareness of the event
- create or enhance a positive image
- position the event relative to its competition
- inform target markets of pertinent details of the event
- generate demand for the event
- remind target markets of the event's details.

Decisions on promotional strategy must focus on the target market. For example, an event with a large, mass market such as an agricultural show (e.g. the Sydney Royal Easter Show) can use television advertising as a promotional device, whereas a small community festival's promotional mix would use publicity and advertising in the local paper. Each of the promotional techniques and their advantages and disadvantages are shown in table 6.6 on the following page.

When the appropriate type of promotion and medium have been chosen, the next step is to decide on the message(s). George and Berry (1981) have some advice that has been adapted for event directors:

- advertisements should feature the event's artists and staff, rather than models
- provide tangible clues to counteract the intangible nature of the event by showing physical facilities at the event site
- seek continuity over time by use of recognisable symbols, spokespersons, trademarks or music
- promise what is possible to foster realistic expectations.

Other guidelines worthy of consideration are:

- make the service more tangible and recognisable by using representatives of the target market enjoying the event product to illustrate the benefits of the event
- ensure all promotion is integrated with all other aspects of the marketing mix. Use one consistent image or message so that the target market is not confused.

A question that many event directors find difficult to resolve is the amount to be spent on promotion — the budget. Ray's (1982) advice on three methods of deciding the budget is a useful framework for thinking through this question.

■ Table 6.6 *The advantages and disadvantages of different types of promotion*

PROMOTIONAL TYPE	MEDIUM	ADVANTAGES	DISADVANTAGES	USE FOR
Advertising	Television	Wide reach, conveys excitement and colour, can lend credibility	Expensive to produce and transmit	Large, mass market events
	Radio	Can be targeted by music tastes, quick to produce, cheaper	Difficult to cut through the clutter of other radio advertisements and programs	Musical events
	Newspapers	Wide reach, short lead time; suburban newspapers tightly target a community	Can be expensive; widely distributed papers may not tightly target the audience	Community festivals
	Magazines or newsletters	Tightly targeted	Long lead times for events	Special interest events
	Posters/ outdoor	Cheap; can be displayed where target market congregates	Can deface buildings, can be ripped down	Youth, community, special interest events
	Flyers	Cheap, effective if well designed, tightly targeted	Need volunteers to distribute	Youth, special interest
Sales promotion	Price discounts for particular types of customers	Generates revenue	Can dilute revenue if groups not carefully chosen	Large, mass market events
	Cross-promotion with a sponsor	Generates sales for the sponsor, can result in additional sales	Sponsor's image may overtake the event's	Most events
Publicity	Television	Adds credibility; large audience	Must have a televisual angle	All events
	Press	Gives credibility; can be a large or targeted audience	Must be of interest to the general reader	All events
	Speciality magazine or paper	Audience is tightly targeted	Has a long lead time	Special interest events
Direct to target market	Mail, phone or e-mail	Little waste, can be very cost effective	Results depend on quality of mailing list	Special interest events
	Internet	Cheap to produce as can usually be done by a volunteer; easy to change messages; can be used to sell tickets direct	Penetration is currently quite small; many people wary of giving credit card information through the Internet	A target market that is technologically advanced

Judgemental approaches can either be arbitrary or a percentage of sales. An arbitrary decision may be based on what was spent last year or for a similar type of event. Alternatively, the amount can be decided as a percentage of sales — either last year's or anticipated sales. As Ray points out, this is analogous to putting the cart before the horse because the promotional strategy is to produce sales, not to control the amount spent on promotion. What these budgeting methods can do is to give the event director a comfort zone in which to work. That is, they are less open to criticism because that was the amount spent last year.

The *competitive parity approach* consists of budgeting at least the same, if not more, than what the competition is spending. The competition for an event is all other leisure activities, so this may prove very difficult to establish. It is important to have sufficient voice not to get lost in the 'clutter', but matching the budgets of other leisure activities is certainly not recommended as:

- the leisure market is complex and it is probably impossible to establish what all possible competitors are spending
- it is doubtful if many events have the revenue potential to support such a costly exercise.

The *objectives and strategy* approach comes from the marketing process of setting marketing objectives, then communication objectives, then deciding what strategies are needed to achieve these objectives. For example, a marketing objective of selling 10 000 tickets flows to a communication objective of telling a potential market of 100 000 people of the benefits of the event. The strategies to be decided are the creative, the make-up of the promotional mix and the medium (or media) to be used. From this process comes a cost that must be realistic. It would be very foolish to spend $5000 on promotion for an event that has a forecast revenue of $7000.

PLACE

Place refers to both the site where the event takes place (which was dealt with earlier) and the place at which consumers can purchase their tickets. For most events, this means deciding whether to use a ticketing agency. Ticketing agencies widen the distribution network, make it easier for customers to purchase tickets, speed up the entry of customers at the venue, and provide a credit card acceptance service and a telephone booking service. However, they charge both the event organisation and the customer. Their use depends on the type of event, any other purchase facility that can be used, the willingness of the target market to pay for a ticketing service and its relative affordability.

However, selling tickets via a ticketing agency, or some other distribution network such as the Internet, does have distinct advantages for the event producer. Ticket sales can be monitored and decisions made regarding the amount of promotion necessary to achieve marketing objectives based on hard information. The security problems inherent in accepting cash at the door are alleviated. As customers pay in advance, the cash flow to the event producer occurs weeks or even months before production, with obvious advantages for the financial health of the event organisation.

The need for market research in event organisations is based on one simple premise: the lower the quality (or indeed, the complete absence) of data used for marketing decisions, the higher the risk of marketing failure. The data collection is usually organised into a marketing information system that Stanton, Miller and Layton define as 'an ongoing, organised set of procedures and methods designed to generate, analyse, disseminate, store and later retrieve information for use in making marketing decisions' (1994, p. 48). The type of information required by event managers varies according to the type of event. Table 6.7 shows some useful categories of marketing research. The table, however, looks a little more complex than it really is, as most, if not all, of the information requirements shown in table 6.7 can be collected from a simple survey of a random sample of event customers as they leave the event. (For those interested in learning more about this topic, an excellent book on research methods is Veal 1997, *Research Methods for Leisure and Tourism*).

■ Table 6.7
Categories of event marketing research

RESEARCH CATEGORY	USES	TYPICAL MARKETING USE
Market analysis	Marketing planning	Measurement and projections of market volume and target market size
Consumer research	Segmentation and positioning	Quantitative measurement of customer attitudes, profiles and awareness; qualitative assessment of consumer needs and perceptions
Promotion studies	Effectiveness of communication	Measurement of consumer reaction to all types of marketing communications
Performance evaluation	Control device	Measurement of customer satisfaction with event

Figure 6.11 shows a simple survey that can be used or modified by event managers to collect market research data. A randomly selected sample of about 100 attendees should be sufficient to obtain useable data that can be processed into meaningful marketing information. In this context, random means that all event customers have an equal chance of being selected for the survey. For example, as customers exit the event, every tenth customer is asked to participate, rather than selecting those thought most likely to respond favourably to the request. The information obtained can be analysed using a computer software package such as Statistical Package for the Social Sciences (SPSS), or simply by using a pocket calculator and a piece of paper.

One final caveat. Creativity, good judgement and courage to make decisions are important qualities for the event manager. Do not succumb to paralysis through analysis. Market research aids competent event management, but does not replace it.

■ **Figure 6.11**
*Sample
customer
details and
satisfaction
survey. This
survey would
be completed
by the
interviewer.*

Sample customer details and satisfaction survey

Introductory remarks: 'Excuse me, we are carrying out a survey to establish how satisfied our customers are with the festival/event. Could you spare a few minutes to answer a few questions?'

1. On a scale of one to five where one is completely dissatisfied and five is very satisfied, could you tell me how you rate

the venue	1	2	3	4	5
entertainment	1	2	3	4	5
food and drink	1	2	3	4	5
toilet facilities	1	2	3	4	5
access/parking	1	2	3	4	5
ticketing arrangements	1	2	3	4	5
cost	1	2	3	4	5
helpfulness of staff	1	2	3	4	5

2. How did you hear about the festival/event?

   advertisement ☐   friends told me ☐   went last year ☐   mail ☐

   saw a poster ☐   other ☐

3. Will you come next year?

   Yes ☐   No ☐

4. Do you have any other comments about the event? ....

   ....

5. What is your postcode? ....

6. What educational level have you achieved?

   year 10 ☐   year 12 ☐   TAFE qualification ☐   bachelor's degree ☐

   post graduate ☐

7. What is your occupation? ....

8. Gender   Male ☐   Female ☐

9. Age group   15–19   ☐

   20–29   ☐

   30–59   ☐

   60+   ☐

THE MARKETING PLAN

The next and final step in the marketing planning process is to incorporate marketing objectives and strategies into the strategic plan for the event. Figure 6.12 illustrates this process. The marketing plan is not separate from the strategic plan, but part of it. Figure 6.12 also shows that a sound understanding of marketing principles is essential knowledge for an event manager.

■ **Figure 6.12**
Incorporating marketing into the strategic plan

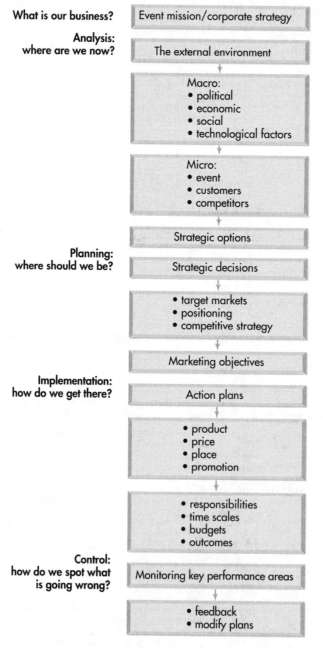

What is our business? — Event mission/corporate strategy

Analysis: where are we now? — The external environment

Macro:
- political
- economic
- social
- technological factors

Micro:
- event
- customers
- competitors

Strategic options

Planning: where should we be? — Strategic decisions

- target markets
- positioning
- competitive strategy

Marketing objectives

Implementation: how do we get there? — Action plans

- product
- price
- place
- promotion

- responsibilities
- time scales
- budgets
- outcomes

Control: how do we spot what is going wrong? — Monitoring key performance areas

- feedback
- modify plans

(**Source:** *adapted from Morgan 1996*)

A common misconception held by many in the festival and event area is that marketing means nothing more than advertising. As this chapter has shown, marketing is a structured way of thinking about managing an event or festival to achieve the objectives of customer satisfaction and either profit or increased awareness of a cause or movement.

The core of the marketing concept is a focus on the customer, in this case the event attendee. This implies that good marketing flows from a complete understanding of the customers — who they are, where they live and what their needs are. This comes from good research and event managers communicating with and observing their customers. From this knowledge comes appropriate marketing strategies that can achieve an event's objectives. Given this understanding of the customer and the external environments in which the event operates, appropriate product, price, promotion and distribution strategies can be implemented.

Questions

1 Why should event managers focus on the needs of their customers, rather than the needs of the event organisers?

2 What are the advantages of market segmentation to an event manager?

3 Name five needs that can be satisfied by attending a community festival.

4 What essential ingredients must a publicity campaign contain to be effective?

5 What considerations other than costs must be considered when deciding on price for an event?

6 What factors must be considered when deciding place (distribution) strategies for an event?

7 What happens to the strategic plan once it is written? Why?

8 What are the advantages of conducting consumer research?

9 What elements constitute an effective marketing communication?

10 Why is it important to show representatives of the target market in marketing communications messages?

St George Floriade,
Canberra

The Australian Capital Territory Parks and Conservation Service, the custodians of Canberra's parks and gardens, originally conceived the St George Floriade event as a one-off presentation for the Australian Bicentenary. It was to be Canberra's special birthday gift to the people of Australia. Several of their senior employees had a vision of re-creating a massed floral display along the lines of the world-famous Keukenhoff in Holland, which attracts more than one million visitors per year.

The success of the first presentation led to the decision that Floriade would be presented annually in Canberra. Visitors to Floriade in Commonwealth Park, on the shores of Canberra's Lake Burley Griffin, have increased from only 80 000 to more than 500 000. Of those visiting, the percentage of tourists has increased markedly to more than 50 per cent. Floriade is now a major national tourist attraction and is estimated to bring more than $25 million into the Australian Capital Territory economy.

Fundamental to the success of Floriade in 1997 was the targeted use of print and electronic media, and the application of paid and unpaid promotional and marketing strategies combined with a 'one-stop shopping' approach. As with any event, increasing awareness and ease of purchase were critical to both the success of the event and the significant growth in tourist numbers.

The nature of the event ensured that four television lifestyle programs were sufficiently interested to produce 'free' segments, which aired during the event's crucial lead up and opening stages. Consequently, an aggregate audience of 1.5 million people in key New South Wales markets was exposed to Floriade at minimal cost to the organisers.

Such free publicity was crucial to exposing the event to a large segment of its potential consumers. It was also critical to establish a link between event awareness, the desire to travel and the actual decision to travel. From a marketing perspective, it was therefore critical to understand the consumer travel decision-making process in order to convert underlying awareness to action.

There are two trends evident when people are deciding to travel: consumers seek perceived value for their travel purchase and consumers look for an easily accessible means of purchase. In order to cater for this consumer demand, it was decided to add value to the event by offering Floriade 'packages' which encompassed entry to the event, free parking, local maps and a range of accommodation choices for a single, affordable price.

With value added to the event through the packages and awareness being raised via television segments and other media exposure, the next step in the marketing strategy was to provide potential consumers with the means to purchase the package easily. This step involved a mixture of paid advertisements and 'advertorial' (advertisements written as journalist copy) placements in major national and regional newspapers, as well as pieces in a number of general 'glossy' magazines and specialist horticultural magazines. Each advertisement highlighted both the value of Floriade packages and also the ease with which they could be purchased via the free Floriade hotline telephone number through which consumers could organise and pay for all their travel arrangements.

As with any special event or festival that is designed to attract tourists, it is essential that consumer wants and needs are both well understood and catered for. The 1997 Floriade event achieved its core objectives of increasing the number and yield of tourists visiting the Australian Capital Territory. This was a direct result of targeted marketing and promotional campaigns.

Evi Prin
Research Manager
Chris Hamon
Director Events
Canberra Tourism and Events Corporation

Questions

1 What are the advantages and disadvantages of the promotional strategies used by Floriade?

2 What consumer needs and wants did Floriade identify?

3 What alternative distribution (place) strategies could Floriade use?

4 Why, do you think, was Floriade successful in receiving publicity on television lifestyle programs?

5 What other media could the Floriade directors have used to achieve the same or similar results?

6 The Floriade product was packaged with accommodation and transport to appeal to non-residents of Canberra. Could any other elements be included in the Floriade package to attract other market segments? How could Floriade be packaged to appeal to Canberra residents?

The Woodford
Folk Festival

From 27 December 1997 to late on 1 January 1998, the Woodford Folk Festival had an aggregate attendance of almost 80 000 and a box office take of almost $1.4 million. It was a festival that allowed the organiser, the Queensland Folk Federation, to pull out of an insolvent trading position after three very difficult years that followed a decision to purchase and build infrastructure on its own 240 acre block. In just three years, the festival had purchased its own venue.

The Woodford Folk Festival, which began as the Maleny Folk Festival, has emerged as a major Australian cultural event, attracting more than a third of its patrons from interstate and more than one in every hundred from overseas. The festival is an unusual success story. At the time the festival started, the folk scene was very small — a handful of enthusiasts, one or two small monthly folk clubs, and concerts and events attracting a couple of hundred people at best.

What follows is a discussion of those vital marketing elements that have made this festival such a success. It is written by Bill Hauritz, the Festival Director, who was instrumental in its birth and who, at the time of publication, remains at the helm.

Last year our office got a call from a Port Macquarie business, asking me if we could send them some papers to let them know how to get a folk festival happening in their area. The people would be behind it, it was a tourist area and they needed a folk festival like Woodford's to boost the town's economy. One of our most passionate workers and dreamers, Peter Auty, was in my office at the time. His suggestion was: 'Bill, just send them the magic powder and tell him to sprinkle it at the site and it will all just happen'. After years of seemingly scaling mountains to get where we were, someone wanted all that information and experience in a letter — such is the perception of many people on the degree of difficulty of the task.

There is a common thread running through all successful businesses, though, and it is simple: 'a good idea and a single-minded stubbornness not to give up until it has been achieved'. While there are many things to learn, we do not need to reinvent the wheel. However, without that single-mindedness and hard work, whatever it is will not work.

One of the lessons I had learnt watching P&C associations raise funds has become central in all our planning. We were taught that if you want many people to come to the school musical, have a lot of people in the cast. The second one was that the more salespeople you have, the more tickets you will

sell. We matched these ideas with the hard-earned information that the most powerful criterion for success is the number of people who attend.

As a musician, I had performed for many years in bands. We did many gigs where organisers were disappointed with the attendance, and this happened more often than not. I have been involved in many committees and have witnessed the fatal flaw of most organising committees for events: the marketing is the last item on the agenda and it usually gets five minutes attention. 'Buy an ad on TV and everyone will be there'. Everyone has been to those perfectly organised functions to which no-one came. There is a huge belief in the festival organising community that if it is promoted in the media then the people will automatically show up. They do not. A full-colour front-page advertisement in the *Sydney Morning Herald* will not sell tickets to a function on its own. Advertising agencies and media will not like me saying this but it does not work. You are wasting your time. If your selling campaign is working then media will be ringing you. People sell tickets, not the electronic media. A good 'word of mouth' is no accident.

If there is one thing we got right in the early days, it was the marketing of our festival. We felt greatly complimented at a marketing seminar I attended last year when the speaker, in answering a question about promotion, said folk festivals get a lot of people… they don't need promoting. Yet ten years earlier, I expect that the same speaker would have said selling tickets to a folk festival would be extremely difficult; no-one goes to folk festivals. Woodford had changed his perspective.

At the 1997 festival, we sold $1.4 million dollars worth of tickets to people to come along to an ill-prepared site without proper amenities, in the hottest month of the year, to listen to obscure musicians do their thing. The promotional budget was $200. Nevertheless, the marketing of Woodford has always been number one on all the agendas of all the meetings. The whole festival team is constructed the way it is for marketing purposes. Marketing drives everything.

The objective of the marketing plan of our festival since the beginning has been: *get as many people to come as we can, give them a fantastic time so that next year they'll come back and they'll bring their friends.* However, getting people to come is the hardest part. Nevertheless, good attendance is really the only criterion for success and we prioritise things accordingly. The successful application of this priority, more than anything else, has been the cornerstone of our success.

Looking back on the last 12 years, I doubt whether we would change anything about the way we have sold the festival. First was the structure of the organising group. The idea was to get as many people involved as we could. When we have an organisers' meeting, we have enough people to open a bar and put on a band. Once, before our third festival, we had a weekend mini-fest. The aim was to get hundreds and hundreds of people armed with sales tools (posters and programs) and encourage them to talk their workmates, neighbours and families to help sell the festival.

We also convinced all the stallholders that their living depended on bringing their friends, relatives and neighbours. When we arranged the program of events, we booked lots of large choirs, large dance groups and the like, instead of soloists. A 50-voice choir was booked, and all their spouses came and bought tickets. Instead of one production company supplying all the stages, we hired individual groups to supply and mix each stage and then involved them in selling the festival to their mates.

Getting hundreds of salespeople armed with sales tools, and making them enthusiastic and motivated was the key to success. To do that required us to sell our concept widely, to share our vision. Principal organisers divided the tasks up into as many areas of responsibility as they could and then pushed the responsibilities downward as far as they would go; we had more than 80 section heads, each with their own people and area of responsibility. We discovered that the more meetings we had to discuss what we were doing and why we were doing it, the more the vision grew and the more it was shared. By the time the festival started there were several hundred organisers plus spouses, hundreds of stallholders and their families, hundreds of suppliers and their families, a huge special invitation list, a thousand performers and their spouses, and so on. When the first ticket buyer arrived there were thousands already wandering around and a festival economy that was already trading strongly. In people's minds it was already a success.

We had already undertaken a lot of research on the history of the folk movement and had already fairly well developed philosophical ideas on what we were about. We felt there were flaws in the folk movement and we moved to fix them. Right from the beginning, we made a real attempt to involve Aboriginal people and, later on, migrant groups. One year we introduced women MCs in order to even up the gender balance. This, and many other innovations introduced by the organisers, widened the margins of the folk movement and created a missionary zeal in the organising group.

Each year we conducted surveys. We distributed questionnaires to everyone, asking for their comments and ideas on how we could improve the festival. We would read them and each new idea adopted would be a small triumph: the involvement of more people. We put everyone's name on the mailing list. Moreover, each year we would reduce the cost of the tickets for those who purchased early. We wrote to everyone as if they were our friends, updated them with the news and asked them to pre-purchase their tickets. We still do this. In 1997, half of our entire ticket sales were purchased before the festival opened. Most of those people had bought before the publication of our program of events. The mailing list has become very valuable, too. However, we learnt that it is a very expensive method of advertising, so we ended up putting on the mailing list only those people who we thought were most likely to buy tickets: our friends the patrons.

By the time the third or fourth festival came along, there was such a huge growth in attendance that it was difficult keeping up with infrastructure requirements. The original venue at Maleny was suddenly too small and the

group made the decision, a couple of years later, to purchase a beautiful block of land at Woodford and move the festival to it. The organising group moved into Woodford on 2 September 1994. In sixteen weeks the organisers, staff and volunteers built roads and bridges, sewerage lines and dams, sullage and water lines, tanks and drains, cut and filled earth; it was an extraordinary period of time. The water was turned on just hours before people started arriving on 27 December 1994.

The festival has become more professional now, with more staff, and has its own Web site. As it gets bigger, the margin for error reduces. The basic structure, though, has not changed. There is still wide consultation and a wide sense of ownership. The method in building the organising group also gave the festival another unplanned attribute. It is resilient. It can take a bad weather year, it can take the knocks and survive.

The Woodford Folk Festival organising group has made many mistakes, but these have been our education. Twelve years later, a lot of the central people are still heavily involved and there is a general sense of excitement and strong ambition for the next step: developing the Woodford land for folklore, arts and the humanities. There are 30 projects on the drawing board and it is more exciting than ever. Each of these projects will, of course, aim to culminate its work at the year's festival. The festival itself will always be a major focus. It has become a beautiful event with great diversity and depth to its proceedings. You should come.

Bill Hauritz,
Director of the Woodford Folk Festival

Questions

1 List three types of market research that would be appropriate for the festival in its early stage of development.

2 Describe the festival's promotional strategy in a paragraph.

3 Describe the festival's product strategy.

4 What was the festival's distribution strategy? Why is it both effective and efficient?

5 What is the festival's pricing strategy? What other pricing strategies can they use?

REFERENCES

Ansoff, I. 1957, 'Strategies for diversification', *Harvard Business Review*, September–October, pp. 113–24.

Cowell, D. 1984, *The Marketing of Services*, Heinemann, London.

Dickman, S. 1997, 'Issues in arts marketing', in *Making It Happen: The Cultural and Entertainment Industries Handbook*, ed. R. Rentschler, Centre for Professional Development, Kew, Victoria.

George, W. & Berry, L. 1981, 'Guidelines for the advertising of services', *Business Horizons*, July–August, pp. 52–6.

Getz, D. 1991, *Festivals, Special Events and Tourism*, Von Nostrand Reinhold, New York.

Getz, D. 1997, *Event Management and Event Tourism*, Cognizant Communications, New York.

Hall, C. M. 1997, *Hallmark Tourist Events: Impacts, Management and Planning*, John Wiley & Sons, Chichester.

Levitt, T. 1980, 'Marketing myopia', in *Marketing Management and Strategy*, eds K. Kotler & C. Cox, Prentice Hall, Englewood Cliffs, New Jersey.

Loane, S. & Horin. A. 1998, 'Most still tie the knot, but much later', *Sydney Morning Herald*, 20 April, p. 4.

Lovelock, C., Patterson, P. & Walker, R. 1998, *Services Marketing: Australia and New Zealand*, Prentice Hall, Sydney.

McCarthy, E. & Perreault, W. 1987, *Basic Marketing*, Irwin, Homewood, Illinois.

Middleton, V. T. C. 1995, *Marketing in Travel and Tourism*, Butterworth-Heinemann, Oxford.

Mohr, K., Backman, K., Gahan, L. & Backman, S. 1993, 'An investigation of festival motivations and event satisfaction by visitor type', *Festival Management and Event Tourism*, vol. 1, pp. 89–97.

Morgan, M. 1996, *Marketing for Leisure and Tourism*, Prentice Hall, London.

Ray, M. 1982, *Advertising and Communication Management*, Prentice Hall, Englewood Cliffs, New Jersey.

Roslow, S., Nicholls, J. & Laskey, H. 1992, 'Hallmark events and measures of reach and audience characteristics', *Journal of Advertising Research*, July/August, pp. 53–9.

Saleh, F. & Ryan, C. 1993, 'Jazz and knitwear: factors that attract tourists to festivals', *Tourism Management*, August, pp. 289–97.

Stanton, W., Miller, K. & Layton, R. 1994, *Fundamentals of Marketing*, 3rd edn, McGraw Hill, Sydney.

Torkildsen, G. 1983, *Leisure and Recreation Management*, Spon, London.

Uysal, M., Gahan, L. & Martin, B. 1993, 'An examination of event motivations', *Festival Management and Event Tourism*, vol. 1, pp. 5–10.

Veal, A. 1997, *Research Methods for Leisure and Tourism*, Pitman, London.

Zeithaml, V., Parasuraman, A. & Berry, L. 1990, *Delivering Quality Service: Balancing Customer Perceptions and Expectations*, The Free Press, New York.

3 EVENT
ADMINISTRATION

7 Sponsorship
of events

LEARNING OBJECTIVES

After studying this chapter, you should be able to:

- define sponsorship in the context of festivals and events

- understand why organisations use sponsorship as a promotional medium

- identify appropriate sponsors for an event

- construct an appropriate sponsorship proposal

- plan activities that satisfy a sponsor's needs.

WHAT IS SPONSORSHIP?

To anybody who has not tried to obtain sponsorship, it may seem that it is a simple process of asking a rich, usually transnational, company for money because the company has a philanthropic bent. In return, the company's name can be included (usually among many others) in the festival or event's marketing communications. However, the process of securing sponsorship is not such a simple undertaking. This chapter outlines a number of strategies that can be used in attempting to secure a sponsor for an event.

Sponsorship is a promotional technique used by businesses, both large and small, for purely commercial reasons. It has nothing to do with philanthropy and is never a donation. It is a commercial transaction that the sponsoring organisation enters into because it believes that the festival or event will offer a communication link to its target market that is more effective than or complementary to other promotional opportunities, such as advertising.

Getz (1997) defines sponsors as 'companies or individuals who provide money, services or other support to events and event organisations in return for specified benefits'. Geldard and Sinclair (1996, p. 6), in their comprehensive work on sponsorship, define it as:

■ the purchase of the, usually intangible, exploitable potential (rights and benefits), associated with an entrant, event or organisation which results in tangible benefits for the sponsoring company (image/profit enhancement). ■

This definition includes the involvement of government agencies, which can be major sponsors of festivals and events. They are not philanthropists, but are seeking an intangible benefit in return for their sponsorship. These benefits may include:
• enhancing the economic development of a region or State (e.g. Australian Grand Prix)
• enhancing a community's identity (e.g. Australia Day)
• increasing social interaction and community development (e.g. Brisbane River Festival)
• sharing ideas and developing a sense of togetherness (e.g. Science Week)
• developing a community's infrastructure (e.g. Sydney Olympic Games)
• winning popular support for the ruling government.

Companies, on the other hand, usually use the sponsorship of public activities such as festivals and events to:
• generate consumer goodwill towards the company
• generate or increase the sales of their products
• increase brand awareness and acceptance
• align a particular brand to a lifestyle
• access niche markets
• provide opportunities for the entertainment of clients
• demonstrate product capabilities
• create merchandising opportunities.

Crompton (1994, p. 65) stresses the reciprocal aspect of sponsorship. He defines it as 'a reciprocal relationship that involves an organisation and a business engaging in an exchange which offers commensurate benefits to each entity'. The reciprocity element of the sponsorship process is illustrated in figure 7.1. For the reciprocity element to be effective, sponsorship must benefit both the event committee and the sponsoring corporation.

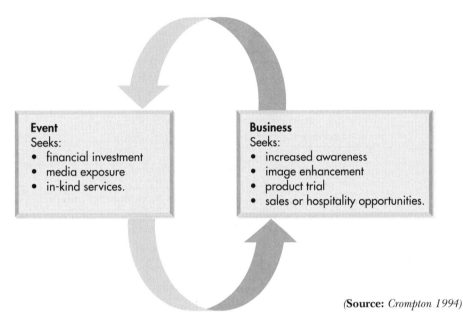

(Source: *Crompton 1994)*

Interestingly, the first recorded instance of sponsorship was undertaken by the Medici family who ruled Florence from 1434–1637. Cosimo the Elder (1389–1464) and his grandson, Lorenzo the Magnificent (1448–1492), sponsored painters, artists, sculptors and scholars. It is reasonable to assume that they sponsored these artists, many of whom featured in events produced by the family, for much the same reasons that Esso Australia sponsored the Australian Opera. That is, the aim of the sponsorship was to generate goodwill towards them from a target audience, to generate awareness and acceptance of their family enterprises and to entertain their clients with hospitality centred on these artistic endeavours.

CORPORATE SPONSORSHIP OF FESTIVALS AND EVENTS

As discussed in chapter 6, organisations need to communicate to potential customers about how their products can satisfy a particular need. Commonly, this is accomplished by advertising in either print or electronic media, sales promotion, generating publicity or personal selling. The sponsoring of festivals and events gives businesses another medium, which, if carefully constructed by the festival or event organisation, can allow businesses to reach a target market in an effective manner that also complements their existing promotional mix. In other words, the sponsorship of an event or festival can become an integral part of the marketing plan of a business.

In their review of the literature on this topic, Sunshine, Backman and Backman (1995) discovered:

- of the top 200 United Kingdom corporate sponsors, the principal benefit they sought from sponsorship was access to specific target audiences followed by corporate image enhancement
- a chain of book stores sponsors college events to develop brand loyalty among new customers who have the potential to be lifelong customers
- another study that reported that the benefits expected from sponsorship were:
  — increased awareness of company and product
  — increased product identification with a particular lifestyle
  — a means of product and market differentiation
  — a means of entertaining key clientele
  — a means of providing merchandising opportunities
  — a means of product or corporate image building
  — an opportunity to represent commitment to a particular community.

According to Geldard and Sinclair (1996), the benefits sought by companies from sponsorship include all of those previously listed, with the addition of:

- exclusivity — the ability to lock a competitor out of an activity
- the opportunity to demonstrate product attributes
- the opportunity to generate sales.

There is no doubt that sponsorship of festivals and events as a promotional medium has increased over recent years. Crompton (1995) suggests that these changes in the operating environment of business have contributed to that growth.

1. The increase in media outlets (including pay TV channels, and new radio stations and specialist magazines) has made it difficult for product messages to 'cut through the clutter'. One way to be seen by consumers every day is to use sponsorship as a promotional medium.

2. The cost of television advertising has increased, while the proliferation of channels has fragmented the viewing audience. The introduction of the remote control, which allows viewers to change channels whenever an advertisement appears, and the video tape recorder, which allows viewers to fast-forward commercials in pre-recorded programs, has further reduced the effectiveness of using television advertising as a promotional medium. Some companies therefore see sponsorship as a more cost-effective medium. However, the consequence of more and more sponsorship of events may be that they too become too cluttered to be effective for communication with a target audience.

3. Colour television and the increase in the number of channels caused by the introduction of pay TV has provided many more opportunities for events, especially sporting events, to be televised, which has consequently provided more opportunities for the exposure of event sponsors.

4. The banning of certain types of direct television advertising can increase sponsorship opportunities. Tobacco companies once provided valuable sponsorship of events because the advertising of tobacco on television was banned. The use of sponsorship allowed their brand image to be reinforced with their target market. This sponsorship by tobacco companies, of course, is now also banned in Australia, with the exception of some international events such as the Australian Formula One Grand Prix. Liquor products can still be advertised on Australian television, although for how long is a matter for conjecture, particularly if the example of the United States is followed in Australia. As liquor companies seek to access the youth market as the next generation of consumers, they are therefore frequent sponsors of music and sports events.

5. Sport has become increasingly commercialised, which has become accepted as vital to sport's well-being. It is common to see a sporting team run onto an arena with the uniforms, the fence and the ground itself emblazoned with sponsors' names. The acceptance of this seems to have reached all levels of sport, with even the most amateur of events being sponsored. A much commented on exception to this proliferation of brand names on sporting fields was the 1998 World Cup. The pitches on which the games were played were verdant green, in contrast to the usually multi-logoed pitches on which Australian professional sport is played. The enormous success of sponsorship activity associated with the 1984 Los Angeles Olympic Games showed corporations how effective corporate sponsorship could be. This exercise gave the corporations concerned an enormous amount of media coverage and the Olympic Games were a financial success.

6. Sponsorship has also become an effective medium to use to communicate with discrete market segments. Until the 1970s, market segmentation was not widespread and companies moved their products by mass marketing techniques. With the advent of the concept of market segmentation, companies needed media through which they could communicate with these target markets. As sports or music or arts fans are spread across the full range of demographics, festivals or events offer an effective medium for this communication. As Sleight (1989, p. 42) notes 'sponsorship works because it fulfils the most important criterion of a communications medium — it allows a particular audience to be targeted with a particular set of messages'.

7. The increase in the number of products and services on the market has been accompanied by a drop in the number of companies because of mergers and take-overs. This has increased the need for producers to enhance their relationships with the retailers of their products. Sponsorship offers innovative and interesting ways to offer entertainment and hospitality to these retailers.

8. Many councils and government services have adopted a user-pays policy. This means that the cost of staging festivals has increased, as the event organisers have to pay for services such as police security, garbage collection, ambulance protection and rental of the council-owned venue. These extra costs have forced festival and event producers to seek sponsorship to cover these increased costs.

It is difficult not to agree with this diagnosis by Crompton (1995). Since sponsorship has become more attractive to potential sponsors, provided the festival or event manager is careful in selecting an appropriate sponsor(s) and is methodical and creative in constructing the sponsorship package of benefits, mutually satisfying rewards for all parties can result.

DECIDING ON THE APPROPRIATE SPONSORSHIP FOR AN EVENT

Geldard and Sinclair (1996) warn that sponsorship is not for all events. Firstly, obtaining sponsorship is both time-consuming and can be damaging to the ego when the inevitable refusals occur. Sponsorship is a commercial contract in which the event promises to deliver certain benefits and rights to the sponsor in return for cash or goods and services in kind, which is known as contra. To ensure these benefits are given to the sponsor requires event management time, planning and effort. It is not a process to be entered into lightly.

If an event can not offer a sponsor appropriate benefits, then a donation to the event may be appropriate. A donation is a gift with no obligation for benefits to be given in return. In other words, it is philanthropy, which is not sponsorship.

Geldard and Sinclair (1996) propose the following check list to establish if an event is suitable for sponsorship.

■ **Figure 7.2**
Check list to establish if an event is suitable for sponsorship

Is the event suitable for sponsorship?

☐ Does the event have some benefits that can be offered to a potential sponsor?

☐ Does the target audience approve of commercial sponsorship?

☐ Are there any companies that are not suitable for sponsoring the event (e.g., tobacco or liquor companies should not be asked to sponsor events for teenagers)?

☐ Does the event organisation have people with the expertise and time to construct and produce sponsorship packages?

☐ Does the event have a policy on sponsorship?

A sponsorship policy sets out what the event organisation can and can not do in terms of attracting and delivering sponsorship benefits. The policy should give details of:

- the event's objectives for seeking sponsorship
- the rules for entering into sponsorship
- the level at which accountability and responsibility for sponsorship lies
- which types of sponsors are unsuitable for the event

- how the sponsorship plan is constructed
- how the value of contra goods and services is established (usually at the retail price the event would have to pay if they were not sponsored)
- how the benefits gained from a sponsorship are to be valued
- who is the approving authority for sponsorship (e.g. the marketing manager or the event director or the board of directors).

IDENTIFYING APPROPRIATE SPONSORSHIP

As the decision to sponsor an event is usually made because it is part of a corporate marketing strategy, Sunshine, Backman and Backman (1995) suggest that the first step in successfully obtaining an appropriate sponsor is to understand the factors that influence the decision-making process. These factors are illustrated below in figure 7.3.

■ **Figure 7.3**
Corporate strategy flow chart

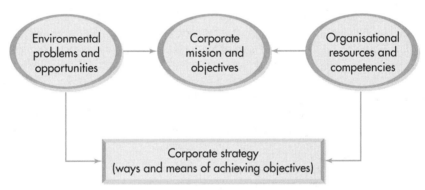

(**Source:** *adapted from Sunshine, Backman & Backman 1995*)

To fully understand how a corporation develops marketing strategies, the event manager can undertake research into the corporation and the environments in which it operates. A reading of the annual report will reveal its corporate mission and generally the objectives that flow from this statement. The annual report also may reveal the perceived competencies of the company and the resources available to it to achieve its objectives. Event managers must always monitor the business, social, cultural, political and economic environments in which they and business operate. This monitoring enables the astute event manager to identify changes in the operating environments of corporations that can make a sponsorship effective for a company. For example, a manager of a community festival in Wollongong may notice the chairperson of a building products company announcing to the financial press a decision to build a corrugated iron plant in Illawara and how the company is looking forward to building links with the community. A carefully constructed sponsorship proposal stressing the effectiveness of the community festival as a communication medium to the citizens of Illawara would have a good chance of success.

Another way to identify potential sponsors is to examine the sponsorship proposal from the sponsor's perspective. Crompton (1993) proposes a memorable acronym of CEDAR EEE which summarises the screening process that businesses use when evaluating sponsorship proposals. The acronym is derived from:

Customer audience

Exposure potential

Distribution channel audience

Advantage over competitors

Resource investment involvement required

Event's characteristics

Event organisation's reputation

Entertainment and hospitality opportunities.

These criteria are expanded in figure 7.4. The task for event managers is to analyse their event using these criteria and then find companies whose marketing needs can be satisfied by the benefits offered by their event.

■ **Figure 7.4**
Screening criteria used by businesses to determine sponsorship opportunities

1. Customer audience

Is the demographic, attitude and lifestyle profile of the target audience congruent with the product's target market?

What is the on-site audience?

Is sponsorship of this event the best way to communicate about the product to this target audience?

2. Exposure potential

What is the inherent news value of the event?

What extended print and broadcast coverage of the sponsorship is likely?

Will the extended coverage be local, regional or national? Is the geographical scope of this media audience consistent with the product's sales area?

Can the event be tied into other media advertising?

Can the company's products be sold at the event?

What is the life of the event?

Are banners and signage included in the sponsorship? How many and what size? Will they be visible during telecasts?

Will the product's name and logo be identified on promotional material for the activity?
- Event posters — how many?
- Press releases — how many?
- On tickets — how many?
- Point-of-sale displays — how many?
- Television advertisements — how many and on what station(s)?
- Radio advertisements — how many and on what station(s)?
- Print advertisements — how many and in what publications?

Where will the product name appear in the event program? Front or back cover? Number and size of program advertisements?

How many programs?

Will the product's name be mentioned on the public address system? How many times?

Can the sponsor have display booths? Where will they be located? Will they be visible during telecasts?

3. **Distribution channel audience**

Are the sponsorship's advantages apparent to wholesalers, retailers or franchisees? Will they participate in promotions associated with the sponsorship?

4. **Advantage over competitors**

Is the event unique or otherwise distinctive?

Has the event previously had sponsors? If so, how successful has it been in delivering the desired benefits to them? Is it strongly associated with other sponsors? Will clutter be a problem?

Does the event need co-sponsors? Are other sponsors of the event compatible with the company's product? Does the company want to be associated with them? Will the product stand out and be recognised among them?

If there is co-sponsorship, will the product have category and advertising exclusivity?

Will competitors have access to signage, hospitality or event advertising? Will competition be allowed to sell product on site?

If the company does not sponsor it, will the competitor? Is that a concern?

5. **Resource investment involvement required**

How much is the total sponsorship cost, including such items as related promotional investments, staff time and administrative and implementation effort?

Will the sponsorship investment be unwieldy and difficult to manage?

What are the levels of barter, in-kind and cash investment?

Does the event guarantee a minimum level of benefits to the company?

6. **Event's characteristics**

What is the perceived stature of the event? Is it the best of its kind? Will involvement with it enhance the product's image?

Does it have a 'clean' image. Is there any chance it will be controversial?

Does it have continuity or is it a one-off?

7. **Event organisation's reputation**

Does the organisation have a proven track record in staging this or other events? Does it have the expertise to help the product achieve its sponsorship goals?

Does the organisation have a reputation and an image with which the company desires to be associated?

Does it have a history of honouring its obligations?

Has the company worked with this organisation before? Was it a positive experience?

Does it have undisputed control and authority over the activities it sanctions?

How close to its forecasts has the organisation been in delivering benefits to its sponsors?

How responsive is the organisation's staff to sponsors' requests? Are they readily accessible?

Is there insurance and what are the company's potential liabilities?

8. **Entertainment and hospitality opportunities**

Are there opportunities for direct sales of product and related merchandise, or for inducing product trial?

Will celebrities be available to serve as spokespeople for the product? Will they make personal appearances on its behalf at the event, in other markets, or in the media? At what cost?

Are tickets to the event included in the sponsorship? How many? Which sessions? Where are the seats located?

Will there be access to VIP hospitality areas for the company's guests? How many will be authorised? Will celebrities appear?

Will there be clinics, parties, or playing opportunities at which the company's guests will be able to interact with the celebrities?

(**Source:** *adapted from Crompton 1993*)

Obviously, not all the criteria outlined are used by all companies when assessing sponsorship proposals. A company may seek to achieve a different range of outcomes or benefits from a sponsorship arrangement. Crompton (1993) stresses that companies usually establish measurable objectives for their sponsorship investments. This suggests that it is in the event's best interests to work with the sponsoring company to establish some sort of measurable objective for their sponsorship of the event.

When sponsorship of festivals and events was in its infancy, many decisions regarding corporate sponsorship reflected the personal interests of senior management. This decision base is now obsolete. Event managers must find companies that have promotional needs that sponsorship can satisfy, understand the sponsorship decision-making process, construct sponsorship proposals that answer the questions raised in that process, and act to ensure what is promised is delivered to the sponsors.

CONSTRUCTING AN EFFECTIVE SPONSORSHIP PROPOSAL

Once organisations that have marketing links to the target market are identified, the next step is to construct a sponsorship package that can satisfy both the organisations' communication needs and the objectives of the event. These benefits are usually a combination of the following elements and are dependent on the type of event.

- **A promotional medium.** Sponsorship is a more efficient means of effectively communicating with a targeted audience (i.e. more target market receivers of the messages at lower cost per impact) than other media. Techniques used include naming rights, where the event is given the name of the sponsor or the sponsor's product (e.g. the Fosters Melbourne Cup); advertisements on banners or posters at the venue; advertisements in a program; or a logo shown on all material produced for the event, such as tickets, entry forms, eating and drinking utensils, signs, displays, floats, merchandise or the venue itself.

- **Publicity.** Sponsorship provides an opportunity to be associated with an event that is viewed favourably by the target audience. The sponsor's involvement in the event needs to then be mentioned in the various media that are read, listened to or watched by the target audience.

- **Networking.** Sponsorship provides opportunities for the sponsor's management and staff to meet people important to their business. These people can either be potential clients, suppliers of product to their business, regulatory authorities or opinion makers.

- **Product sales or demonstration.** Sponsorship provides opportunities for product sales or product demonstrations to a target market.

- **Entertainment facilities.** Sponsorship provides opportunities for the sponsor to entertain clients. The sponsorship package needs to be constructed so that it allows the sponsor to offer preferential seating, quality food and beverages, preferential parking and access to unusual or sought after entertainment to its clients or potential clients. The package can also include introduction to celebrities involved in the event.

- **Access to an event by a sponsor's staff.** Sponsorship can improve staff morale and provide a wider awareness of the sponsorship when staff can be given access to the event at a reduced price. Such a benefit is likely to help maintain good relationships between the event and the sponsor, thereby increasing chances of the sponsorship being continued.
- **Price.** The cost of the sponsorship should be no more than the cost of using another promotional medium. For example, if the cost to reach a similar target market using television is $55 000, a sponsorship price of $35 000 may be viewed as an attractive proposition by a company.

Establishing the range of benefits to offer the sponsor can come only from research into each of the sponsor's needs, and then customising a package of benefits at a competitive price that will satisfy the needs of that potential sponsor by using all the communication and entertainment benefits the event offers.

CONTACTING POTENTIAL SPONSORS

Fairly casual research (an observant eye and informal questioning) will provide a list of providers of goods and services designed to satisfy the needs of the target market for the festival or event. The next step in the sponsorship process is to select appropriate sponsors from this list for the event and conduct in-depth research on their marketing strategies. For example, if the organisation uses television advertising to promote its products, can the event complement this advertising program in some way? Is the organisation currently sponsoring an event? If so, is that event complementary or competitive to this event?

The next step is to contact the potential sponsor organisation to establish:
- the name and address of the person to whom the proposal should be addressed
- how the event can complement the organisation's current marketing communication strategies
- any special needs the organisation may have.

Once this is done, a customised formal written proposal can be sent to the decision maker incorporating all the potential sponsor's special requirements. After a decent interval (about five days), this can be followed up by a telephone call requesting a meeting to present the proposal in person. If, after the meeting, the potential sponsor declines the opportunity to sponsor the event, select another potential sponsor from the list and carry out the steps again.

Once an organisation that will agree to sponsoring the festival or event has been found, a sponsorship business plan outlining both parties' responsibilities should be drawn up.

CONSTRUCTING A SPONSORSHIP BUSINESS PLAN

The first step to ensure that sponsor expectations are met is to construct a sponsorship business plan. Geldard and Sinclair (1997) state that once an agreement has been reached with the sponsor(s), a sponsorship business plan should be constructed that includes:

- a quantifiable outcome for the sponsorship package
- corporate or brand image objectives, if applicable
- a time line (or Gantt chart) that details all the activities that need to take place and the time of their implementation
- a forecast of the sponsorship program's costs
- details of the human resource costs needed to carry out the program.
  A sponsorship business plan will generally consist of these components.
- **Introduction.** This puts the plan into context by describing the history, mission and objectives of the event and the role of the sponsor(s) in the event. It names the sponsor(s), their needs and expected outcomes.
- **Background.** This section details the social, cultural, economic and political environment in which the event is to operate, the business and competitive environment of the sponsors, their involvement in the event and the length of the sponsorship contract. It also includes details of the target market for the event.
- **Objectives.** This section outlines the desired outcomes of the sponsorship expressed in specific, measurable, achievable, relevant and time-specific terms. It is helpful to include the reasons why these objectives have been chosen.
- **Target audiences.** This section lists all those organisationally affected by the plan (both in the event's and the sponsor's organisations), the event's target market, the event's stakeholders, television audience (if applicable), etc.
- **Action list/time line/accountability.** Shown here are all activities that need to be completed to achieve the sponsorship objectives, the deadline for completion of these activities, and who is responsible for their completion.
- **Budget.** All sponsorship activities incur costs, including human resource costs, to the event organisation. In this section all anticipated costs by cost centre (e.g. prize money, communication costs, promotional costs to support the sponsorship, staff hours spent on sponsorship matters, signage manufacture, professional fees, promotional material, sponsor entertainment) and the revenue from the sponsorship (either cash or contra) should be listed. This then shows the income from the sponsorship and the costs incurred in supporting it. Figure 7.5 provides a check list of items to be included in a sponsorship budget. (See chapter 8 for more information on budgets.) All of the details, except perhaps the profit element of the budget, should be given to the sponsor to show the event's managerial competencies.

- **Evaluation.** Shown in this section are the key result areas (KRAs) by which the success or otherwise of the sponsorship is to be measured. Obviously, this has to be written in a form that is measurable.

Items that will incur cash outlays or person hours to support the sponsorship	Cost ($)
☐ Event programs	
☐ Additional printing	
☐ Signage production	
☐ Signage erection	
☐ Support advertising	
☐ Hospitality — food and beverage	
☐ Telephone and facsimile	
☐ Public relations support	
☐ Tickets for sponsors	
☐ VIP parking passes	
☐ Cost of selling sponsorship (staff time at $ ____ per hour)	
☐ Cost of servicing sponsorship (staff time at $ ____ per hour)	
☐ Legal costs	
☐ Travel costs	
☐ Taxis and other transport	
☐ Evaluation research	
☐ Media monitoring	
Total costs	
Profit margin (must be at least 100%)	
Minimum sponsorship sale price	

The construction of the sponsorship business plan is a creative and rewarding task that is essential if the objectives of the sponsor are to be met. It shows the sponsor that the organisation is managerially competent and engenders confidence in the event's ability to achieve mutually rewarding outcomes.

It requires a good understanding of marketing concepts and principles, the corporate and marketing needs of the sponsor, and creativity to produce innovative and exciting ways for the sponsor to get its message across to the target market.

SERVICING THE SPONSOR'S NEEDS

Before proceeding to discuss how to appropriately service sponsors, it is appropriate at this stage to reinforce the mutual obligations of the event and its sponsor. Geldard and Sinclair (1996) list these as follows:

The event's obligations to the sponsor
- to deliver all the benefits promised and outlined in the contract without constant prodding from the sponsor
- to be genuinely committed to positive sponsorship outcomes for all stakeholders
- to protect the rights of the sponsor
- to acknowledge the sponsor at every appropriate opportunity
- to provide innovative programs to assist the sponsor meet its objectives
- to ensure all members of the event organisation are aware of the event's obligations to the sponsor and are enthusiastic about them being met
- to keep the sponsor fully informed on all relevant matters occurring in the event organisation
- to warn the sponsor in advance of potential unpleasant publicity

The sponsor's obligations to the event
- to provide the cash payment or in-kind goods and services agreed to in a timely manner
- to be genuinely committed to the sponsorship
- to promote the interests of the sponsorship whenever possible
- to commit sufficient promotional funds to ensure the sponsorship is a success

In order to ensure that the event does satisfy the sponsor's marketing needs listed in the sponsorship agreement, it is essential that the event organisation services (that is, looks after) the sponsor. This can include everything from maintaining harmonious relationships between the sponsor's staff and the staff of the event organisation to ensuring the sponsor's signage is kept in pristine condition. Following is a list of important activities, adapted from Geldard and Sinclair (1996), which will assist in exceeding the sponsor's expectations, thereby improving future sponsorship relationships.
- **One contact.** One person from the event organisation needs to be appointed as the contact point for the sponsor. That person must be readily available (a mobile phone helps), have the authority to make decisions regarding the event, and be able to forge harmonious relationships with the sponsor's staff.

- **Understand the sponsor.** A method of maintaining harmonious relationships is to get to know the sponsor's organisation, its staff, its products and its marketing strategies. By doing this, it becomes easier to understand all the needs of the sponsor and thus easier to satisfy these needs.
- **Motivate the event organisation's members about the sponsorship.** Keeping members informed of the sponsorship contract, the objectives of the sponsorship and how the sponsor's needs are to be satisfied will help ensure that the sponsorship works smoothly to the benefit of both parties. However, if members are not wholly supportive of the sponsorship and the actions necessary to fulfil the needs of the sponsor, the sponsorship can founder very quickly. For example, if members fail to wear a uniform that bears the logo of the sponsor while being televised, the sponsor has every right to be peeved.
- **Use of celebrities associated with the event.** If the event includes the use of artistic, sporting or theatrical celebrities, ensure that the sponsors have an opportunity to meet them in a social setting. Most people enjoy immensely the opportunity to tell anecdotes about their brush with the famous!
- **Acknowledge the sponsor at every opportunity.** The use of all the available media to acknowledge the sponsor's assistance is not only courteous, but probably part of the sponsorship contract. Media that can be used include the public address system, newsletters, media releases, the annual report and staff briefings.
- **Sponsorship launch.** Have a sponsorship launch to tell the target market that brand x is to sponsor the event. The style of the launch depends on the type of sponsorship and the creativity of the event director.
- **Media monitoring.** Monitor the media for all stories about the event and provide copies to the sponsor. This shows the sponsor that the event takes an interest in the sponsorship and is alert to the benefits the sponsor is receiving.
- **Principal sponsor.** If the event is such that it has many sponsors, ensure that the logo of the principal sponsor (that is, the sponsor who has paid the most) is seen on everything that the event does. This includes stationery, uniforms, flags, newsletters, stages, etc.
- **Naming rights.** If the event has given naming rights to a sponsor, it has an obligation to ensure that these rights are used in all communications emanating from the event organisation. This includes making every endeavour to ensure that the media are aware of and adhere to the name of the event. This sometimes is difficult, but must be attempted.
- **Professionalism.** Even though many events are managed by volunteers, this does not mean that staff can act like amateurs. Sponsors expect to be treated efficiently and effectively, with their reasonable demands met in a speedy manner. Sponsorship is a partnership. Loyalty to that partnership will be repaid.
- **Undersell and over-deliver.** Do not promise what cannot be delivered. Be cautious in the proposal and then ensure that the expectations raised by the cautious proposal are at a minimum met, but probably exceeded.

SUMMARY

The importance of securing sponsorhip for a festival or event presents a range of benefits both for the event management and the sponsoring company. In order to attract the most appropriate sponsors to an event, an event committee must research thoroughly those companies and their products that it feels would be most likely to benefit from sponsoring the event. The committee must also prepare a proposal outlining to the sponsor(s) the objectives of the event and the perceived sponsor benefits, and ensure that the working relationship is productive and honours the contract between the two parties. The components of the sponsorship process have been summarised below in table 7.1.

■ Table 7.1
Stages in the corporate sponsorship process

STAGE	CHARACTERISTIC
Research	Market research and environmental monitoring to identify suitable corporation(s) for event sponsoring.
Preparation	Preparation of sponsorship proposal that includes: • details of event, including its target markets • identification of benefits for the sponsor and their value • cash or contra requested for the sponsorship • responsibilities of each partner in the sponsorship.
Consideration	Stages of consideration by potential sponsors are: • initial contact with event organisation by telephone • informal discussions between event organisation and marketing personnel of potential sponsor • formal presentation to potential sponsor's decision maker(s).
Decision	If no, try the next corporation on the list. If yes, proceed to the next stage.
Agreement	Contract between sponsor and event organisation detailing responsibilities of both parties.
Implementation	Carry out activities prescribed in contract.
Evaluation and feedback	Feedback to sponsor detailing performance in agreed key result areas.

(**Source:** *adapted from Hall 1997*)

Questions

1 Define sponsorship from the perspective of an event organiser and the marketing manager of a fast-moving consumer goods firm.

2 Define philanthropy and explain why it is not sponsorship.

3 Why do governments sponsor events?

4 Name an event for which sponsorship may be inappropriate and list the reasons for this.

5 What is meant by monitoring the social, cultural, political and technological environments in the context of event sponsorship? Name an example of this process.

6 Construct a CEDAR EEE analysis for an event with which you are familiar.

7 Construct a sponsorship proposal for an event known to you.

8 Construct a sponsorship budget for the sponsorship of an event known to you.

9 List the key result areas for the sponsorship of the event you used for the previous question.

10 Give details of how you would brief the event's contact person for the event you used in question 8.

CASE STUDY

Melbourne's
Moomba festival

Melbourne's Moomba festival is well over 40 years old and it is still regarded as the largest outdoor annual event in Australia, with a 1.5 million attendance in 1997. When Moomba was first invented, there was minimal competition for audience, resources and cash but, these days, the 10-day festival is surrounded by a litany of other events, many of which occur at the same time.

In order to survive, Moomba has had to adapt over the years and, like everything else around it, the festival is constantly looking for new methods of gaining and maximising the benefit of financial partnerships.

Speaking opportunities, logo acknowledgment, sophisticated entertainment occasions, advertising and general promotion through a variety of media sources are some of the benefits offered to all of the entities associated with the festival. As we enter the 21st century, however, the festival and event sector needs to offer more and think creatively about what specific attributes of the industry can be packaged to attract increased support from the commercial arena.

Many years ago, large companies used to compete with each other to produce the most memorable float for presentation in the annual Moomba Parade. The Gas & Fuel Corporation and Myer Melbourne are two of the organisations that committed enormous resources to creating a new grandiose float every year.

Those who recall the spectacular parades of times gone by bemoan the loss of the giant-scale legendary floats but, in reality, no commercial organisation can justify spending excessive amounts of time and dollars to produce such a spectacular image when it is viewed for only a few hours. It is just not a sensible use of the marketing budget. These days, from a business point of view, a corporate organisation's involvement with a festival that is as big as Moomba is best done through other means.

In order to maintain itself as a 'meaningful event', Moomba has made changes along the way; for instance, the traditional street parade now occurs at night and is a very different gig compared to what it was five years ago. While Moomba's program is never designed with sponsorship as its first priority, the festival is always on the lookout for logical financial partners to support various aspects of the activities.

Festivals provide interesting and challenging marketing opportunities; a point that the corporate sector is starting to recognise. Unlike a sports event, where half of the attendees are disappointed when their team loses, most festival audiences are out purely to have a good time and to be entertained, so they are more likely to be interested in tasting a new product or receiving a sponsor's message.

Food and beverage suppliers are an integral element of any event and, in Moomba's case, it is this category of partners which has created some of the most interesting and rewarding sponsorship opportunities for both the festival and the supplying companies.

A few years ago, Peters, as the principal sponsor of Moomba, paid for the creation of the Peters Troupe, a group of musicians who perform throughout the festival at different important events. Carefully costumed, they present Peters' image in a fun style that promotes the sponsor's products in a positive and appropriate manner. Not only does this add value to Peters' relationship with Moomba, it also provides additional entertainment for the festival at no cost to the programming budget and it increases product sales on site.

Product suppliers and partners have increasingly become involved with the marketing of the festival and this benefits everyone. During the lead-up period to the festival, Pura Milk devotes one side of its milk cartons to Moomba. Milk cartons are great vehicles for promotion as they have a long shelf life and, just as important, there is a carton of milk in practically everybody's house! This promotion clearly links Pura and Moomba and assists in advertising the dates of the festival.

Montana Wines, Moomba's official wine supplier, has devised some smart point-of-sale materials which again benefit Moomba because the promotions add to the overall marketing activity without generating any additional expense for the festival. Promotions that reinforce the link between a sponsor and the event are beneficial to all parties and allow the corporate entity to expand its marketing beyond mere signage or program advertising.

Moomba utilises the Yarra River in Melbourne in many creative and diverse methods and presents a nightly Aquascreen show, which incorporates lasers, projections and giant barges. The festival's partnership with 101.1 TTFM, a popular Victorian radio station, has been enhanced by using the technology that is in place for the river spectacular. At the conclusion of the Aquascreen presentation, the projector rolls one of the station's commercials, which were originally designed for television. The audience appreciates seeing a message they usually view in their living rooms being beamed onto a water wall in the dark and the radio sponsor gains an unusual form of access to the huge crowds which gather nightly on the banks of the river.

All of the sponsorship partners associated with Moomba work closely with the staff to ensure all opportunities are identified and explored. While this is time consuming, it creates a stronger partnership and offers commercial organisations new ideas and opportunities to reach Moomba's vast number of attendees.

A sponsorship is a business relationship and neither party should ever lose sight of that. Moomba has worked hard to build the business opportunities it can offer to its commercial partners and new concepts are constantly being sought and examined. As the program and entertainment develops and alters in line with what contemporary audiences seek and expect, so too does the range of corporate partners which are involved and that is a healthy state for a festival to be in.

by Maggie MacGuire, Festival and Event Industry Consultant
Maggie MacGuire & Associates

Questions

1 Describe the target market for Moomba in demographic and socio-economic terms.

2 What benefits can Moomba offer potential sponsors?

3 Besides those mentioned in the case study, what other companies would find sponsorship of Moomba a worthwhile investment of marketing resources?

4 Given that more than 500 000 residents of Melbourne will see the Aquascreen show, what is a reasonable price to ask for sponsorship of the show?

5 Why are promotions that reinforce the link between a sponsor and the event beneficial to both parties?

REFERENCES

Crompton, J. 1993, 'Understanding a business organisation's approach to entering a sponsorship partnership', *Festival Management and Event Tourism*, vol. 1, pp. 98–109.

Crompton, J. 1994, 'Benefits and risks associated with sponsorship of major events', *Festival Management and Event Tourism*, vol. 2, pp. 65–74.

Crompton, J. 1995, 'Factors that have stimulated the growth of sponsorship of major events', *Festival Management and Event Tourism*, vol. 3, pp. 97–101.

Geldard, E. & Sinclair, L. 1996, *The Sponsorship Manual*, The Sponsorship Unit, Victoria.

Getz, A. 1997, *Event Management and Event Tourism*, Cognizant Communication Corporation, New York.

Hall, C. M. 1997, *Hallmark Tourist Events: Impacts, Management and Planning*, John Wiley and Sons, England.

Sleight, S. 1989, *Sponsorship: What It Is and How To Use It*, McGraw-Hill, Maidenhead, England.

Sunshine, K., Backman, K. & Backman, S. 1995, 'An examination of sponsorship proposals in relation to corporate objectives', *Festival Management and Event Tourism*, vol. 2, pp. 159–166.

8

Control
and budgets

LEARNING OBJECTIVES

After studying this chapter, you should be able to:

- understand the use of control by management

- identify the control systems used in special events and festivals

- analyse the factors that create successful control mechanisms

- identify the key elements of budgetary control and explain the relationship between them

- understand the advantages and shortcomings of using a budget.

WHAT IS CONTROL?

Control consists of making sure that what happens in an organisation is what was supposed to happen. The control of an event can range from the event manager simply walking the site and discussing daily progress with staff to implementing and monitoring a detailed plan of responsibilities, reports and budgets. The word 'control' comes from the Latin *contrarotulare*, meaning 'against the roll': in ancient Rome, it meant comparing something to the official records, which were kept on paper cylinders or rolls. In modern times, the word has retained some of this meaning, and the control of any business activity involves comparing the progress of all key functions against a management plan to ensure that projected outcomes are met.

Event planning can be effective only if the execution of the plan is carefully controlled. To do this, it is necessary to develop proper control mechanisms. These are methods which are designed to keep a project on course and return it to plan if it wanders. Control affects every aspect of the management of events, including logistics, human resources and administration, and its basic nature remains the same in every area.

The nature of control is described by Beniger (1986), who identified two complementary activities:

- **Information processing:** This is necessary for all planning. When it is goal-directed, it allows the continual comparison of an organisation's stated goals against reality.
- **Reciprocal communication, or feedback:** There must be a constant interchange between the controller and the areas being controlled.

These two activities depend on an effective communication system.

This chapter explores control in the context of festivals and special events. It will demonstrate that the choice of workable control mechanisms is central to the success of an event, and discuss budgets, which are the main control system used in event management.

ELEMENTS AND CATEGORIES OF CONTROL

The process of control involves establishing standards of performance and ensuring that they are realised. This can be a complex process, but consists of three main steps:

- **Establishing standards of performance:** These can come from several sources, including standard practices within the event management industry; guidelines supplied by the board of management of the event; specific requirements of the client and sponsors, and audience or guest expectations. Standards must be measurable.
- **Identifying deviations from standards of performance:** This is done by measuring current performance and comparing it with the established standards. Since the event budget is expressed in measurable terms, it provides an important method of highlighting areas that are straying from the plan and which require attention.

- **Correcting deviations:** Any performance that does not meet the established standards must be corrected. This can entail the use of many types of problem-solving strategies, including renegotiating contracts and delegating.

These three steps are also called the control cycle (Burke 1993) and are central to the successful delivery of an event. Such a cycle would be applied with varying frequency, depending on the size and complexity of the event itself.

Generally, events are characterised by two types of controls: operational and organisational. Operational controls are used for the day-to-day running of the event. Organisational controls relate to the overall objectives of the event organisation, for example whether the event is profitable and satisfies the client's brief. Hicks (1976) suggests a further category of controls according to when they are applied:

- **Predictive control** tries to anticipate and identify problems before they occur. Predicting cash flows for an event is an important area because expenses are not concurrent with income. For example, venue hire is usually paid in advance of the event. Similarly, for an event with a small budget, briefing a lawyer is another example of predictive control. Some companies, for instance, may be less likely to pay promised fees to a small company than they would to a larger, more powerful company. Also, the organisers of a small one-off event are not in a position to threaten a defaulting company with withdrawal of further work opportunities. In these, and similar situations, a swift letter from a solicitor who has been briefed beforehand can often hasten payment. Another term for predictive controls is feedforward.
- **Concurrent control** measures deviation from the standards as they occur. The event manager's informal question of 'How's it going?' falls into this category. The monitoring of food stalls during an event for instance is essential to ensure that health and safety regulations are being followed. It may be difficult to predict just how a food provider will deviate from the guidelines. (At one festival, for example, tea and coffee urns were placed against a canvas dividing wall. On the other side, a children's play group was in operation.)
- **Historic controls** are mostly organisational controls and can include analysis of major deviations from an event plan so that the next event runs more closely to plan. Such controls review the concluded event and are concerned with the question: 'How were objectives met?'

In order to compare actual and planned progress in managing an event, points of comparison are necessary. These include the following:

- **Benchmarks** are identifiable points in the organisation of the event where a high standard is achieved. Benchmarks emphasise quality and best practice. For example, catering of a high standard could be a benchmark for a corporate party. Attaining a benchmark is often a cause for celebration by the event company.
- **Milestones**, or key dates, are intermediate achievement dates that stand as guideposts for monitoring an event's progress. They mark particularly critical completion times. For example, the arrival of the headline performers at the venue is a critical time, and the submission date of a grant proposal is a key date.

Figure 8.1
The control process

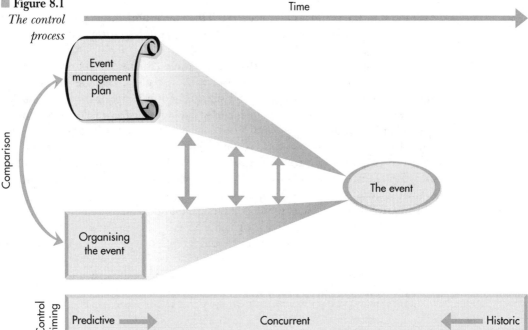

Event control can be expensive in time and money. Its cost and effectiveness depend on the choice of the control mechanisms that make up the control system. Control mechanisms must be:

- **meaningful and efficient:** They should be directed only at those areas that contribute to the success of the event. These significant areas have to be identified in advance, and addressed in the event plan. A limited amount of time is available for measuring and comparing — this process must be streamlined so it does not become an end in itself.
- **simple:** Controls should not be any more complicated than is necessary. Their aim is practical and they have to be able to be communicated to many levels within an event. An excessively complicated system of controls can alienate a broadly based festival committee.
- **relevant:** Controls must be prepared to match each area of event management, and they should be distributed to those who have the responsibility of carrying them out. For example, there is no point in the publicity section having data that concern the budget of the performers.
- **timely and flexible:** Deviations from the plan should be identified early and addressed before they develop further. Concurrent controls should allow sufficient time to correct any gaps with the plan. Flexibility is essential, as the controls may need to respond to revision of the event plan up until the last moment. Sometimes, milestones must be moved to accommodate changes in the event. For example, a benchmark may be an attendance of

1000 people, but if only 800 chairs were delivered, it is no longer a best practice benchmark and must be dropped lest it create a logistical problem.

- **able to suggest action:** The most useful control mechanisms provide corrective actions to be taken when members of the event team find a gap between the plan and reality. Without these suggestions for action, inexperienced staff or volunteers can become confused and the festival manager can be swamped by problems that could readily have been solved by others if guidance had been provided.

When deviations or gaps are identified, the event manager can make a reasoned choice — either to close the gap, or leave it alone and revise the plan. Historic organisational controls, for example, may show a gap between the festival objectives and what actually happened. The festival manager can choose to change the objectives themselves or change aspects of the event instead.

CONTROL METHODS

Some of the control methods used in events are very straightforward, while others are complex and require a high level of financial reporting skills. However, they all have the same aim: to highlight areas that have strayed from the plan so that management can take appropriate action.

■ Reports *and meetings*

Reports that evaluate the progress of an event are perhaps the most common control method. The reports are presented at management or committee meetings. The frequency of these meetings will depend on the proximity of the event date. Many event management companies hold weekly meetings with reports from the teams (or subcommittees) and individuals responsible for particular areas. The meetings are run using standard meeting rules, such as those described in Renton (1994), with a time for subcommittee reports. The aim of these reports is to assist the meeting in making decisions.

Typically, an annual community festival would have monthly meetings throughout the year leading up to the event, and increase these to weekly meetings two months before the festival is scheduled to begin. For example, the Broome Shinju Matsuri Festival of the Pearl has weekly meetings that alternate between the festival committee and those of the general community (which discuss major decisions by the festival committee). In this way, the public has some control over the planning of the festival. At the committee meetings, the subcommittees dealing with publicity, sponsorship, entertainment, youth and community relations report their actions. The reports expose any gaps so that the event coordinator can take action to close them. This is also called management by exception, because it assumes everything is flowing well, that routine matters are handled by the subcommittee and that the event coordinator need only step in when significant deviations from the plan demand it.

■ Delegation *and self-control*

The use of subcommittees at a festival is an example of delegating activities to specialist groups. Part of the responsibility of each subcommittee is to solve problems before they report. Since it is impossible for the event manager to monitor all the areas of an event, this method is valuable because it allows delegated groups to control their own areas of specialisation. However, the subcommittee must confine its actions to its own event area and the event manager must be aware of possible problems arising across different subcommittees. For example, solving a problem in the entertainment part of an event could give rise to problems in the sponsorship areas.

■ Quality

There are various systems to control the quality of an event and the event company itself. In particular, quality control is dependent on gaining and responding to customer feedback, and on the role played by event personnel in delivering quality service. Integrating the practical aspects of controlling quality with the overall strategy of an event is called total quality management (TQM). It seeks to create an event company that continually improves the quality of its services. In other words, 'feedback, change and improvement' are integral to the company's structure and operations. Various techniques of TQM are used by event companies. One technique is finding and rewarding quality champions — volunteer programs often have awards for quality service at an event. Different professional organisations, such as the International Special Events Society (ISES) and the International Festival and Events Association (IFEA), share the same aim: to strive to improve the quality of festivals and events. They do this by disseminating information and administering a system of event evaluation and awards for quality.

■ The break-even *chart*

This simple graphic tool can highlight control problems by finding the intersection of costs and revenue. Figure 8.2 shows a simple but effective break-even chart for an event that is dependent on ticket sales. For example, a Neil Cameron Fire Event (Cameron 1993) would have fixed costs of stage, pyrotechnics and administration. But the greater the attendance, the larger the cost of security, seating, cleaning, toilets and so forth. However, at one point the revenue from ticket sales exceeds the costs. At this point, the break-even point, the event starts making a profit. If a fixed cost such as venue hire is increased, the extra number of people needed 'through the door' can quickly be calculated. How would the organisers attract those extra people to the event? One means might be increased promotion.

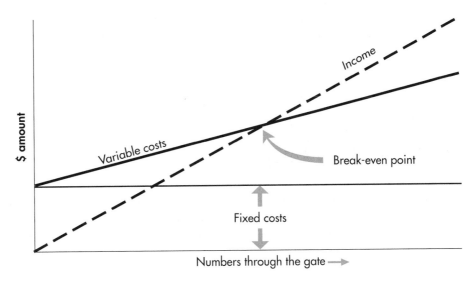

■ **Figure 8.2**
The break-even chart

[Chart: Y-axis labeled "$ amount", X-axis labeled "Numbers through the gate →". Shows "Income" (dashed line), "Variable costs" (solid line), "Break-even point" where they cross, and "Fixed costs" between the two lower horizontal levels.]

■ Ratio *analysis*

There are several ratios that can be used to identify any problems in the management of an event. They can also be used for predictive control as in the earlier example. Their main function is as indicators of the health of the event organisation. In particular the ratio of

$$\frac{\text{Current assets}}{\text{Current liabilities}}$$

indicates the financial strength of the organisation. However, calculation of assets can be difficult, since special events by their nature have few current assets except those intangible qualities: goodwill and experience. In a similar way to a film production company, an event company may be formed to create and manage a one-off festival where every asset is hired for the duration of the event.

Return on investment is a significant ratio for any sponsors or investors in an event. This is expressed as

$$\frac{\text{Net revenue}}{\text{Investment}}.$$

The revenue for a sponsor may be expressed in advertising dollars. For example print press exposure can be measured by column centimetres and approximated to the equivalent cost in advertising. This ratio is most often used for events that are staged solely for financial gain. An entrepreneur of a major concert performance must demonstrate a favourable ROI to potential investors to secure financial backing.

Other ratios can provide valuable data. As Brody and Goodman (1988) explain in their discussion of fundraising events, the ratio between net and gross profit is important in deciding the efficiency of an event for fundraising and provides a means to compare one event to another. This ratio is called the percentage of profit or the profit margin. Another useful ratio is that of free publicity to paid advertising, particularly for concert promoters.

By performing a series of appropriate ratio analyses, an event management company can obtain a clear picture of the viability of the organisation and identify areas requiring more stringent control.

THE BUDGET

A budget can be described as a quantified statement of plans (in other words, the plan is expressed in numerical terms). The budget process includes costing and estimating income and the allocation of financial resources. The budget of an event is used to compare actual costs and revenues with projected costs and revenues. In particular, maximum expenditure for each area of the event's operation is estimated. To achieve this efficiently, a budget can take many forms. For instance, it may be broken into sub-budgets that apply to specific areas of a complex or large event such as the staging, logistics, merchandising and human resources. Budgets are of particular importance to the management of events because most aspects of the event incur costs requiring payment before the revenue is obtained. Cash flow needs special attention. Most funding or sponsorship bodies need to see a budget of the proposed event before they will commit their resources. This second part of the chapter expands on these points and provides an example to illustrate them.

CONSTRUCTING THE BUDGET

Two types of budget process can be used in event management. The line-item budget, as the name suggests, focuses on each cost and revenue item of the total event, and the program budget that is constructed for a specific program element (Getz 1997). An example of the latter is a budget devised for a festival that concerns only the activities of one of the performance areas or stages. Such a budget effectively isolates this area of the event from the general festival finance. In this way individual budgets can be used to compare all the performance areas or stages. The line-item budget is illustrated in figure 8.3. The line-items are venue costs, artist fees and so on.

The creation of a budget has the advantage of forcing management to establish a financial plan for the event and to allocate resources accordingly. It imposes a necessary financial discipline, regardless of how informally an event may be organised. In a similar way to the Gantt chart, it can be used for review long after the event is over.

HUNTER VALLEY FESTIVAL
Musica Viva Australia

Budget
Income and expenditure

Income		$	Expenditure	$
Box office		26 000	Artist fees and expenses	21 752
Subscription — 5 concerts				
80 @ $150		12 000	*Venue costs*	
Single sales			Stage and lighting	13 600
40 @ $35 Adult	1 400		Booking charges	2 602
30 @ $15 Concession	450		Marketing and publicity	15 000
	1 850		Front of house staff	5 600
× 5 concerts		9 250		
Sale of merchandise		5 000		
Sponsorship		7 500		
Total income		**59 750**	**Total expenditure**	**58 554**

SURPLUS/DEFICIT	1196

■ **Figure 8.3** *Hunter Valley Festival 1991*

Preparing a budget is illustrated by figure 8.4. The process begins by establishing the economic environment of the event. The economics of the region and the nation (and even world economics) may impinge on the event and significantly change the budget. An example of this is the effect of the fall in the value of the Australian dollar on the major arts festivals. Within a week the cost of the entertainment imported for the festivals rose by over 10 per cent. To determine the economic environment, it is useful to ask the following questions. What similar events can be used as a guide? Will changes in the local or State economy affect the budget in any way? If it involves international performers or hiring equipment from overseas, will there be a change in the currency exchange rates? These, and many more questions, need to be answered before constructing a budget that will result in reasonable projections of costs and revenue.

The next step is to obtain the guidelines from the client, sponsors or event committee. For instance, a client may request that only a certain percentage of their sponsorship be allocated to entertainment, with the rest to be allocated to hospitality. Guidelines must fit with the overall objectives of the event and may require constructing sub-budgets or program budgets. This is both an *instructive phase*, in that the committee, for example, will instruct the event manager on the content of the budget and a *consultative phase* as the event manager would ask the advice of other event specialists and the subcontractors.

The third step is to identify, categorise and estimate the cost areas and revenue sources. The categories become the line items in the budget. A sample of the categories is given in table 8.1. This is a summary, or a first-level budget, of the cost and revenue areas. The next level down expands each of these line items and is shown in tables 8.2 and 8.3. The use of a computer-generated spreadsheet enables a number of levels in the budget to be created on separate sheets and linked to the first-level budget. Cost items take up the most room on a budget and are described below.

■ Table 8.1
Generic budget — first level

INCOME	AMOUNT	EXPENDITURE	AMOUNT
Grants		Administration	
Donations		Publicity	
Sponsorship		Venue costs	
Ticket sales		Equipment	
Fees		Salaries	
Special programs		Insurance	
Concessions		Permits	
TOTAL		Security	
		Accounting	
		Cleaning	
		Travel	
		Accommodation	
		Documentation	
		Hospitality	
		Community groups	
		Volunteers	
		Contingencies	
		TOTAL	

Once the costs and possible revenue sources and amounts are estimated, a *draft budget* is prepared and submitted for approval to the controlling committee. For example, this may be the finance subcommittee of a large festival. The draft budget is also used in grant submissions and sponsorships.

The Federal Government funding bodies, including the Australia Council and Festivals Australia, have budget guidelines and printed forms that need to be completed and included in the grant application.

The final step involves preparation of the budget and financial ratios that can indicate deviations from the initial plan. An operating business has a variety of budgets including capital expenditure, sales, overheads and production. Most special events will require only an operation budget or cash budget.

Figure 8.4   *The budget process*

The special nature of events and festivals requires close attention to the flow of cash. Goldblatt (1997), Getz (1997), and Catherwood and van Kirk (1992) all emphasise the importance of the control of cash to an event. Goldblatt (1997) stresses that it is imperative for the goodwill of suppliers. Without prompt payment the event company faces immediate difficulties. Payment terms and conditions have to be fully and equitably negotiated. These payment terms can ruin an event if they are not given careful consideration beforehand. To obtain the best terms from a supplier Goldblatt suggests the following.

- Learn as much as possible about the suppliers and subcontractors and the nature of their business. Do they own the equipment? What are the normal payment terms in their business? Artists, for instance, expect to be paid immediately, whereas some information technology suppliers will wait for 60 days.
- Be flexible with what can be offered in exchange — including sponsorship.
- Try to negotiate a contract that stipulates a small deposit before the event and full payment after it is over.

- Suggest a line of credit, with payment at a set time in the future.
- Closely control the purchasing.
- Ensure that all purchases are made through a purchase order that is authorised by the event manager or the appropriate finance personnel. A purchase order is a written record of the agreement to supply a product at a prearranged price. All suppliers, contractors and event staff should be informed that no purchase can be made without an authorised form. This ensures that spending is confined to what is permitted by the budget.
- Obtain a full description of the product or service and the quantities required.
- Itemise the price to a per unit cost.
- Calculate any taxes or extra charges.
- Determine payment terms.
- Clarify delivery details.
- Consider imposing penalties if the product or service delivered is not as described.

As figure 8.5 shows, the ability of an event coordinator to effect any change diminishes rapidly as the event draws closer. The supply of goods and services may, of necessity, take place close to or on the actual date of the event. This does not allow organisers the luxury of reminding a supplier of the terms set out in the purchase order. Without a full written description of the goods, the event manager is open to all kinds of exploitation by suppliers and, as the event may be on that day, there may be no choice but to accept delivery.

Figure 8.5
Control, cost and time

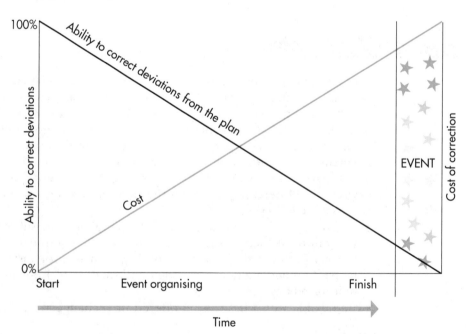

(**Source:** *Burke, R. 1993, Project Management: Planning and Control, John Wiley & Sons, New York, 2nd edn*)

When considering cash flow, the advantage of the ticketing strategies of events such as the Port Fairy Folk Festival are obvious. As tickets are sold months before the event, the management is able to concentrate on other areas of planning. A similar advantage is obtained by event companies that specialise in the corporate area. Generally they are paid up-front. This allows the event manager or producer the freedom to negotiate terms and conditions with the suppliers without having to worry about the cash flow. A cash flow timing chart similar to the Gantt chart is often helpful in planning events. This shows the names of the suppliers and their payment requirements. It includes deposit dates, payment stages, payment on purchase, monthly fixed cost payments and 30, 60 or 90 day credit payments.

COSTING

The cash flow at an event is heavily dependent on the cost of goods and services. These are estimated for the construction of the budget. The prediction, categorisation and allocation of costs is called the costing. In relation to the break-even chart (see figure 8.2) two types of costs have been identified. These are described in the following text.

Fixed costs or overheads are costs associated with the event that occur regardless of how many people come to the event. They include the unchanging expenses concerned with the operation of the event management company, for example rent, staff salaries, telephone and other office expenses. At a large festival these expenses may include rates, land tax and interest on loans. When deciding on a budget, these costs should be apportioned reasonably to the various event areas. This process is called absorption of the overheads by the cost centres. Cost centres, for example, include entertainment, catering, staging or travel. The publicity costs of the Hunter Valley Festival included a part cost of the general publicity for the work of the event company, Musica Viva. If the fixed costs are incorrectly absorbed the cost centre will be wrongly described. For a correct financial picture of the future event, the overheads have to be reasonably spread to all areas. The aim of an event company is to reduce the fixed costs without affecting the quality of the event.

Variable costs are expenses that pertain solely to the event and are directly related to the number of people who attend the event. Food and beverage costs are linked directly to the number of people attending an event. If more people attend an event more tickets need to be printed, more staff may need to be hired, and certainly more food provided.

This division of costs is not as clear-cut in the event industry as in other industries. It is sometimes clearer instead to talk in terms of direct costs (the costs directly associated with the event, whether variable or fixed) and overheads (costs associated with the running of the event company). In this case the direct costs are the major costs — and the aim of the event company is to control these costs. Table 8.2 lists the detailed budgeted costs of a one-off event.

Table 8.2 Projected costs — second level		$			$
Administration	Office rental			Communication	
	Fax/photocopy			First aid	
	Computers			Tents	
	Printers			Tables and chairs	
	Telephone			Wind breaks	
	Stationery			Generators	
	Postage			Technicians	
	Office staff			Parking needs	
	SUBTOTAL			Uniforms	
Publicity	Artwork			SUBTOTAL	
	Printing		Salaries	Coordinator	
	Poster and leaflet distribution			Artists	
	Press kit			Labourers	
	Press ads			Consultants	
	Radio ads			Other	
	Programs			SUBTOTAL	
	SUBTOTAL		Insurance	Public liability	
Venue	Hire			Workers' compensation	
	Preparation			Rain	
	SUBTOTAL			Other	
Equipment	Stage			SUBTOTAL	
	Sound		Permits	Liquor	
	Lights			Food	
	Transport			Council	
	Personnel			Parking	
	Toilets			Children	
	Extra equipment			SUBTOTAL	

Table 8.2
(*continued*)

		$			$
Security	Security check		Documentation	Photo/video	
	Equipment			SUBTOTAL	
	Personnel		Hospitality	Tent	
	SUBTOTAL			Food	
Accounting	Cash and cheque			Beverage	
	Audit			Personnel	
	SUBTOTAL			Invitations	
Cleaning	Before			SUBTOTAL	
	During		Community	Donations	
	After			SUBTOTAL	
	SUBTOTAL		Volunteers	Food and drink	
Travel	Artists			Party	
	Freight			Awards and prizes	
	SUBTOTAL			SUBTOTAL	
Accommodation			Contingencies		
	SUBTOTAL			SUBTOTAL	

Catherwood and van Kirk (1992) divide the costs of an event into four main categories:

- operational or production costs including hiring of event staff; construction; insurance and administration
- venue/site rental
- promotion — advertising, public relations, sales promotion
- talent — costs associated with the entertainment.

To obtain the correct cost of each of the elements contained in the budget categories (sometimes called cost centres) there is a common costing process involved. The steps are described in the following text.

Conceptual estimate or 'ball park figure': This would be used in the conceptual development stage of the event to give management an idea of what costs are involved. Generally this would have an accuracy of +/− 25 per cent.

Feasibility study: This includes comparing costs in similar events. For example the cost of headline speakers varies according to their popularity and type of career. Asking other event managers about current speaker fees gives the event producer a basis for negotiating a fair price and a more realistic budget estimation.

Quote or definitive estimate: This is the cost quote in reply to the tender. The larger festivals will put out to tender many of the elements of the event including sound, lights and security. A near-correct estimate can be made on this basis. For small events, the quote may be obtained by phoning a selection of suppliers and comparing the costs. However, it is rarely the case that the costs are comparable, as there are so many unusual features or special conditions. Once an event company has built up a relationship with a supplier, it tends to stay with that supplier.

TIPS ON REDUCING COSTS

With careful and imaginative planning, costs can be reduced in a number of areas. They are discussed below.

Publicity: An innovative event may need a large publicity budget that is based on revenue from ticket sales. The event manager's aim should be to reduce this wherever possible. Established festivals may need very little publicity as 'word of mouth' will do all the necessary work. For instance, the annual Woodford Folk Festival with a budget of $2.3 million spends very little on publicity because it has built up a strong reputation with its target audience. The more innovative the event the greater the possibility for free publicity. The Tropicana Festival of Short Films in Sydney, for example, gains enormous free publicity as it attracts film stars to the event.

Equipment and supplies: Suppliers of products to events have down times during the year when their products may be hired cheaply. In particular, theatrical productions at the end of their run are a ready source of decoration and scenery. Annual events like the Sydney Gay and Lesbian Mardi Gras often have equipment in storage that can be hired.

In-kind gifts: Many organisations will assist events to achieve cross-promotional advantages. Entertainment can be inexpensive if there is a chance that an organisation can promote a performance or product at the event. For instance, at the Macquarie Marshes concert the boutique wine company, Bloodwood, agreed to supply their wine freely to the party for the media and friends held prior to the event — in exchange for the rights to sell their product at the concert.

Hiring charges: The hire costs of large infrastructure components such as tents and generators and headline acts can be reduced by offering work at other festivals and events. For example, the large cultural festivals around Australia, including the Melbourne International Festival and the Adelaide Festival of the Arts, can offer a festival circuit to any overseas performer. Costs are amortised over all the festivals.

Priorities cost centres: At some time it will be necessary to cut costs. You will need to anticipate the effect on the overall event if one area is significantly changed or eliminated. In project management this is called sensitivity analysis (Burke 1993). Estimates are made of the effect of cost changes on the event and the costs centres are placed in a priority list according to the significance of the effect. For instance, a sensitivity analysis could be applied to the effect of imposing a charge on a program that was previously available free. While this could significantly increase revenue, it may produce a negative effect in sponsorship and audience satisfaction, which may well be translated into the reduction of revenue.

Volunteers: Costs can be reduced by using volunteers instead of paid staff. It is important that all the skills of the volunteers are fully utilised. These skills should be continually under review as new skills may be required as the event planning progresses. For charitable functions, volunteers will often absorb many of the costs as tax deductible donations.

REVENUE

Anticipating potential sources of revenue should be given as much attention as projecting expenses. The source of the revenue will often define the type of event, the event objectives and the planning. A company product launch has only one source of revenue — the client. Company staff parties, for example, are paid by the client with no other source of revenue. The budget then has only one entry on the left hand side. A major festival, on the other hand, has to find and service a variety of revenue sources such as sponsors and participants. This constitutes a major part of festival planning.

Revenue can come from the following sources:
- Ticket sales — most common in entrepreneurial events
- Sponsorship — common in cultural and sports events
- Merchandising
- Advertising
- 'In-kind' arrangements
- Broadcast rights — an increasingly important source of revenue in sport events.
- Grants — federal, State and local government
- Fund-raising — common in community events
- The client — the major source for corporate events.

Table 8.3 features an expanded list of revenue sources. For many events, admission fees and ticket prices need careful consideration. The revenue they generate will impact on the cash flow and the break-even point. The ticket price can be decided by one or more of three methods:

Covering costs: All the costs are estimated and added to the projected profit. To give the ticket price, this figure is then divided by the expected number of people that will attend the event. The method is quick, simple and based on knowing the break-even point. It gives a 'rule of thumb' figure that can be used as a starting point for further investigations in setting the price.

Market demand: The ticket price is decided by the prevailing ticket prices for similar or competing events. In other words, it is the 'going rate' for an event. Concert ticket prices are decided in this way. In deciding on the ticket price, consider elasticity of demand. For instance, if the ticket price is increased slightly will this affect the number of tickets sold?

Perceived value: The event may have special features that preclude a price comparison to other events. For instance, for an innovative event the ticket price must be carefully considered. By its nature this kind of event has no comparison. There can be variations in the ticket price for different entertainment packages at the event (at many multi-venued events the ticket will include admission only to certain events), for extra hospitality or for special seating. Knowing how to grade the tickets is an important skill in maximising revenue. There are market segments that will not tolerate differences in pricing, whereas others expect it. It can be a culturally based decision and may be part of the design of the event.

■ **Table 8.3**
Revenue sources — second level

INCOME		$	INCOME		$
Grants	Local		Ticket Sales	Box office	
	State			Retail outlets	
	Federal			Admissions	
	Arts			SUBTOTAL	
	Other		Merchandise	T-shirts	
	SUBTOTAL			Programs	
Donations	Foundations			Posters	
	Other			Badges	
	SUBTOTAL			Videos	
Sponsorship	In kind			SUBTOTAL	
	Cash		Fees	Stalls	
	SUBTOTAL			Licences	
Individual contributions				Broadcast	
	SUBTOTAL			SUBTOTAL	
Special programs	Raffle		Advert sales	Program	
	Auction			Event site	
	Games			SUBTOTAL	
	SUBTOTAL		Concessions		
				SUBTOTAL	

■ Ticket *scaling*

There are many ticketing strategies that strive to obtain the best value from ticket sales. The most common strategy is to vary the pricing, according to seat position, number of tickets sold and time of sale. Early-bird discounts and subscriptions series are two examples of the latter. Another strategy involves creating a special category of attendees. This could include patrons, special clubs, 'friends of the event', people for whom the theme of the event has a special meaning or those who have attended many similar events in the past. For example, for a higher ticket price, patrons are offered extra hospitality, such as separate viewing area, valet parking and a cocktail party.

■ In-kind support *and bartering*

One way to increase income is to scrutinise the event cost centres for areas that could be covered by an exchange with the supplier or bartering. For example, the advertising can be expanded for an event with a program of 'give-aways'. These are free tickets to the event given away through the press. Due to the amount of goodwill surrounding a fund-raising event, bartering should be explored as a method of obtaining supplies.

■ Merchandising

The staging of an event offers many opportunities for merchandising. The first consideration is 'Does the sale of goods enhance the theme of the event?'. The problems of cash flow at an event, as stated earlier in this chapter, can give the sale of goods an unrealistic high priority in event management. It is easy to cheapen a 'boutique' special event with the sale of 'trinkets'. However, the attendees may want to buy a souvenir. For example, a large choir performing at a one-off spectacular event may welcome the opportunity to purchase a video of their performance. This could be arranged with the choir beforehand and result in a guaranteed income. As a spin-off the video could be incorporated into promotional material for use by the event management in bidding for future events.

■ Broadcast *rights*

An increasingly important source of revenue, particularly in sporting events, is the payment for the right to broadcast. A live television broadcast of an event is a lucrative area for potential — but it comes at a price. The broadcast, rather than the needs and expectations of the live audience, becomes master of the event. Often the live audience becomes merely one element in the televising process. At the ARIA (Australian Record Industry Association) Awards the audience includes 'fillers' — people who fill any empty seats so that the camera will always show a capacity audience.

If the entire event is recorded by high-quality video equipment, future broadcast rights should also be investigated. For instance, in many countries there is a constant demand for worthwhile content for pay television (cable or satellite). At the time of writing, Internet broadcast is in its infancy. There have been a number of music and image broadcasts but they are limited by the size of the bandwidth. There can be no doubt that this will become an important medium for the event industry.

■ Sponsorship *leverage*

Leverage is the current term for using event sponsorship to gain further support from other sponsors. Very few companies or organisations want to be the first to sponsor a one-off event. However, once the event has one sponsor's support, sufficient credibility is gained to enable an approach to other sponsors. For example, gaining the support of a major newspaper or radio station allows the event manager to approach other sponsors. The sponsors realise that they can obtain free publicity.

■ Special *features*

When an event is linked to a large population base, there are many opportunities for generating income. Raffles, for example, are frequently used to raise income. At a concert dance in England, all patrons brought along a prize for a raffle to be drawn on the night. Everyone received a ticket in the raffle as part of the entry fee to the event. The prizes ranged from old ties to overseas air tickets. Every person received a prize and the raffle became part of the entertainment of the evening.

Holding an auction at an event is also an entertaining way to increase income. Prior to the Broome Fringe Festival (held in June, 1998), the event manager organised an innovative auction. The items auctioned included haircuts, 'slave for a day', body work and massages. The sale of players' jerseys, complete with the mud stains, after a major football match, has also proved a lucrative way of raising revenue.

REPORTING

The importance of general reporting on the progress of event planning has already been described in this chapter. The budget report is a means of highlighting problems and suggesting solutions. It is an effective form of communication to the event committee and staff and should be readily understood. It is important that appropriate action is taken in response to the report's suggestions. Table 8.4 is a list of guidelines for a straight-forward report.

■ **Figure 8.6**
Reporting guidelines

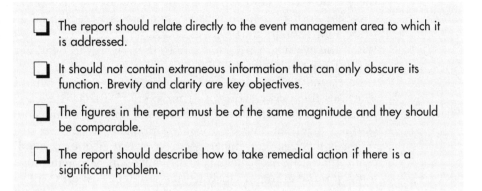

☐ The report should relate directly to the event management area to which it is addressed.

☐ It should not contain extraneous information that can only obscure its function. Brevity and clarity are key objectives.

☐ The figures in the report must be of the same magnitude and they should be comparable.

☐ The report should describe how to take remedial action if there is a significant problem.

The most common problem in an event is the cost 'blow out'. Special event planners often encounter unforeseen circumstances that can cost dearly. For example the subcontractor who supplies the sound system can go bankrupt; the replacement subcontractor may prove far more expensive. One of the unwritten laws of project management is that the closer the project is to completion the more expensive any changes become. Appropriate remedial action may be to use cheaper catering services or to find extra funding. This could take the form of a raffle to cover the extra costs. Figure 8.5 graphically shows how the cost of any changes to the organisation of an event escalate as the event date nears.

A major problem associated with a budget, particularly for special events, may involve blind adherence to it (Hicks 1979). It is a tool of control and not an end in itself. The elegance of a well laid-out budget and its mathematical certainty can obscure the fact that it should be a slave to the event objectives, not its master. A budget is based on reasonable projections made within an economic framework. Small changes in the framework can effect large changes in the event's finances. For instance, extra sponsorship may be found if the right products are added to the event portfolio. A complicated, highly detailed budget may consume far more time than is necessary to make the event a success.

Time is a crucial factor in special event management. Keeping rigidly within budgetary standards can take up too much time and energy of the event management, limiting time available for other areas.

Finally, a budget that is constructed by the event management may be imposed on staff without adequate consultation. This can lead to losing valuable specialist staff if they find themselves having to work to unreasonable budgetary standards. In particular, an innovative event requires the creative input of all the staff and subcontractors. At these events, informal financial control using a draft budget is often far more conducive to quality work than strict budgetary control.

There is little point in expending effort in creating a plan for an event if there is no way to closely monitor it. The event plan is a prerequisite for success. The control mechanisms to keep the project aligned to the plan need to be well thought out and easily understood by the management team. When the event strays from the plan there needs to be ways to bring it back into line or to change the plan.

An estimate of the costs and revenues of an event is called the budget and it acts as the master control of an event. With a well-reasoned budget in place, all sections of an event know their spending limits and can focus on working together. The cash flow of an event needs special considerations. When is the cash coming in? Moreover, when does it need to go out? An event that does not have control mechanisms, including a well-planned budget, is not going to satisfy its stakeholders. Not only will it fail, but organisers will never know the reason for its failure. A sound budget gives management a solid foundation on which to build a successful event.

Questions

1. What controls do you use to get from home to work or school?

2. List the milestones for a Rough Water Swim event involving at least 1000 competitors.

3. Identify the best practices for a corporate conference dinner.

4. Identify the cost centres and revenue sources for
   (a) a corporate staff party
   (b) a concert (include a break-even chart)
   (c) a wine and food festival
   (d) the Sydney Olympics.

5. If it was necessary to cut costs at the above events, which areas would be the first to feel the effects?

6. What 'economies of scale' can be expected from multi-venued festivals?

7. Anticipate the possible cash-flow problems at a large cultural festival in a State capital.

Sydney Gay and
Lesbian Mardi Gras

Sydney Gay and Lesbian Mardi Gras is a community-based organisation that has just reached its 20th anniversary. Our organisation was formed from the diverse lesbian and gay communities of Sydney to enable us to explore, express and promote the life of our combined community through a cultural focus. We affirm the pride, joy, dignity and identity of our community and its people through events of celebration.

Mardi Gras provides resources and opportunities for our community — for creative expression and the development of cultural and political skill. It enhances the potential of both.

There is a volunteer Board of 14 that is elected by the membership, a full-time staff of 14, volunteer committees and thousands of volunteers who work on the Parade, in the office, in the workshop and at our numerous events.

The organisation has a budget of over $4 million. The main sources of income are the two parties, the Sleaze Ball and the Mardi Gras Party, as well as membership fees from over 8000 members. Sponsorship contributes approximately five per cent in cash to the budget and a further five per cent 'in-kind' arrangements.

Committees are chaired by board directors and it is these directors, along with relevant members of staff, who are responsible for events and activities, such as marketing, coming in on budget. With the size of the organisation growing at a rate of 15 per cent per annum, keeping budgets under control is a challenge.

For all expenditure, purchase orders are raised and are kept in check with the budget figures and the cash flow projections. Regular reviews occur to ensure projections are accurate and realistic.

Mardi Gras has found it invaluable to have accounts presented at board meetings once a month, that include income and expenditure, cash flow and cash at bank information. This ensures that decisions in regard to extraordinary expenditure can be made using the most accurate and up-to-date information.

An administration committee has been in operation for some years. It deals with all staff issues, the general management of the company and the administration budget that includes membership, wages, ticketing, maintenance, capital costs and other general costs.

Sydney Gay and Lesbian Mardi Gras is a not-for-profit organisation that is limited by guarantee. However, the company has established cash reserves to maintain the future of the organisation.

Overall the financial structure of the Mardi Gras is secure, due mostly to the strong income base the parties provide the organisation.

Bev Lange, President, Sydney Gay and Lesbian Mardi Gras

Questions

1 As a fast-growing organisation and major event, the Sydney Gay and Lesbian Mardi Gras has had to develop its budget and financial control systems as it has evolved. From what you have been told in the case study, do you think these systems are adequate for the event? What changes, if any, would you suggest to these systems?

2 How would you describe the organisational framework of the Sydney Gay and Lesbian Mardi Gras? What other organisational structures could it employ? Do you think it has the best structure for its needs?

3 The Sydney Gay and Lesbian Mardi Gras is one of the largest internationally known events in Australia. What factors do you think have led to its rapid growth and success?

REFERENCES

Beniger, J. 1986, *The Control Revolution*, Harvard University Press, Cambridge.

Bennett, R. 1994, *Managing: Activities and Resources*, Kogan Page Limited, London, 2nd edn.

Brody, R. & Goodman, M. 1988, *Fund-Raising Events: Strategies and Programs for Success*, Human Sciences Press Inc, New York.

Burke, R. 1993, *Project Management: Planning and Control*, John Wiley & Sons, New York, 2nd edn.

Cameron, N. 1993, *Fire on the Water*, Currency Press, Paddington, Australia.

Catherwood, D. & Van Kirk, R. 1992, *The Complete Guide to Special Event Management*, John Wiley & Sons, New York.

Getz, D. 1997, *Event Management and Event Tourism*, Cognizant Communications, New York.

Goldblatt, J. 1997, *Special Events: Best Practices in Modern Event Management*, Van Nostrand Reinhold, 2nd edn.

Hicks, H. & Gullet, C. 1976, *The Management of Organisations*, McGraw-Hill Kogakusha Ltd, Tokyo.

Renton, N. 1994, *Guide for Meetings and Organisations: Volume 2, Meetings*, The Law Book Company Ltd Sydney, Sixth Edition.

9

Legal and
risk management

LEARNING OBJECTIVES

After studying this chapter, you should be able to:

■ explain the central role of event ownership in event administration

■ identify the necessary contracts for events and their components

■ construct a risk management plan

■ understand the variety of rules and regulations governing events

■ describe the process of gaining insurance.

LEGAL ISSUES

A key question in event administration is: 'who owns the event?' The legal owner of an event could be the event coordinator, the committee, a separate legal entity or the sponsors, but it is important to recognise that the ownership of the event entails legal responsibility and therefore liability. The members of an organising committee can be personally held responsible for the event. This is often expressed as 'jointly and severally liable'. The structure of the event administration must reflect this, and the status of various personnel, such as the event coordinator, the subcontractors and other stakeholders, must be clearly established at the outset. Likewise, sponsorship agreements will often have a clause as to the sponsor's liability, and therefore the extent of their ownership of the event. All such issues need to be carefully addressed by the initial agreements and contracts.

The organising committee for a non-profit event can become a legal entity by forming an incorporated association. Such an association can enter into contracts and own property. The act of incorporating, under the relevant association incorporation act in each State, means that the members have limited liability when the association incurs debts. It does not grant them complete exemption from all liability such as negligence. By law, an association must have a constitution or a list of rules. Such documents state the procedures and powers of the association, including auditing and accounting matters, the powers of the governing body and winding-up procedures. In many cases, community and local festival events do not form a separate incorporated association as they are able to function under the legal umbrella of another body such as a local council. This gives the event organising committee considerable legal protection as well as access to administrative support. For a one-off event, this administrative support can save time and resources, because the administrative infrastructure, such as fax machine, phone lines, secretarial help and legal and accounting advice, is already established.

Establishing an appropriate legal structure for an event management company is an exercise in liability minimisation. Several structures are possible for an event company, which could operate as a sole trader, partnership or a company limited by liability. Each of these legal structures has different liability implications. Legal advice may be required to determine the most appropriate structure for a particular circumstance.

CONTRACTS

A contract is an agreement between two or more parties that sets out their obligations and is enforceable by law. It describes the exchange to be made between the parties. A contract can be a written or an oral agreement. In the world of event management, an oral contract is of little use if problems occur in the future. Therefore, it is appropriate to put all contractual agreements in writing. This may frequently take the form of a simple letter of agreement, not more than a page in length (see figure 9.1). However, when large amounts of money and important responsibilities are involved, a formal contract is necessary.

As Goldblatt (1997) explains, a typical event industry contract will contain:
- the names of the contracting parties, their details and their trading names
- details of the service or product that is offered (e.g. equipment, entertainment, use of land, expert advice)
- the terms of exchange for such service or product
- the signature of both parties indicating understanding of the terms of exchange and agreement to the conditions of the contract.

Figure 9.1
An example of a letter of agreement

Festival copy (sign and return)

Date:

To:

PERFORMER AGREEMENT

This agreement is between the Folk Federation of South Australia Inc (hereafter referred to as the Festival) and _____ (hereafter referred to as the Performer).

The Festival and Performer(s) agree that:

1. **Performances:** The Festival engages the Performer(s) for the following days and times to perform at the 1998 Victor Harbor Folk Festival):
   (See Timetable attached)

   and the Performer(s) accept the said engagement.

2. **Payment:** Provided that the Performer(s) fulfil the obligations set out in the agreement, the Festival shall pay the Performer(s) an agreed fee of
   $ _____ .

3. **Time of payment:** Payment will be made *by cheque* within 10 days of the Festival (unless otherwise arranged).
   Cheque to be made out to: _____ name of person/company

4. **Other commitments:** to the Performer(s) include the following: *(n/a denotes not applicable)*
   Number of passes to performers: _____

   Travel: _____

   Transit: _____

   Accommodation: _____

5. **Travel arrangements** made by the Festival are final and the cost of any changes not agreed to during the negotiations of this contract shall be borne by the Performer(s).

(continued)

Figure 9.1
(*continued*)

6. **Outside performances:** The performer shall inform the Festival of any other engagements taken during the period 2–5 October within 50 km of the Victor Harbour Folk Festival.

7. **Cancellation:** If any performances by the Performer(s) are cancelled or prevented for any reason, including but not limited to, public calamity, strike, lockout, Act of God or due to reasons beyond the control of the Festival, the Festival shall not be liable to the Performer(s) for fees, costs, expenses or damages of any kind.

8. **Publicity:** The Performer(s) agree to allow *short* takes of their performances to be photographed, recorded or video taped by the Festival or by Festival approved media to assist in promotion of the Festival and Performer(s) may obtain copies of such recordings or photography at their own expense. The Performer(s) shall provide the Festival as requested with the necessary materials required to adequately promote the Festival and the Performer. This may take the shape of recordings, photographs, biography and appearances or media interview subject to availability of such materials.

9. **Deductions:** The Festival shall have the right to deduct or withhold from the Performer(s) any amounts required to be deducted by law. The Festival does not take responsibility for the payment of any taxes and any amounts payable under superannuation guarantee legislation relating to the artists' income from this engagement.

10. **Merchandise:** The artist agrees that any merchandise items offered for sale by the artist at the Festival shall be sold solely through the Festival shop operated on behalf of the Festival. The artist further agrees that a 15% commission will be deducted from the reconciled gross sales.

11. **All notices:** regarding this agreement shall be in writing and served by mail, email, telegram, or facsimile addressed to the parties at their respective addresses.

12. **In the event of a dispute:** this agreement shall be governed by and construed in accordance with the laws of the province of South Australia.

13. **Alterations:** This agreement may not be changed without consent of both parties; however, the Festival shall have the power to make changes to Performer(s) program times under special circumstances.

Please sign **BOTH** copies of this agreement and **RETURN ONE** to the Festival office.

* A signed copy of this contract is required for issue of cheque to the performer(s).

Signed for the Festival _____ 1998

Signed for the Performer(s) _____ 1998

To make this mutual obligation perfectly clear to all parties, the contract would set out all key elements. These would consist of the following: financial terms, including a payment schedule; a cancellation clause; delivery time; the rights and obligations of each party; and an exact description of the goods and services being exchanged.

Event management companies may need a wide range of contracts to facilitate their operation. Some of these are shown in figure 9.2.

An event of medium size would require a set of formal contracts covering:
- the event company or coordinator and the client
- the entertainers
- the venue
- the suppliers (e.g. security, audiovisual, caterers)
- the sponsor(s).

For smaller events these may be arranged by letters of agreement, without going into too much detail.

Different contracts have different 'styles' and the event manager must be familiar with them. Some of these contracts are discussed in the following text.

■ Entertainment

A common feature of entertainment contracts is the 'rider'. This is an attachment to the contract, usually on a separate piece of paper. Hiring a headline performer may necessitate signing a twenty to thirty page contract. The contract often contains a clause requiring the event company to provide the goods and services contained in the rider, as well as the performance fee. The rider can list such things as food, extra accommodation, transport and set-up assistance. The event company ignores this at its peril. The rider can be used by the entertainer's agent as a way of increasing the fee in real terms, which can have serious consequences for the budget of an event. For example, a university student union that employs a well-known rock group at a minimal fee for a charity function would find its objectives greatly damaged by a rider stipulating reimbursal of food, accommodation and transport costs for 30 people.

Another important clause in any entertainment contract is exclusivity. For example, a headline act may be the major attraction for an event. If the act is also performing nearby this could easily detract from the uniqueness of the event. A clause to prevent this is therefore inserted into the contract. It indicates that the performer cannot perform within a specified geographic area during the event or for a certain number of days prior to and after the event. The intricacies of entertainment contracts led Freedman (1991) to suggest that event managers obtain legal advice about contracts when planning a celebrity concert.

The contract must contain a clause that stipulates the signatories have the right to sign on behalf of the contracting parties. An entertainment group may be represented by a number of agents. The agents must have written proof that they exclusively represent the group for the event.

■ Venue

The venue contract will have specialist clauses, including indemnifying the venue against damages, personnel requirements and provision of security staff. The contract can also contain these elements:

- **security deposit:** an amount, generally a percentage of the hiring fee, to be used for any additional work such as cleaning and repairs that result from the event.
- **cancellation:** outlining the penalty for cancellation of the event and whether the hirer will receive a refund if the venue is rehired at that time.
- **access:** including the timing of the opening and closing of the doors, and actual use of the entrance ways.
- **late conclusion:** the penalty for the event going overtime.
- **house seats:** the free tickets reserved for venue management.
- **additions or alterations:** the event may require some changes to the internal structures of the venue.
- **signage:** this covers the signs of any sponsors and other advertising. Venue management approval may be required for all promotional material.

When hiring a venue, it is important to ascertain exactly what is included in the fee. For example, just because there were chairs and tables in the photograph of the venue does not mean that they are included in the hiring cost.

■ Sponsor

The contract with the sponsor would cover issues related to quality representation of the sponsor such as trademarks and signage, exclusivity and the right of refusal for further sponsorship. It may specify that the sponsor's logo be included on all promotional material, or that the sponsor has the right to monitor the quality of the promotional material. Geldard and Sinclair (1996), advise that the level of sponsor exclusivity during an event will need to be reflected in the contract between the event committee and the sponsor. Possible levels are: sole sponsor, principal sponsor, major or minor sponsor and supplier. The contract would also describe hospitality rights, such as the number of complimentary tickets supplied to the sponsor.

Broadcast

Broadcast contracts can be very complex, due to the large amounts of money involved in broadcasting and the production of resultant merchandise such as videos and sound recordings. The important clauses in a broadcast contract address the following key components:

- **territory or region:** The broadcast area — local, State or international — must be defined. If the attached schedule shows the region as 'World', the event company must be fully aware of the rights it is bestowing on the broadcaster, and their value.
- **guarantees:** The most important of these is the one stating that the event company has the rights to sign for the whole event. For example, some local councils require that an extra fee be paid for broadcasting from their area. Also, performers' copyright can preclude any broadcast without written permission from their record and publishing companies. Comedy acts and motivational speakers are particularly sensitive about broadcasts and recordings.
- **sponsorship:** This area can present difficulties when different levels of sponsorship are involved. Sometimes the rights of the event sponsor and the broadcaster's sponsors can clash.
- **repeats, extracts and sub-licenses:** These determine the allowable number of repeats of the broadcast, and whether the broadcaster is authorised to edit or take extracts from the broadcast and how such material can be used. The event company may sign with one broadcaster, only to find that the rights to cover the event have been sold on for a much larger figure to another broadcaster. In addition, a sub-license clause may annul many of the other clauses in the contract. The sub-licenser may be able to use its own sponsors, which is problematic if they are in direct competition with the event sponsors.
- **merchandising:** The contract may contain a clause that mentions the rights to own products originating from the broadcast. The ownership and sale of such recordings can be a major revenue source for an event. A clause recently introduced in these sorts of contracts concerns future delivery systems. Multimedia uses, such as CD-ROMs, cable television, and the Internet are all relatively recent, and new communications technologies continue to be developed. It is easy to sign away the future rights of an event when the contract contains terms that are unknown to the event company. It is wise to seek out specialist legal advice.

- **access:** The physical access requirements of broadcasting must be part of the staging and logistic plan of the event. A broadcaster can easily disrupt an event by demanding to interview performers and celebrities. It is important to specify how much access the broadcaster can have to the stars.
- **credits:** This establishes, at the outset, the people and elements that will be listed in the titles and credits.

The broadcaster can offer all kinds of assistance to the event company. It has an interest in making the event presentable for television and will often help decorate the site. The level of assistance will depend on its stake in the event. For example, Channel Ten's involvement in the Uncle Toby's Iron Man series has led to many kinds of synergies between the event, the sponsors and the broadcaster.

CONSTRUCTING A CONTRACT

The process of constructing a contract is shown in figure 9.3 and comprises five main steps: the intention, negotiation, initial acceptance, agreement on terms, and signing. This process can be facilitated if the event management has standard contracts, where the name of the supplier and any special conditions can be inserted. This saves the event company going through unfamiliar contracts from sponsors, suppliers and entertainers, which can be very time consuming.

■ **Figure 9.3**
The process of constructing a contract

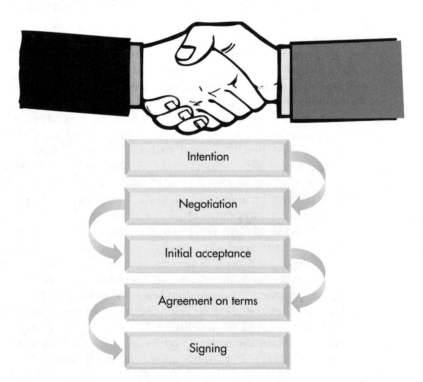

Intention

Negotiation

Initial acceptance

Agreement on terms

Signing

For large events and more complex contracts a 'heads of agreement' is sent after the negotiations are completed. This is a summary of any important specific points, listing the precise service or product that is being provided. The contract can be renegotiated or terminated with the agreement of all parties. The final should contain a clause that allows both parties to go to arbitration in the advent of a disagreement.

TRADEMARKS AND LOGOS

Another kind of ownership issue for event management is the ownership of trademarks and logos. Recently, a federal court order was granted to the Sydney Organising Committee for the Olympic Games preventing the use of their logo by any other party. This illustrates the importance of the ownership of event symbols.

The event company must also be aware of the risks of misrepresenting its event. There is a danger, when promoting an event, to exaggerate its benefits. Descriptions of the product must always be accurate, as disgruntled consumers may and do take legal action to gain punitive damages when they feel that advertising for an event has made false claims. The Trade Practices Act can be used to argue such cases.

Luci Rafferty, a senior partner at law firm Andersen Legal, advises:

■ Part V of the Trade Practices Act 1974 (Cth) prohibits 'unfair practices' within the marketplace and has, in certain instances, been effectively used to protect those involved in events marketing.

The sections most often relied on are, section 52, which prohibits 'misleading or deceptive' conduct and section 53(c) and (d) which concern representations made by a corporation that it has, or its goods and services have, sponsorship approval or affiliation that it in fact does not have.

These sections are of obvious benefit to individuals and associations alike as they provide the means by which effective action can be taken against those who wish to associate themselves with an event when they have no right to do so.

Section 52 states 'a corporation shall not, in trade or commerce, engage in conduct that is misleading or deceptive or is likely to mislead or deceive.' Section 52 has often been used to restrain the unauthorised use of 'personalities' in advertising and marketing strategies. An instance where section 52 was used to protect the rights of a sporting personality in an advertising and market campaign was in the case of World Series Cricket Pty Ltd v Parish (1977) 17ALR181. A claim was made alleging a breach of section 52 of the Trade Practices Act in relation to the holding of an event. In this case, it was the first year that World Series Cricket was to be held. The Australian Cricket Board commenced proceedings because the Board claimed that the public would be misled through the various advertisements in believing that the particular event has been endorsed by the Board. The claim was upheld (Fewell 1995). ■

DUTY OF CARE

A fundamental legal principal is that of taking all reasonable care to avoid acts or omissions that could injure a 'neighbour'. This is called duty of care, and is covered by an area of law known as torts. A tort is a breach of duty owed to other people and imposed by law, and in this it differs from the duties arising from contracts, which are agreed between contracting parties. Unlike criminal law, which is concerned with deterrence and punishment, the law of torts is concerned with compensation.

For event management, duty of care means taking actions that will prevent any foreseeable risk of injury to the people who are directly affected by, or involved in, the event. This would include event staff, volunteers, performers, the audience or spectators and the public in the surrounding areas.

RISK MANAGEMENT

Special events are particularly susceptible to risks. A unique venue, large crowds, new staff and volunteers, movement of equipment and general excitement are a recipe for potential hazards. The event manager who ignores advice on risk prevention is courting disaster and foreshortening his or her career in the event industry. The sensible assessment of potential hazards and preventative action is the basis of risk management.

Every part of event management has potential risks. Berlonghi (1990) categorises the main areas of risk as follows:

- administration: The organisational structure and office layout should minimise risk to employees.
- marketing and public relations: The promotion section must be aware of the need for risk management. By their nature, marketeers are optimistic about the consequences of their actions and tend to ignore potential risks.
- health and safety: A large part of risk management concerns this area. Loss prevention plans and safety control plans are an important part of any risk management strategy. The risks associated with food concession hygiene and sanitation require specific attention.
- crowd management: Risk management of crowd flow, alcohol sales and noise control. (See the chapter on logistics, chapter 10.)
- security: The security plan for an event involves careful risk management thinking.
- transport: Deliveries, parking and public transport contain many potential hazards that need to be addressed.

A good risk management strategy will also cover any other areas whose operations are crucial to the event and which may need special security and safety precautions, such as ticket sales and other cash points and communications.

In every area the risks must be identified and pre-empted, and their management fully integrated into the event plan.

As with many aspects of event management, risk management can be represented as a cycle. This cycle has four components, which are discussed below.

Identification

Pre-empting problems requires skill, experience and knowledge. Something that appears safe to some of the event staff may well contain hidden dangers. A sponsor's sign at an event may look securely mounted when examined by the marketing manager, but it would require the specialist knowledge of the stagehands to be assured that it is secure. Since the event manager cannot be expert in every field, it is best to pool the experience of all the event staff and volunteers by convening a risk assessment meeting. Such a meeting should aim to gather risk management expertise. For large events a consultant may be hired. The meeting is also an opportunity to train and motivate event staff in the awareness, minimisation and control of risks.

Evaluation

Once the risks are identified they can be listed in order of importance. They are given priority according to the probability of their occurrence and the severity of their results. Risk assessment meetings often reveal the 'prophets of doom' who can bring an overly pessimistic approach to the planning process. This is itself a risk that must be pre-empted. It is important that the meeting be well chaired and focused, since the time needed for risk assessment must always be weighed against the limited time available for the overall event planning. An effective risk assessment meeting will produce a comprehensive and realistic analysis of the potential risks.

Control

After the potential risks have been evaluated, the event manager needs to create mechanisms to control any problem that can arise. Many different strategies are possible.

In his comprehensive manual on risk management for events, Berlonghi (1990) suggests the following risk control strategies:

- **Cancel and avoid the risk:** If the risk is too great it may be necessary to cancel all or part of the event. Outdoor concerts that are part of a larger event are often cancelled if there is rain. The major risk is not audience discomfort, but that of electrocution.
- **Diminish the risk:** Risks that cannot be eliminated need to be minimised. For example, to eliminate all possible security risks at an event may require every patron to be searched. This solution is obviously unworkable and instead a risk minimisation strategy will need to be developed. This might mean installing metal detectors or stationing security guards in a more visible position.

- **Reduce the severity of risks which do eventuate:** A major part of safety planning is preparing quick and efficient responses to foreseeable problems. Training staff in elementary first aid can reduce the severity of an accident. The event manager cannot eliminate natural disasters but can prepare a plan to contain the effects. For example, the Woodford Disaster Plan referred to in the chapter on logistics (chapter 10).
- **Devise back-ups and alternatives:** When something goes wrong the situation can be saved by having an alternative plan in place. For example, in case the juggler does not turn up to the children's party, the host has organised party games to entertain the children. On a larger scale, back-up generators are a must at big outdoor events.
- **Distribute the risk:** If the risk can be spread across different areas, its impact will be reduced if something does go wrong. One such strategy is to spread the cash-taking areas, such as ticket booths, so that any theft is contained and does not threaten the complete event income. Having a variety of sponsors is another way to distribute risk. If one sponsor pulls out, the others can be approached to increase their involvement.
- **Transfer the risk:** Risk can be transferred to other groups responsible for an event's components. Subcontractors may be required to share the liability of an event. Their contracts generally contain a clause to the effect that they are responsible for the safety of their equipment and the actions of their staff during the event. In Australia, most performing groups are required to have public liability insurance before they can take part in an event.

■ Review

Evaluating the successes and failures of the risk control strategy is central to the planning of future events. The event company must be a 'learning organisation'. The analysis of and response to feedback is essential to this process.

*I*NSURANCE

Central to any strategy of liability minimisation is obtaining the correct insurance.

The Community Festival Handbook (1991) contains helpful suggestions regarding insurance. These include the following:

- Allow enough time to investigate and arrange the correct insurance. This may include asking for quotes and professional advice. Finding the right insurance broker is the first priority.
- Make sure that the event committee or company is fully covered for the whole time. That is, from the first meeting.
- Require all the suppliers of products and services to show they have liability cover.

- Be prepared to give the insurance broker all information concerning the event and the companies involved. They may require a list of possible hazards such as pyrotechnics.
- Be prepared to record the details of any damage or injury. Photographs and videos are a help in this.
- Keep all records, as a claimant has six years to formulate a claim.
- Do not accept the transfer of liability of the suppliers to the event management.
- Look at what is included and excluded in the insurance document. For example, rain insurance is specific about the amount and time of the rain. Are the event volunteers covered by the insurance?
- Are there any additional stakeholders insured? These are companies or individuals that are covered by the insurance but not the named insured. For example, the sponsors and the venue may benefit from the insurance policy.

There are many kinds of insurance that can be taken out for events. These include: weather insurance; personal accident insurance for the volunteer workers; property insurance, including money; workers compensation insurance; public liability; directors and officers liability. The choice of the particular insurance cover is dictated by the risk management strategy developed by event management.

REGULATIONS, LICENCES AND PERMITS

There are long lists of regulations that need to be satisfied when staging a simple event. The bigger and more innovative the event, the larger the number of these regulations. The correct procedure in one State may be completely different in another. The principal rule is to carry out careful research, including investigating similar events in the same area and seeking advice on what permits and licences are necessary to allow an event to proceed.

It is always the responsibility of an event company to find out and comply with all pertinent rules and regulations. For example, a street parade through Sydney can come under a wide range of government authorities. The Paddington Festival Parade along Oxford Street required a series of long meetings with the two local councils, police and traffic authorities. The event itself was over in two hours. In Victoria a special licence is required to erect tents over a certain size. This includes tents that are used for only one night. Local noise regulations can change within the same city within the jurisdiction of different councils. Not only that, but event management must make it a practice to pay particular attention to workplace health and safety regulations.

Figure 9.4 describes some of the permits, licences, insurances and regulations with which a community festival must comply to take place on the south coast of Victoria. It is evident that an event manager may need to seek legal advice to ensure that all relevant regulations are taken into account.

■ Figure 9.4

*Legal
requirements
for the Port
Fairy Folk
Festival*

Insurance:

(a) Public liability insurance of $5 000 000. Excess $500. Property damage claims only.

(b) Personal accident insurance covering 550 volunteers
$600 — weekly benefits
$60 000 — death benefits

The policy also covers the committee, charitable and school organisations that provide the food stalls.

(c) Occasionally special insurance is taken out to cover tents with specific risks, for example, the Circus Oz tent.

(d) Car parks are covered against damage to vehicles.

(e) Insurance against theft, fire and other damage to the equipment owned by the festival committee. Equipment includes storage sheds, staging, electrical equipment, tables and chairs.

Legislation to be aware of:

1. Liquor licensing for alcohol.
2. Health — food vans, smoking, toilets.
3. Victorian building regulations — tent construction, people in arena. Tent construction workers must be licensed.
4. Country Fire Authority — fire reels and hoses, extinguishers.
5. Security personnel are governed by a licence.
6. Police Act — vehicle access along streets, crowd control.
7. (a) Local Government Act — leasing of municipal property.
   (b) By-laws of the Moyne Shire Council — drinking alcohol in the streets, fence erection, signage, street closure, planning permits, craft stall permits.
8. Banking Act — control of finances.
9. Insurance legislation.
10. Residential tenancies and caravan parks legislation — accommodation of performers, ticket holders, and guests.
11. Associations Incorporation Act — governing the organising Committee.
12. General contract law — agreements with performers, printing, agreement with the Australian Performing and Recording Artists Association (APRA).
13. Environmental Protection Authority (EPA) noise levels.

(**Source:** *Bruce Leishman, of Conlan and Leishman Pty Ltd, solicitors*)

Permits and licences allow special activities during an event such as the handling of food, pyrotechnics, sale of liquor and road closures. They can even cover the performances. The Australian Performing and Recording Artists Association (APRA) issues licences for the performance of its members' works. APRA functions as a collection society, monitoring and collecting royalties on behalf of its members (music composers and their publishers). So when an event company decides to set fireworks to music, it is not just a matter of hiring a band.

Many regulations, permits and licences change with each local government area and State and new regulations and reinterpretations of the old rules are proclaimed regularly. For example, at the time of writing the complex regulations relating to workers' compensation are under review in NSW. Also, workers' compensation regulations are different in each State. The Public Halls Act is administered by local councils and often its interpretation will vary from council to council. Local councils are also responsible for issuing entertainment licences and open air permits for events. Even event accounting may need permits, and an event company must register a business name before opening an account at a bank.

This complex area needs the close attention of event management. Companies must undertake detailed research into all regulations affecting their event and should allocate time to deal with the results of that research. Government agencies can take a long time to respond to requests. Therefore it is imperative to begin early in seeking any permits and licences, and to factor delays and difficulties with obtaining them into the time frame of the event planning process.

SUMMARY

Event managers have a duty of care to all involved in an event. Any reasonably foreseen risks have to be eliminated or minimised. The process of doing this is central to a risk management strategy. Liability minimisation is part of this strategy. This includes identifying the ownership of the event, careful structuring of the event management, taking out insurance and adhering to all the rules and regulations pertaining to the event. Specific legal issues of concern to the event management team include contracting, trademarks and trade practices. Legal matters can be complex and differ from State to State. It is recommended that any event company seek legal advice when unsure of these matters.

Questions

1 List the areas covered by the contract between the event company and supplier of audiovisuals.

2 What are two methods of minimising liability?

3 Contrast the risks involved in staging an outdoor concert to those involved in producing an indoor food fair. What risk management strategy could be used to reduce or eliminate these risks?

4 What actions can be taken to reduce the cost of overall liability insurance? Should the event company be insured for patrons to be covered after they leave the event?

5 What licences and permits are needed for a street party?

The Shakespeare Festival
Australia

The Shakespeare Festival Australia began as a 12-day festival in April 1997, celebrating the works of William Shakespeare. It is presented by the Southern Highlands Institute for the Performing Arts, a non-profit, incorporated association formed to build a performing arts centre in the southern highlands district of New South Wales. This area has declining rural and manufacturing sectors, shrinking blue-collar industries and increasing youth unemployment. A thriving tourism industry will assist the area's economy.

Most of the information on which the committee based its decision to hold such a festival was sourced from the experience of Shakespeare festivals overseas, especially those held in the USA and Canada. The example of the Shakespeare Festival in Stratford, Ontario was considered especially relevant as it was held in a rural area like the southern highlands — scenically beautiful and about two hours drive from a large population centre. This festival grew from small beginnings in a tent in 1953 to a six-month-long festival with three theatres and a budget of millions of dollars. From the beginning, the Shakespeare Festival Australia was intended to develop into a major national festival like its Canadian predecessor.

The festival was developed with two goals: firstly, as a new arts event to highlight the need for a performance and educational centre and, secondly, to attract visitors to the region during autumn. We decided to hold the first festival to coincide with Shakespeare's birthday on 23 April.

School halls were used for indoor performances. Outdoor performances were held in public spaces and in the grounds of some of the larger hotels. Our limited budget prevented us from producing our own plays, so we brought in productions that had already had a season, or were currently in production. The festival involved the local community through a street parade. Local amateur theatre companies and film and music practitioners also participated. Funding came from cash sponsorship of events by local businesses, as well as in-kind sponsorship. We obtained significant amounts of media coverage, both locally and nationally, as the event captured the imagination of the public. The box office takings reflected this enthusiasm. Capacity audiences attended most events, except those with a high ticket price (which usually involved food).

In its second year the festival was expanded to a month-long event incorporating five weekends, and moved forward to commence in early March. Theatre companies from Victoria and Queensland, as well as Sydney and regional New South Wales, travelled to the highlands to participate. The program was expanded to include mid-week as well as weekend performances and a number of new elements were added.

Despite overall attendance and box office figures being up on the first year, the extra expenses involved in running a much bigger festival did not cover the costs. The earlier timing also clashed with the Sydney Gay and Lesbian Mardi Gras and the Adelaide Festival, which affected non-local media coverage and, surprisingly, the weather was generally too hot. However, the audience feedback was very positive.

Letters of agreement confirmed most of the planning and contractual arrangements for the festival. Two board members with expertise in the area handled all negotiations and agreements for the hire of equipment. All negotiations with performers began with telephone calls to assess their availability. Performance fees and travel and accommodation arrangements were discussed. Accommodation for the performers was arranged at one guesthouse. When agreement was reached with the performers, the performance fee, travel and living expenses, technical requirements and rehearsal facilities were confirmed in a letter of agreement. There was no common agreement document.

Formal contracts were drawn up between the festival and the ticketing agencies. These were standard agreement forms specifying such details as commission, performance dates, times and cancellation of shows. Similar arrangements were made with the supplier of merchandising. The contract covered details including sale or return, commission on sales and payment details.

The sponsorship committee sourced cash sponsorship, which was receipted and documented by the treasurer. In-kind sponsorship was generally agreed upon with a verbal agreement. The only government funding came from Tourism New South Wales. A contract between Tourism New South Wales and the festival was signed.

The event general manager and the local council were kept fully informed about all plans and arrangements. Permission was obtained from the Highway Patrol, the council's traffic manager and the traffic committee for the street closure. A supporting letter was obtained from the Bowral Chamber of Commerce indicating that there would be no opposition to the closure from traders.

The council also gave permission for the use of Corbett Gardens, a formal park in the centre of Bowral. The local Rotary Club, who also ran a food stall during the performances, supplied security during performances. Garbage collection and access to toilets that were normally locked at night were issues we had to consider when using the park as a performance venue.

Milton Park, a large country-style resort hotel, was also used as a site for events during the festival. No council permission was required to use this site as it came under existing usage guidelines. Milton Park donated the use of their outdoor ampitheatre and conference room. The festival provided a port-a-loo at the ampitheatre site. Milton Park arranged for the removal of garbage.

Bradman Museum Theatre is a licensed venue under the Public Halls Act and therefore had all of the facilities we required on site. A staff member was in attendance at every performance to provide security.

The most challenging venue was the Renwick Festival Centre. It is in a remote location, so a lot of signage was needed to direct patrons to the site. Using the site involved negotiation between the Highlands Soccer Club and the New South Wales Department of School Education, who recently purchased the site.

The venue is a poorly maintained multipurpose gymnasium. However, it was transformed with hired seating, a complete lighting rig, masses of black drapes and a huge stage built for the room.

Although we did not achieve all of our goals in the second year of the Shakespeare Festival Australia, we have learned invaluable lessons that will be applied in the following years until Shakespeare becomes synonymous with the southern highlands in the same way that country music is with Tamworth.

Elizabeth Rogers
Festival Director
The Shakespeare Festival Australia
Southern Highlands Institute for the Performing Arts, New South Wales

Questions

1 What characteristics of the southern highlands of New South Wales led to it being chosen as the location for the Shakespeare Festival Australia?

2 Draft an appropriate mission statement and key objectives for the festival.

3 What contracts and permissions were considered necessary by the organisers for the conduct of the festival? From what you know of the festival, do these measures seem adequate? If not, what other areas of the event might usefully have been covered by written agreements?

4 What lessons regarding the program and timing have been learned from the first two festivals, and how would you apply these lessons if you were organising the next festival?

5 Create a marketing plan for the festival designed to exploit its potential to attract tourists and maximise their length of stay and expenditure.

REFERENCES

Berlonghi (1990), *Special Event Risk Management Manual*, Bookmasters, Mansfield, Ohio.

Fewell, Mark 1995 (ed.), *Sports Law: A Practical Guide*, LBC Information Services, Sydney.

Freedman, H. & Smith, K. 1991, *Black Tie Optional*, Fund Raising Institute, Rockville, Maryland.

Geldard, E. & Sinclair, L. 1996, *The Sponsorship Manual*, The Sponsorship Unit, Olinda, Vic.

Goldblatt, J. 1997, *Special Events: Best Practices in Modern Event Management*, 2nd edn, Van Nostrand Reinhold, New York.

PART 4

EVENT
COORDINATION

Logistics

LEARNING OBJECTIVES

After studying this chapter, you should be able to:

- define logistics management and its evolution

- understand the concept of logistics management and its place in event management

- construct a logistics plan for the supply of customers, event products and event facilities

- use event logistics techniques and tools.

WHAT IS LOGISTICS?

'One of the hardest tasks, for logisticians and nonlogisticians alike, is to look at a list and spot what's not there' (Pagonis 1992, p. 73).

Placing the word 'logistics' into its historical context provides an understanding of its use in present event management. Logistics stems from the Greek word *logistikos*, 'skilled in calculating'. The ancient Romans used the term for the administration of their armies. The term evolved to refer to the practical art of the relocation of armies. Given the complexity of modern warfare, logistics became a science that included speed of operations, communications and maintenance of the armed forces. After World War II, modern businesses applied the experience and theory of logistics as they faced similar problems with transport and supply as those faced by the military.

The efficient movement of products has become a specialised study in the management discipline. Within large companies, especially international companies, a section can be devoted to coordinating the logistics requirements of each department. Logistics has become a discipline in its own right. This has led to consolidation into a separate independent function in companies, often called integrated logistics management. Coyle, Bardi and Langley (1988) describe logistics as the planning, implementing and control of the flow and storage of products and their related information from production to the point of consumption, according to consumer requirements.

The value of a company's product can be improved by the efficient coordination of logistics in the company. Gilmour (1993) argues that, due to the special conditions and widespread distribution of customers, services and products in Australia, logistics takes on an importance not found in many other countries. He emphasises that the logistic practices developed in the USA and Europe are not good enough for Australian conditions and, to be competitive in world markets, Australia needs to pay attention to overcoming the disadvantages of vast geographic distances.

For a complete understanding of event logistics, this chapter is divided into sections dealing with the tasks of event logistics and the role of the logistics manager.

THE ELEMENTS OF EVENT LOGISTICS

The various elements of event logistics can be organised into the logistics system shown in figure 10.1. This system is used to organise the logistic elements of an event.

Whereas most logistics theory concerns the supply of products to customers, event logistics includes the efficient supply of the customer to the product, and the supply of facilities to and from the event site. In this sense, it has more in common with military logistics than modern business logistics. Business logistics is an ongoing activity and is part of the continual management of a company. Military and event logistics often concern a specific project or campaign rather than continuing management. There is a defined preparation, lead up, execution and shutdown. As well, issues such as inventory control and warehousing that are the basis of business logistics are not as important to a one-off event.

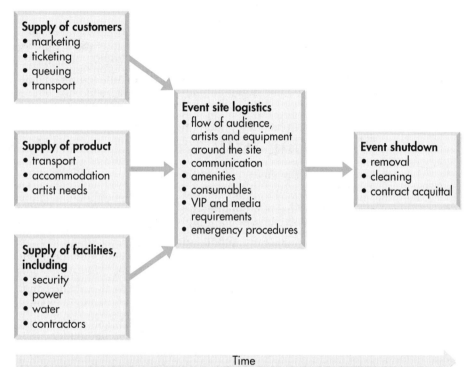

Figure 10.1
Elements of the logistics system

The areas of importance to event logistics can be categorised as:
- *Supply*: this is divided into the three areas of customer, product and facilities. Supply also includes the procurement of the goods and services.
- *Transport*: in Australia, as pointed out by Gilmour (1993), the transport of these goods and services can be a major cost to an event and requires special consideration.
- *Linking*: logistics is part of the overall planning of an event and is linked to all other areas. With large multivenue events, the logistics become so complex that an operations or logistics manager is often appointed. The logistics manager functions as part of the overall network management structure outlined in this chapter.
- *Flow control*: this refers to the flow of products, services and customers during the event.
- *Information networks*: the efficient flow of information during the event is generally a result of efficient planning of the information network. This concept is expanded in the section about on-site logistics.

All these areas need to be considered when creating a logistics plan. Even for small events, such as a wedding or a small product launch, a logistics plan must be incorporated in the overall event plan. For these sorts of events, logistics comes under the title 'staging', which is described in chapter 11.

■ Supply of *the customer*

The customers of an event are those who pay for it. They can be the audience (concerts and festivals), spectators (sport), and the sponsors or clients (corporate events). The customers have expectations that have to be met for a successful outcome. The way the event is promoted will particularly influence their expectations. These expectations will include aspects of logistics.

■ Linking with *marketing and promotion*

The supply of customers is ultimately the responsibility of marketing activities. The numbers, geographical spread and expectations of the customers will affect the logistics planning. The targeting of specialist markets or widespread publicity of an event will require a logistics plan with very different priorities. For example, the transport requirements of the customers will vary according to the distance travelled. The majority of the audience of the Port Fairy Folk Festival drives from Melbourne. Therefore, vehicle access and parking is a priority at the festival site. The Womadelaide festival in Adelaide, with its nationwide publicity campaign, has a large interstate audience. This offers opportunities for special negotiations with the airlines and hotels.

If the publicity of an event is spread nationwide, the logistics will be different to a product launch that concerns only the staff and customers of a company. In this way the logistics are closely linked to the marketing of an event.

■ Ticketing

Ticketing is important to events whose primary income is from the entrance fee. Most corporate events, including office parties and product launches, and many public events are free. However, for other events, such as sports events, the extent of ticket sales can determine success or failure (Graham 1995). Ticket distribution is regarded as the first major decision in event logistics.

The pricing and printing of the tickets is generally not a logistics area. However, the distribution, collection and security are of concern. In Australia, tickets for events can be sold through various distributors like Ticketek for a fee, or they can be sold by mail. The Port Fairy Folk Festival sells out all its tickets at least four months in advance. Selling tickets at the gate gives rise to security problems in the collection, accounting and depositing of funds. The ticket collectors need training to deal with the public, as well as efficiently moving the public through the entrance. The honesty of the staff may also be a security concern. In larger venues, an admission loss-prevention plan is used to minimise the possibility of theft.

It is not unusual in Australia to sell tickets through retail outlets. For the Macquarie Marsh Project, an environmental concert in the wetlands of central New South Wales, the organiser used local tourism information centres as a distribution channel to sell tickets. Inventory control and cash receipts are two areas that require special attention when using retail outlets for ticket distribution. Numbering of the tickets and individual letters of agreement with each outlet are the most efficient methods of control. The letter of agreement would include the range of ticket numbers, level of the tickets (discount or full price) and the method of payment. Depending on the size of the event, the ticketing can be crucial to the event's success and take up a significant amount of the event director's time. Figure 10.2 is a check list of the logistics of ticketing an event.

■ **Figure 10.2**
Ticketing —
logistics check
list

Does the artwork on the ticket contain the following?

☐ number of the ticket

☐ name of the event

☐ date and time of the event

☐ price and level of the ticket (discount, complimentary, full price, early bird)

☐ seating number or designated area (ticket colouring can be used to show seating area)

☐ disclaimer (in particular, this should list the responsibilities of the event promoter)

☐ event information, such as a map, warnings and what to bring

☐ artwork so that the ticket could be used as a souvenir (part of the ticket could be kept by the patron)

☐ contact details for information

Printing schedule

☐ When will the tickets be ready?

☐ Will the tickets be delivered or do they have to be collected?

☐ If there is an error or a large demand for the tickets, will there be time for more to be printed?

Distribution

☐ What outlets will be used — retail, Ticketek, Internet, mail or at the gate?

☐ Has a letter of agreement with all distributors, setting out terms and conditions, been signed?

(continued)

Figure 10.2
(*continued*)

☐ What method of payment will be used (by both the ticket buyer to the distributor and in the final reconciliation) — credit card, cash, direct deposit?

☐ Are schedule of payment and reconciliation forms available?

☐ Does the schedule of communications referring to ticket sales indicate sales progress and if more tickets are needed?

Collection of tickets

☐ How will the tickets be collected at the gate and transferred to a passout?

☐ How experienced are the personnel and how many will there be? When will they arrive and leave?

☐ Is a separate table for complimentary tickets needed at the ticket collection site?

☐ What security arrangements are in place for cash and personnel?

☐ How will the tickets be disposed of?

Reconciliation of number of tickets with revenue received

☐ What method of reconciliation will be used? Is an accountant being used?

☐ Is the reconciliation ongoing, at the conclusion of the event, or at the end of the month?

☐ Has a separate account been set up just for the event to assist the accountancy procedure?

An innovative method of ticketing for festivals is to use the hospital-style wristbands called crowd control bands. These are colour coded to indicate the level of the ticket — a day ticket, a weekend ticket or a special performer's ticket. The use of these wristbands introduces a visual method of control during a large event, as the sale of food and drinks is allowed only if the wristband is shown. In this way, the food vendors become part of the security for the event.

The Internet is increasingly used for the distribution of tickets for large events, concerts and conferences. This use of the Internet illustrates the linking of logistics and marketing. Originally the World Wide Web (WWW) was used to market events by advertising them through a Web site. The introduction of encrypted data enabled an increase in the privacy and security of payment methods and the sale of tickets from a site. The site collaborates with the existing ticketing system and can also be connected to travel agencies.

■ Queuing

Often the first experience of a customer at an event is queuing for tickets or parking. Once inside the event, customers may be confronted with queues for food, toilets and seating. An important aspect of queue theory is the 'perceived waiting time'. This is the subjective time that the customers feel that they have waited. There are many rules of thumb about diminishing the customers' perceived waiting time. In the catering industry, queuing for food can affect the event experience. An informal rule is one food or beverage line for every 75 to 100 people. Figure 10.3 lists some of the factors to consider in the logistics of queuing.

■ **Figure 10.3**
Queuing —
factors to
consider

- How many queues and possible bottlenecks will there be?
- Have an adequate number of personnel greeters, crowd controllers, ticket collectors and security been allocated?
- Is signage (including the estimated waiting time) in place?
- When will the queues form? Will they form at once or over a period of time?
- How can the perceived waiting time be reduced (for example, queue entertainers)?
- What first aid, access and emergency procedures are in place?
- Are the lighting and sun and rain protection adequate?
- Are crowd-friendly barricades and partitions in place?

At the Atlanta Olympics the perceived waiting time at the entrance queues was diminished by the use of entertainers. Exit queuing can be the last experience for the customer at an event and needs the close attention of the event manager. At Sydney's Darling Harbour's New Year's Eve celebrations, the authorities use 'staggered entertainment' to spread the exit time of the crowds.

The oversupply of customers at a commercial event can give rise to a number of security and public safety problems that should be anticipated in the logistics plan. Only presale tickets will indicate the exact number of the expected audience. When tickets are sold at the entrance to an event, the logistics plan has to include the possibility of too many people. Oversubscription may be pleasing for the event promoter, but can produce the logistical nightmare of what to do with the excess crowd.

■ Customer *transport*

Transport to a site is often the first physical commitment by the audience to an event. The method and timing of arrival — public or private transport — is important to the overall logistics plan. The terms used by event managers are 'dump', when the audience arrives almost at once, and 'trickle', when they come and go over a longer period of time. Each of these needs a different logistics strategy. The first impression of the event by the audience can influence all subsequent experiences at the event. For this reason, it is the most visible side of logistics for customers. In their work on sports events, Graham et al. (1995) comment on the importance of spectator arrivals and departures. They stress that arrival and departure is a part of the event hospitality experience. The first and last impression of an event will be the parking facility and the traffic control.

The organisation of transport for conferences takes on a special importance. In a handbook for conference organisers by CIM Rostrum (n.d.), the linking of transport and the selection of the venue is emphasised. The selection of the conference venue or site has to take into account the availability and cost of transport to and from the site. As well, the transport to other facilities has to be considered. A venue that involves a 'long haul' will increase overall costs of a conference or event, as well as adding to the organisational confusion. CIM further points out that it can make the conference seem less attractive to the delegates and therefore impact on delegate numbers.

For large events, festivals and parades, further logistic elements are introduced to the transport of the customer to the event. In particular, permission (council, main roads departments, police) and road closures need to be part of the logistics plan. Figure 10.4 lists the elements of customer transport that need to be considered for an event.

An innovative way of solving many logistics problems (parking, etc.) and enhancing the audience experience was used by the organisers of the Australian Music Festival in Glen Innes, New South Wales. The festival took place at the old Glen Innes railway station and the audience arrived by steam train with the performers. By the time the passengers arrived from Central Station (Sydney) on the Great Northern train, the festival experience had already begun.

The Glen Innes festival also demonstrates how the transport arrangements for the customer (audience) can be linked to the transport of the product (musicians). This can be taken much further and include sponsorship deals with transport companies. In particular, the transport of equipment can be offset against the large number of tickets required to transport the audience. Australian domestic airlines will often negotiate a discount for excess baggage charges incurred by performers if the event account is large enough.

The lack of transport facilities can be used as part of the event experience. As Nick Rigby, Head Ranger at Cape Byron, New South Wales, describes:

■ For our inaugural environmental heritage concert at the Pass we did not allow cars near the site as it would have spoilt the feeling of the evening. The audience had to park a kilometre away and walk along the beach to the Pass. This little journey was part of the environmental experience. We had volunteers steering people in the right direction and welcoming them to Cape Byron. It was quite a sight, over a thousand adults and children strolling along the beach with their picnic 'eskies' and blankets. ■

☐ Have the relevant authorities (e.g. local council, police, Department of Main Roads) been contacted for information and permission?

☐ What public transport is available? Are timetables available?

☐ Has a backup transport system been organised (in case the original transport system fails)?

☐ Is the taxi service adequate and has it been informed of the event? (Informing the local taxi service is also a way of promoting the event.)

☐ What quality is the access area? Do weight and load restrictions apply? Are there other special conditions that must be considered (e.g. underground sprinkler systems under the access area)?

☐ Is there adequate provision for private buses, including an area large enough for their turning circle, driver hospitality and parking?

☐ Is there a parking area and will it be staffed by trained personnel?

☐ Is a towing and emergency service available if required?

☐ Has transport to and from the drop-off point been organised (e.g. from the parking station to the site or venue entrance and back to the parking station)?

☐ At what rate are customers estimated to arrive (dump or trickle)?

☐ Is there adequate access and are there parking facilities for disabled customers?

■ Supply of product — *product portfolio*

Any event can be seen as the presentation of a product. Most events have a variety of products and services — a product portfolio — all of which help to create the event experience for the customer. The individual logistic requirements of the various products need to be integrated into a logistics plan.

For a large festival the product portfolio may include more than 200 performing groups from around Australia and overseas. For a small conference the product may be a speaker and video material. It should be remembered that the product can also include the venue facilities. This is why the term 'the event experience' is used to cover all of the aspects of the customers' experience. It can include, for example, the audience itself and just catching up with friends, in which case the people become part of the product portfolio.

Transport

If the product portfolio includes products coming from overseas, the logistics problems can include issues such as carnet and customs clearance. A carnet is a licence issued by Customs that allows the movement of goods across an international border. A performing artist group coming into Australia is required to have clearance for all its equipment, and needs to pay any taxes on goods that may be sold at the event, such as videos or compact disks.

A large account with an airline can allow the event manager an area of negotiation. Savings, discounts, free seats or free excess charges can be granted by an airline company in exchange for being the 'preferred airline' of the event.

The transport requirements for the performers should be forwarded to the logistics manager by the artistic director well before the event. This illustrates the linking of the various functional areas of a large event.

Importing groups from overseas or interstate provides the logistics manager with an opportunity to communicate with these groups. The 'meet and greet' at the airport and the journey to the site can be used to familiarise the talent with the event. Such things as site map, rehearsal times, accommodation, dressing-room location, equipment storage and transport out can be included in the artist's event or festival kit.

Accommodation

The accommodation requirements of the artists must be treated separately from the accommodation of the audience. The aim of the event manager is to get the best out of the 'product'. Given that entertainers are there to work, their accommodation has to be treated as a way of increasing the value of the investment in entertainment. Substandard accommodation and long trips to the site are certain ways of reducing this value. Often these requirements are not stated and need to be anticipated by the logistics manager.

Artists' needs *on site*

A range of artists' needs must be catered for, including transport on site, storage and movement of equipment, stage and backstage facilities, food and drink (often contained in the contract rider), sound and lights. All these have a logistic element, but are described in detail on pages 261–2 in chapter 11.

As with accommodation, an efficient event manager will anticipate the on-site needs of the artists. Often this can only be learned from experience. In multicultural Australia, the manager needs to be sensitive to requirements that are culturally based, such as food, dressing rooms (separate) and appropriate staff to assist the performer.

SUPPLY OF FACILITIES

The supply of the infrastructure to an event site introduces many of the concepts of business logistics. The storage of consumables (food and drink) and equipment, and the maintenance of equipment become particularly significant. For a small event taking place over an evening, most of the facilities will be supplied by the venue. The catering, toilets and power, for example, can all be part of the hiring of the venue.

Larger festivals or more innovative events require the sourcing of many of the facilities. Some of these are discussed in detail in chapter 11. An inaugural outdoor festival will need the sourcing of almost all the facilities. To find the best information about the availability and cost of the facilities, the event manager should look for a project in the area that required similar facilities. For example, earth moving equipment, toilets, generators, fencing and security are also used by construction and mining companies. Some facilities can be sourced through film production companies. Many of the other facilities travel with the various festivals. Large tents and sound systems need to be booked in advance.

Figure 10.5 is an order sheet listing some of the facilities used for the 1997–98 Woodford Folk Festival in southern Queensland. Note the need for steps and the number of site offices.

Innovative events, like a company-themed Christmas party in an abandoned car park, will require a long lead-time to source the facilities. For example, it may take months to source unusual and rare props and venues for an event. These lead times can significantly affect the way the event is scheduled.

ON-SITE LOGISTICS

The site of an event may vary from an old woolshed for a bush dance to an underground car park for a Christmas party, to a 50 hectare site for a festival. Logistic considerations during the event become more complex with the size of the event. The flow of materials and people around the site and communication networks become the most important areas of logistics.

◼ Flow

With larger festivals and events, the movement of the audience, volunteers, artists and equipment can take a larger part of the time and effort of the logistics manager than the lead-up to the event. This is especially so when the site is complex or multi-venued and there is a large audience. During the lead-up to an event, many of the elements of logistics can be taken care of by the subcontractors. For example, the movement of the electricity generators to the site is the responsibility of the hire company. However, when the facilities are on site, it becomes the responsibility of the logistics manager for their positioning, movement and operation.

Figure 10.5 *Woodford Folk Festival order sheet*

VENUES	Hoecker	Marquee	Shade	Backstage	Floors	Site office	Stage size	Extensions
Big top		160' × 110'		12' × 12'			9.6 × 4.8 × 0.9 m	(2) PA wings 3.6 × ?
Concert	20 × 30 m			12' × 12'			9.4 × 4.8 × 0.6 m	
Folkloric theatre	20 × 30 m			6 × 9 m 3 × 6 m	6 × 9 m 3 × 6 m		9.6 × 4.8 × 0.6 m	Foldback risers at ?
Forum	15 × 20 m						5 × 4 × 0.45 m	
Blues	20 × 20 m			24' × 24'			8.4 × 4.8 × 0.6 m	
Dance	15 × 20 m				12 × 9.6 m		7.2 × 4.8 × 0.6 m	
Murri	10 × 20 m						8.4 × 4.8 × 0.6 m	
Children's festival Workshop Cafe		40' × 60' 24' × 36'	(2) 13 × 15 m	12' × 12' (7) 12' × 12'		4 × 4 m	6 × 4.8 × 0.3 m	
Cooroboree ground			13 × 18 m	12' × 12'				
Talking circle				12' × 12'				
Visual arts				(12) 4 × 4 m TT (2 sides each)	3.6 × 3.6 m	Penny to organise		
Greenhouse		48' × 60'					5.6 × 3.6 × 0.45 m	
Fire event		(3) 36' × 36'	8 × 10 m			2.4 × 4.8 m 2.4 × 3.6 m		
Amphitheatre	20 × 15 m			5 × 10 m 12' × 24'	18 × 13 m			
Troubadour		40' × 60'					4.8 × 2.4 × 0.3 m	
The Wok House							5.4 × 3.6 × 0.3 m	
Bim Bamboo!!								
Lantern factory		36' × 36'						

FACILITIES

	Hoecker	Marquee	Shade	Backstage	Floors	Site office	Stage size	Extensions
Administration		36' × 36'				2.4 × 6 m A/C		
Signology		15' × 15'						
Green room		(2) 30' × 36'						
Street theatre		(2) 12' × 12'						
Sponsors' lounge	10 × 10 m				10 × 10 m			
Front gate	5 × 10 m					2.4 × 4.8 m A/C		
Camping gate	6 × 6 m					JS caravan		
Welcome tent		4 × 4 m TT						
Organisers' green room	10 × 15 m							
Treasury						3.4 × 6 m A/C		
Cashiers						2.4 × 4.8 m A/C		
Security						2.4 × 4.8 m A/C		

BARS

	Hoecker	Marquee	Shade	Backstage	Floors	Site office	Stage size	Extensions
Guinness		48' × 60'			10 × 10 m	2.4 × 4.8 m	4.8 × 3.6 × 0.3 m	
Session		48' × 48'						
Carnival		(2) 30' × 36'						
The Club		48' × 60'					5.4 × 3.6 × 0.4 m	
The Cafe		30' × 36'	8 × 10 m					
Blues		(2) 30' × 36'						

MURRI CAMP

	Hoecker	Marquee	Shade	Backstage	Floors	Site office	Stage size	Extensions
Kitchen		30' × 36'	8 × 10 m					
Accommodation		(3) 6 × 9 m				(3) 6 × 9 m		
		(3) 6 × 9 m				(3) 6 × 3 m		

TOTALS

	Chrs	8' T	3' Rnd	6' Rnd	Cold room	Cool cube	Tubs	Electricity	Plumbing	Pickets	Hessian	Extras
0 mm	1100	4										
0 mm	500	3										
0 mm	350	2										
	40	3	6									small fridge small urn
0 mm	300	2										
0 mm	350	2										
	150	2										
0 mm	250	2										
	150	2										4 tiered seats/2 fans
	60	12										4 × 4 m sandpit
	48	4	12		small fridge							12 hay bales
		1										
	100	40						1 switchboard	1 tap			
	200	4										
	30	10										
	10	4										
	20	4	3									fridge
	140	6	15	2								
		2								60 (20 × 4'3"s)	80 m	
	12	6										
	20	15										
	2	2										
	40	60										
	12	2						caravan		6	30 m	2 floods in punchbowl
	20		6									fridge
	10	10										
	5	4										
	4	4										
	100	15										
	10	8										
	4	3										
	200	4	20	2	1	1	6					
	120	4	20		1	1	6					
	120	3	20		1	1						
	200	4	20		1	1	6					
	120	3	20		1	1	4					
	150	4	25		2	1	6					
	120	3	20		1 (small)	1	4					gas BBQ
												gas rings
	150	4	25		2	1	6					
	3847	**256**	**167**	**4**	**7**	**6**	**28**					
ER	5000	280	180									

The access roads through a large festival and during the event have to accommodate:

- artist and equipment transport
- garbage removal
- emergency fire and first aid access and checking
- stall set up, continual supply and removal
- security
- food and drink supplies
- staging equipment set up, maintenance and removal, and
- site communication.

As illustrated by figure 10.6, even during a straightforward event, many factors of the traffic flow must be considered. The performers for an event will need transport from their accommodation to the stage. Often the performers will go via the equipment storage area to the rehearsal rooms, then to the stage. At the conclusion of the performance, the performers will return their equipment to storage, then retire for a well-earned rest in the green room. For a community festival with four stages, this to-ing and fro-ing can be quite complex.

At the same time as the performers are transported around the site, the media, audience and VIPs are on the move. Figure 10.6 does not show the movement of the food vendors' suppliers, water, security, ambulances and many more. When any one of the major venues empties there is further movement around the site by the audience. This results in peak flow times when it may be impossible to move anything around the venue except the audience. These peaks and lows all have to be anticipated in the overall event plan.

Figure 10.6

Some of the traffic patterns to consider when planning an event

1. Performers' accommodation ⟶ equipment storage area ⟶ rehearsal area ⟶ stage ⟶ equipment storage area ⟶ social (green room)
2. Media accommodation ⟶ media centre ⟶ stages ⟶ social area
3. VIP accommodation ⟶ stages ⟶ special requests
4. Audience pick-up points ⟶ specific venue

Each event contains surprising factors in traffic flow. For the Easter Show which was formerly held at the Sydney Showground, for example, the narrow gate that allowed entrance to the performers was also the gate that was used for the various animals. Each day of the two week show had a queue that contained a mix of school orchestras, dancers, bands, sound equipment, Brahmin bulls, sheep trucks, camels and horses moving in both directions. This flow was coordinated by one gatekeeper.

Communication

On-site communication for the staff at a small event can be with the mobile phone or the loud hailer of the event manager. With the complexity of larger events, however, the logistics plan must contain an on-site communications plot (CP). The Woodford site communications plot (figure 10.7) shows the complexity of communications at a festival that attracts 90 000 admissions.

Figure 10.7
Woodford Folk Festival 1997 communications plot

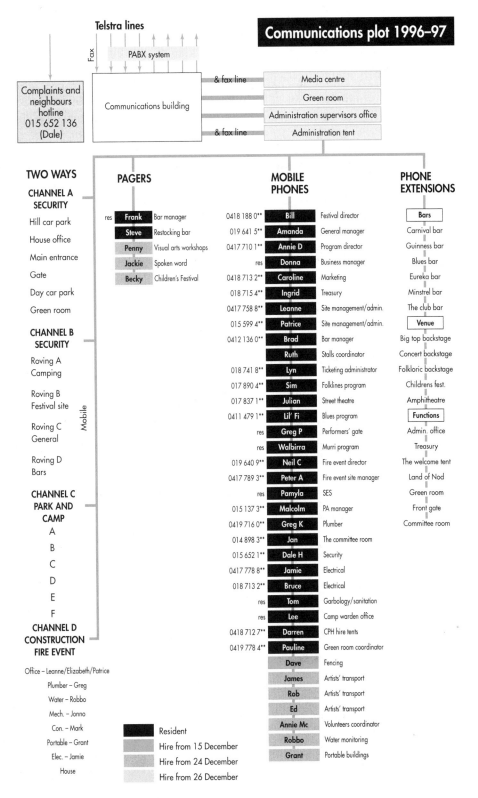

Telstra lines

PABX system

Fax

Complaints and neighbours hotline
015 652 136
(Dale)

Communications building

& fax line

Media centre

Green room

Administration supervisors office

& fax line

Administration tent

Communications plot 1996–97

TWO WAYS

CHANNEL A SECURITY

Hill car park
House office
Main entrance
Gate
Day car park
Green room

CHANNEL B SECURITY

Roving A
Camping

Roving B
Festival site

Roving C
General

Roving D
Bars

CHANNEL C PARK AND CAMP

A
B
C
D
E
F

CHANNEL D CONSTRUCTION FIRE EVENT

Office – Leanne/Elizabeth/Patrice
Plumber – Greg
Water – Robbo
Mech. – Jonno
Con. – Mark
Portable – Grant
Elec. – Jamie
House

PAGERS

res	Frank	Bar manager
	Steve	Restocking bar
	Penny	Visual arts workshops
	Jackie	Spoken word
	Becky	Children's Festival

Resident
Hire from 15 December
Hire from 24 December
Hire from 26 December

MOBILE PHONES

0418 188 0**	Bill	Festival director
019 641 5**	Amanda	General manager
0417 710 1**	Annie D	Program director
res	Donna	Business manager
0418 713 2**	Caroline	Marketing
018 715 4**	Ingrid	Treasury
0417 758 8**	Leanne	Site management/admin.
015 599 4**	Patrice	Site management/admin.
0412 136 0**	Brad	Bar manager
	Ruth	Stalls coordinator
018 741 8**	Lyn	Ticketing administrator
017 890 4**	Sim	Folklines program
017 837 1**	Julian	Street theatre
0411 479 1**	Lil' Fi	Blues program
res	Greg P	Performers' gate
res	Walbirra	Murri program
019 640 9**	Neil C	Fire event director
0417 789 3**	Peter A	Fire event site manager
res	Pamyla	SES
015 137 3**	Malcolm	PA manager
0419 716 0**	Greg K	Plumber
014 898 3**	Jan	The committee room
015 652 1**	Dale H	Security
0417 778 8**	Jamie	Electrical
018 713 2**	Bruce	Electrical
res	Tom	Garbology/sanitation
res	Lee	Camp warden office
0418 712 7**	Darren	CPH hire tents
0419 778 4**	Pauline	Green room coordinator
	Dave	Fencing
	James	Artists' transport
	Rob	Artists' transport
	Ed	Artists' transport
	Annie Mc	Volunteers coordinator
	Robbo	Water monitoring
	Grant	Portable buildings

PHONE EXTENSIONS

Bars

Carnival bar
Guinness bar
Blues bar
Eureka bar
Minstrel bar
The club bar

Venue

Big top backstage
Concert backstage
Folkloric backstage
Childrens fest.
Amphitheatre

Functions

Admin. office
Treasury
The welcome tent
Land of Nod
Green room
Front gate
Committee room

The communications plot includes fax, two-way radios, pagers, mobile phones and landline extensions. The Woodford communications plot also contains the title of each manager, as well as the complaints and neighbours' hotline.

On-site signage is an important part of communicating to all of the attendees of the event. Signage may be as simple as messages on a whiteboard in the volunteers' dining area, or involve large, on-site maps showing the public the location of facilities. Two important issues in on-site signage are position and clarity. A direction sign that is obscured by such things as sponsors' messages diminishes its value. The most effective way of communicating with the audience at an event is to have the necessary information in the program. Figure 10.8 shows an example of the audience information included in the program for a small festival in northern New South Wales.

■ **Figure 10.8**
Festival information from the Northern Rivers Folk Festival program, 3–5 October 1997

~Festival Information~

Staying at the festival Limited on-site camping is available at a flat rate of $10 per person. N.B. this fee is not for profit, it's to cover the costs of providing facilities.

Other accommodation There are three caravan parks in Lismore, delightful rural cabins, B&Bs, hotels, motels and backpacker accommodation. You can book your stay in or around Lismore through the Lismore Tourist Information Centre, 1300 369795 (no booking charge). Please tell them you are coming to the festival.

People with disabilities Facilities are provided for people with disabilities. If you have special needs please contact us first and we will do our best to help you.

Volunteers Our heartfelt thanks to all the wonderful folk who have given their time and energy to create this very special event.

This festival is run entirely by volunteers, who appreciate a helping hand! If you can put in a couple of hours to help it would be great, just check in at the festival office.

Festival workers put in even more time. If you would like to help with setting up or clean-up, etc., please call us on 02 66 217 537.

The bars The festival is a licensed event, run strictly according to licensing regulations! Under 18s and anyone who seems intoxicated will not be served. No BYO. Photo ID required.

First aid The Red Cross will be on site throughout the festival.

Car parking We welcome back the Tuncester Bush Fire Brigade to take care of the car park.

(Donations to these two essential voluntary services would be appreciated.)

Lost and found care for children and things — located in the club house.

Tickets Please bring your ticket to exchange for a wristband which must be worn throughout the festival. Spot checks will happen!

We suggest you bring your own mug for soft drinks, etc. to save on disposables. Sunscreen and hats are strongly recommended and you may need a jumper for the cool spring nights.

The Lismore Folk Trust Inc.

A not-for-profit organisation run solely by volunteers, the Trust produces this annual festival, the Lismore Lantern Festival and other events throughout the year. Membership entitles you to concessions at all Folk Trust events, newsletters (vacancy for an editor!) and is essential support for the festival. You can find out more about the Trust, and how to join, at the festival office.

Proudly supporting Summerland House, Alstonville

■ **Amenities and** *solid waste management*

For large festivals and events, the layout of the amenities is always included in the logistics site map. Figure 10.9 is an example of a large festival logistics site map that shows the layout of amenities.

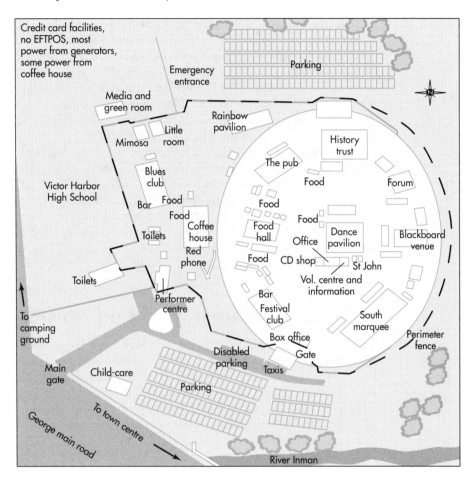

The site map is an indispensable tool for the event manager and is described in more detail later in this chapter. The schedules for the maintenance and cleaning of the amenities are part of the plan. For smaller events, these areas may be the sole responsibility of the venue management and part of the hiring contract.

Responsibility for cleaning the site and restoring it to its original condition is of particular importance to an event manager, as it is generally tied to the nature of the event. For example, the Sound Cloud event in 1988 at Sydney's Royal Botanic Gardens attracted a huge audience to a delicate area. The mere movement of the audience destroyed the grass and resulted in the Gardens administration being suspicious of any further events in their area. If a national park is used as the site for an event, a Review of Environmental Factors (REF) is mandatory. The REF is a list of criteria the activity must meet to be permitted under various acts and regulations. These include the *National Parks and Wildlife Act 1974* (NSW), the *Endangered Fauna (Interim Protection) Act 1991* (NSW) and the *Threatened Species Conservation Act 1995* (NSW). As well, the REF has to contain descriptions of the future implications of the activity, its impact on the existing environment and land use, and its significance to the local Aboriginal community.

Well maintained toilets, in particular their number, accessibility and cleanliness, can be a very important issue with the audience. A rule of thumb for community festivals is one toilet for every 150 people (Neighbourhood Arts Unit 1991). Respondents to the Port Fairy Folk Festival audience survey (see figure 10.16) stressed the state of the toilets was important for return visits to the festival. The logistics manager has to be aware of 'peak flows' during an event and the consequences for vehicle transport of waste and the opening times of treatment plants.

The collection of solid waste can range from making sure that the venue manager has enough bins, to calling for a tender and subcontracting the work. The number of bins and workers, shifts, time lines for collection and removal of skips should all be contained in the logistics plan, as it interrelates with all of the other event functional areas. This is a further example of the linking of the elements of logistics. A plan for primary recycling (recycling at collection point) would include both the education of the public (signage) and special bins for different types of waste (aluminium, glass, paper).

▨ Consumables: *food and beverage*

The logistics aspects of food and beverage on a large, multivenue site primarily concern its storage and distribution. Food stalls may be under the management of a stall manager as there are State and local regulations that need to be followed. The needs of the operators of food stalls, including transport, gas, electricity and plumbing, are then sent on to the logistics manager. The sale of alcoholic beverages particularly can present the logistics manager with security issues.

At a wine and food fair, the 'consumables' are the attraction. The collection of cash is often solved by the use of presale tickets that are exchanged for food and wine samples. The tickets are bought at one place on the site, which reduces possible problems with security, cash collection and accounting.

Figure 10.10 lists some of the main factors to consider when including food and beverage outlets at an event.

As well as feeding and watering the public, logistics includes the requirements of the staff, volunteers and performers. The catering area for the staff and performers, often called the green room, provides an opportunity to disseminate information to the event staff. At the Northern Rivers Folk Festival, a strategically placed, large whiteboard in the green room was used to communicate with volunteers.

Last, but not least, is the catering for sponsors and VIPs. This generally requires a separate plan to the general catering. In some festivals, a hospitality tent is set aside for special guests. This aspect of events is covered in chapter 11.

- Have local and State liquor licences been granted?

- What selection criteria for stall applicants (including the design of the stall and menu requirements) will be used?

- What infrastructure will be needed (including plumbing, electrical and gas)?

- Does the contract include provisions for health regulations, gas supplies, insurance and workers' compensation?

- What position on the site will the stalls occupy?

- Have arrival, set up, breakdown and leaving times been set?

- What cleaning arrangements have been made?

- Do stallholders understand the need for ongoing inspections, such as health, electricity, plumbing, garbage (including liquids) disposal and gas inspection?

- Are there any special security needs that must be catered for?

- How and when will payment for the stall be made?

- Will the stallholder provide in-kind support for the event (including catering for VIPs, media and performers)?

■ VIP and *media requirements*

The effect on event logistics by media coverage of the event cannot be over-estimated. Even direct radio broadcasts can disrupt the live performance of a show, both in the setting up and the actual broadcast. The recording or broadcast of speeches or music often requires separate microphones or a line from the mixing desk. This cannot be left until just before the performance. Television cameras require special lighting, which often shines directly into the eyes of the audience. The movement of a production crew and television power requirements can be distracting to a live performance, and need to be assessed before the event.

Media organisations work on very short time lines and may upset the well planned tempo of the event. However, the rewards in terms of promotion and even finance are so large that the media logistics can take precedence over most other aspects of the event. These decisions are often made by the event manager in consultation with event promotions and sponsors. This is an area that illustrates the need for flexible negotiations and assessment by the logistics manager.

The requirements of VIPs can include special security arrangements. Once again it is a matter of weighing up the benefits of having VIPs with the amount of extra resources that are needed. This, however, is not the logistic manager's area of concern; the event manager or event committee should deal with it. Once the VIPs have been invited, their needs have to take precedence over the public's.

■ Emergency *procedures*

Emergency procedures at an event can range from staff qualified in first aid, to using the St John Ambulance service, to the compilation of a comprehensive disaster plan. The location of first aid should be indicated on the site map and all the event staff should be aware of this. Large events require an emergency access road that has to be kept clear. These issues are so important that a local council will immediately close down an event that does not comply with their regulations about emergencies.

Festivals in the countryside can be at the mercy of natural disasters, including fires, storms and floods. Figure 10.11 shows just one page of the disaster plan of the Woodford Folk Festival 1997. The lines of authority and necessary procedures are stressed in the disaster plan. These procedures include the partial evacuation of the festival site in the event of a disaster (particularly prolonged, heavy rain). It notes that rescuers should concentrate on personnel in immediate danger when conducting an evacuation.

■ **Figure 10.11**
Extract from the Woodford Folk Festival 1997 disaster plan

AUTHORITY
This plan is written under the authority of the *State Counter Disaster Organisation Act 1974–78*.

AIM
The aim of this plan is to set out the policies and procedure to be followed by State Emergency Service personnel in times of major incidents, disasters or emergencies that may occur during the Woodford Folk Festival.

In matters where this document is silent, then the Caboolture Shire Disaster Plan will come into effect and be enacted.

OBJECTIVES
To establish the general guidelines to be followed for all incidents and/or emergencies.
To set the guidelines to be followed in the event of a fire.
To set the guidelines to be followed in the event of a multicasualty incident.
To set the guidelines to be followed in the event of a lost person.
To set the guidelines to be followed in the event of a flood in the festival site.
To set the guidelines to be followed in the event of a severe storm causing damage.
To set the general guidelines to be followed for any other event that may occur.

COMMAND AND CONTROL
The control organisation for emergencies and searches is the Queensland Police Service.

The control organisation for fire incidents is the Queensland Fire and Rescue Service.

The control organisation for medical and multicasualty incidents is the Queensland Ambulance Service.

The support and management organisation for the above is the Queensland State Emergency Service.

The control organisation for storm damage operations is the Queensland State Emergency Service.

The Maleny State Emergency Service Group activities at the Woodford Folk Festival are overseen by the training officer and are conducted as training.

In the event of an incident or emergency occurring, the Maleny training officer or delegate must be informed immediately, regardless of the time of day.

As Pagonis (1992) points out, military logistics is divided into three phases: deployment, combat and redeployment. Redeployment often takes the most effort and time. The amount of time and effort spent on the shutdown of an event are in direct proportion to the size of the event and its uniqueness. Repeated events, like many of the festivals mentioned in this chapter, have their shutdown schedule refined over many years. Shutdown can run quickly and smoothly. All the subcontractors know exactly how to get their equipment out and where they are placed in the order of removal. The event manager of a small event may only have to sweep the floor and turn off the lights.

Most difficulties arise in inaugural events, large events and mutivenued events. In these cases, logistics can be as important after the event as at any other time and the need for planning most apparent. The breakdown and removal of site structures, the collection of equipment and the exits of the various traders should all be part of the schedules contained in the logistics plan. The plan for the breakdown of the event is part of the initial meeting and negotiation with contractors. A major part of working out a Gantt chart (see pages 231–2) or a critical path is the acquittal of equipment, which includes removing, repairing and cleaning the equipment.

As emphasised in the Port Fairy example at the end of this chapter and by Catherwood and Van Kirk (1992), the shutdown of an event is the prime security time. The mix of vehicles, movement of equipment and general feeling of relaxation provides a cover for theft. The smooth flow of traffic leaving an event at its conclusion must also be considered. Towing services and the police may need to be contacted.

Very large events may require the sale of facilities and equipment at a post-event auction. Some events in Australia find that it is more cost effective to buy or make the necessary equipment and sell it after the event. Finally, it is often left to the person in charge of logistics to organise the final thank-you party for the volunteers and staff.

TECHNIQUES OF LOGISTICS MANAGEMENT

We will now consider the role of the logistics manager and their relation to the other functional areas and managers of an event.

■ The event logistics *manager*

As mentioned throughout this chapter, the logistics manager has to be a procurer, negotiator, equipment and maintenance manager, personnel manager, map maker, project manager and party organiser. For a small event, logistics can be the direct responsibility of the event manager. Logistics becomes a separate area if the event is large and complex. Multivenued and multiday events usually require a separate logistics manager position.

Part of the role of the logistics manager is to efficiently link all areas of the event. Figure 10.12 shows the lines of communication between the logistics manager and various other managers for a large, complex, multivenued event. It is a network diagram because, although the event manager or director has ultimate authority, decision-making authority is usually devolved to the various submanagers who work at the same level of authority and responsibility as the event manager.

The information required by the logistics manager from the other festival managers is shown in table 10.1. The clear communication between managers in this network is also partly the responsibility of the logistics manager.

■ **Figure 10.12**
The lines of communication between the logistics manager and other managers for a multivenued event

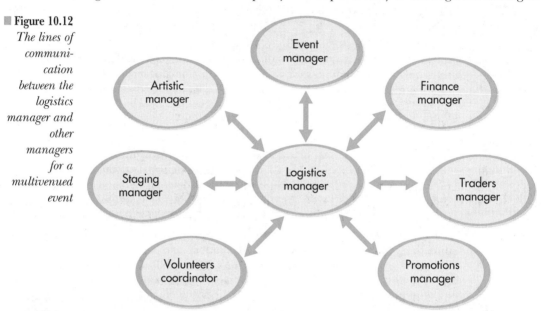

■ **Table 10.1** *Information required by the logistics manager from the other festival managers*

POSITION	GENERAL ROLE	INFORMATION SENT TO LOGISTICS MANAGER
Artistic director	Selection of and negotiation with artists	Travel, accommodation, staging and equipment requirements
Staging manager	Selection of and negotiation with subcontractors	Sound, lights and backstage requirements and programming times
Finance director	Overseeing budgets and contracts	How and when funds will be approved and released and the payment schedule
Volunteers coordinator	Recruitment and management of volunteers	Volunteers selected to assist Requirements of the volunteers (e.g. parking, free tickets)
Promotions manager	Promotion during the event	Requirements of the media and VIPS
Traders manager	Selecting suitable traders	Requirements of the traders (e.g. positioning, theming, electricity, water, licence agreements)

The tools used in business and military logistics can be successfully adapted to event logistics. Because an event takes place at a specific time and specific place, the tools of scheduling and mapping are used. The dynamic nature of events and the way that the functional areas are so closely linked means that a small change in one area can result in crucial changes throughout the event. For example, the incorrect placement of an electric generator can lead to a mushrooming of problems. If the initial problem is not foreseen or immediately solved, it can grow so much that the whole event is affected. This gives initial negotiations and on-going assessment a special significance in event logistics. The logistics manager needs to be skilled in identifying possible problem areas and needs to know what is *not* on the list.

■ Scheduling: *bar chart*

One of the most important tools used in logistics is the bar chart or time line, or the Gantt chart. Gantt charts are bar charts that are used in project management as a visual representation of the schedule. Following are the steps in creating a Gantt chart.

- *Tasks*: break down the logistics of the event into manageable tasks or activities. For example, one of the tasks of the security for the event is the erection of the perimeter fence. This can be further broken down into the arrival of the fencing material, the arrival of volunteers and equipment, and the preparation of the ground.
- *Time lines*: set the time scale for each task. Factors to consider are the starting and completion times. The availability, hiring costs, possible delivery and pick-up times and costs are other considerations in constructing a time scale. For example, a major factor in the arrival of large tents is their hiring costs. These costs can depend on the day of the week on which they arrive, rather than the amount of time they are hired for.
- *Priority*: set the priority of the task. What other tasks need to be completed before this task can start? Completing this priority list will create a hierarchy of tasks or a work breakdown structure.
- *Grid*: draw a grid with the days leading up to the event across the top and a list of the tasks down the left-hand side of the grid. A horizontal bar that corresponds to each task is drawn across the grid. For example, the task of preparing the ground for the fencing is dependent on the arrival of materials and labour at a certain time and takes one day to complete. The starting time will be when the prior tasks are completed and the length of the time line will be one day. The horizontal bars or time lines are often colour-coded so that each task may be easily recognised when the chart is completed for all activities.
- *Milestones*: as the chart is used for monitoring the progress of the event, tasks that are of particular importance are designated as milestones and marked on the chart. For example, the completion of the security fence is a milestone as it acts as a trigger for many of the other event preparation activities.

Figure 10.13
Simplified
Gantt chart
of a small
festival

Figure 10.13 shows an example of a simplified Gantt chart. This chart is common to most small rural Australian festivals.

Tasks	F	S	S	M	T	W	T	F	S	S	M	T	W	T	F	S	S
Clear and prepare site		▓	▓	▓	▓						opening night				◇		
Generators arrive						▓											
Lighting on site											▓	▓	▓	▓	▓	▓	▓
Tents arrive												▓	▓	▓			
Stages arrive and set up													▓	▓			
Site security															▓	▓	▓
Sound system arrives															▓		

◇ **Milestone:** start of festival

In his work on the human factors in project management, Dinsmore (1990) stresses that this display of project tasks and time requirements has high communication value to an event. It forestalls unnecessary explanations to the staff and sponsors and gives a visual representation of the event. Time lines are used in events no matter what their size. The arrival of goods and services on time even at a small event can add significant value to the event.

The advantages of a Gantt chart are it:
• visually summarises the project or event schedule
• is an effective communication and control tool (particularly with volunteers)
• can point out problem areas or clashes of scheduling
• is readily adaptable to all event areas
• provides a summary of the history of the event.

For the Gantt chart to be an effective tool, the tasks must be arranged and estimated in the most practical and logical sequence. Underestimation of the time needed (length of the time line) can give rise to cost blow out and render any scheduling ineffective. As Lock (1988, p. 89) points out:

> ■ Extended schedules produced in this way are an ideal breeding ground for budgetary excesses according to Professor Parkinson's best-known law, where work is apt to expand to fill the time available. ■

■ Network analysis: *critical path*

One important aspect of any logistic plan is the relationship of tasks to each other. This can be difficult to show on a chart. With larger events, the Gantt chart can become very complex, and areas where there is a clash of scheduling may be obscured by the detail of bars and colours. A vital part of logistics is giving tasks a priority. For example, the arrival and set-up of the main stage in an event is more important than finding an extra extension cord. However, on a Gantt chart all of the tasks are given equal importance. The tool of network analysis was developed to overcome these problems.

Network analysis was created and developed during defence force projects in the USA and UK in the 1950s and now has widespread use in many project-based industries. The basis of network analysis is critical path analysis, which uses circles to represent programmed events and arrows to illustrate the flow of activities. Thus, the precedence of programmed events is established and the diagram can be used to analyse a series of sub-events. From the diagram, the most efficient scheduling can be found. This is known as the critical path. Figure 10.14 illustrates a network derived from the Gantt chart shown in figure 10.13. The critical path is shown as an arrow. This means that, for example, if the generator did not arrive on time, everything along the critical path would be directly affected. The lights would not be put up and, without evening light or electricity to run the pneumatic hammers, the tents could not be erected. Without the protective cover of the tents, the stage could not be constructed and so the sound system could not be set up. The critical path is indeed critical.

Figure 10.14
Gantt chart represented as a network

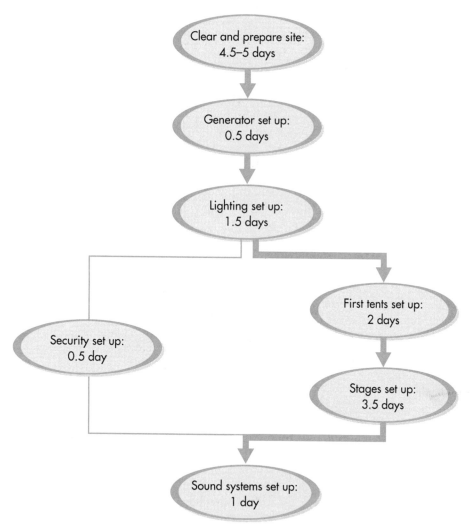

There are a number of software packages available to help create the Gantt chart and critical path. These are project management programs, which are usually used in the construction industry. Unfortunately, most of these packages are based on a variable completion time or completion within a certain time. In the event industry, the completion time (i.e. when the event is on) is the most important factor and every task has to relate to this time. The event manager cannot ask for an extension of the time to complete all of the tasks.

Time charts and networks are very useful as a control and communication tool; however, like all logistics techniques, they have their limitations. Graham (1995) describes how the Los Angeles Olympic Organising Committee gave up on the critical path chart as it became too unwieldy. There were 600 milestones. Rather than assisting communication and planning, it only created confusion. The solution was for the committee to return to a more traditional method of weekly meetings.

■ Site or *venue map*

A map of the event site or venue is a necessary communication tool for the logistics manager. For small events, even a simple map can be an effective tool that obviates the need for explanations and can quickly identify possible problem areas. The map for larger festivals can be an aerial photograph with the logistic features drawn on it. For smaller events, it may be a sketch map that shows only the necessary information to the customer. The first questions to ask are 'what is the map for?' and 'who will be reading it?'. A logistics site map will contain very different information than the site map used for promotional purposes. The map needs to filter information that is of no interest to the logistics plan. Monmonier (1996, p. 25), in his highly respected work on mapping, summarises this concept thus:

> ■ A good map tells a multitude of little white lies; it suppresses truth to help the user see what needs to be seen. Reality is three-dimensional, rich in detail, and far too factual to allow a complete yet uncluttered two-dimensional scale model. Indeed, a map that did not generalize would be useless. But the value of a map depends on how well its generalized geometry and generalized content reflect a chosen aspect of reality. ■

The three basic features of maps — scale, projection and the key (showing the symbols used) — have to be adapted to their target audience. Volunteers and subcontractors, for example, must be able to clearly read and understand it. The communication value of the site map also depends on where it is displayed. Some festivals draw the map on the back of the ticket or program.

The check list for items to be included on a site map can be very detailed. Figure 10.15 shows a standard check list of the logistics for a small festival.

☐ scale and direction (north arrow)	☐ food and market stalls
☐ a list of symbols used on the map (key)	☐ tents and marquees
☐ entrance and exits	☐ equipment storage areas
☐ roads and parking	☐ off-limit areas and danger spots (e.g. creeks, blind corners)
☐ administration centre	☐ green room
☐ information booths	☐ maintenance area
☐ first aid and emergency road access	☐ pathways
☐ lost children area	☐ telephones
☐ electricity and water outlets	☐ ATMs
☐ toilets	☐ media area

As the Macquarie Marshes are in outback New South Wales, a sketch map on the ticket showed how to find the site, parking and the location of facilities. Next to the map was a list detailing the behaviour expected of event participants. The festival site shown in figure 10.9 would be used by volunteers, staff, performers and all other personnel at the event. The promotional map for the audience, on the other hand, would be in colour and display points of interest to the public.

For corporate events, a simple map of the venue at the entrance, showing the location of seating, toilets, food areas and the bar, can relieve the staff of having to answer a lot of questions!

*N*EGOTIATION AND ASSESSMENT

No matter what the size of the event, mutual agreement on supply and conditions is vital. In particular, the special but changing nature of one-off events requires the techniques of dynamic negotiation to be mastered by the logistics manager. In his work on negotiation and contracts, Marsh (1984, p. 1) defines negotiation as:

> ■ a dynamic process of adjustment by which two parties, each with their own objectives, confer together to reach a mutually satisfying agreement on a matter of common interest. ■

Logistical considerations need to be covered by the initial negotiations with subcontractors. Agreement on delivery and removal times are an indispensable part of the time lines, as they form the parameters of the critical path.

It needs to be stressed that the management of special events in Australia is a dynamic industry. The special nature of many events means that many aspects cannot be included in initial negotiations. Decisions and agreements need to be continually reassessed. Both parties to the agreement have to realise that the agreement needs to be flexible. However, all possible problems have to be considered at the beginning, and there are logistics tools to enable this to happen.

Having prepared the schedules and site map, an important tool to use is what Pagonis (1992, p. 194) describes as the skull session:

> ■ Before implementing a particular plan, I usually try to bring together all of the involved parties for a collective dry run. The group includes representatives from all appropriate areas of the command, and the goal of the skull sessions is to identify and talk through all the unknown elements of the situation. We explore all possible problems that could emerge, and then try to come up with concrete solutions to those problems. Skull sessions reduce uncertainty, reinforce the interconnection of the different areas of specialisation, encourage collaborative problem solving, and raise the level of awareness as to possible disconnects [sic] in the theatre. ■

Goldblatt (1997) calls this gap analysis. Gap analysis is studying the plan in an attempt to identify gaps that could lead to a weakening in the implementation of the logistics plan. Goldblatt (1997) recommends using a critical friend to review the plan to look for gaps in your logical thinking.

The identification of risk areas, gaps and 'what ifs' is important in the creation of a contingency plan. For example, at the Woodford Folk Festival that takes place in the hottest months of the year in Queensland, the supply of water was identified as a priority area and a contingency plan created for a viable alternative. This included having water carts on call and making sure the nearest water pipe was available to the general public.

CONTROL OF EVENTS LOGISTICS

The monitoring of the logistics plan is a vital part of the overall control of an event. An important part of the plan is the identification of milestones — times when crucial tasks have to be completed. The Gantt chart can be used to compare projected performance with actual performance by recording actual performance times on the chart as the tasks occur. It is a simple monitoring device.

The aim of the logistics manager is to create a plan to enable the logistics to flow without the need for active control. The use of qualified subcontractors with experience in events is the only way to make this happen. This is where the annual festival, with its established relationship with suppliers, has an advantage over the one-off, innovative event. For example, the objective of the director of the Port Fairy Folk Festival was to enjoy the festival without having to intervene in any on-site problems!

EVALUATION OF LOGISTICS

The ultimate evaluation of the logistics plan is the success of the event and the easy flow of event supply and operations. However, the festival committee, event director and/or the sponsors may require a more detailed evaluation. The main question to ask is if the logistics met their objectives. If the objectives as set out in the plan are measurable, then this task is relatively straightforward. If the objectives require a qualitative approach, then the evaluation can become imprecise and open to many interpretations.

An evaluation enables the logistics manager to identify problem areas that enables improvement and therefore adds value to the next event. Techniques used in evaluation are:
- quantitative — meeting measurable objectives; sometimes called benchmarking
- qualitative — discussion with stakeholders.

The term 'logistics audit' is used for a systematic and thorough analysis of the event logistics. Part of the audit concerns the expectations of the audience and whether they were satisfied. The Port Fairy Folk Festival carried out an audience survey that identified areas of infrastructure for improvement and expansion for the growth of the festival. Figure 10.16 is an extract from a detailed survey of the attending audience of the Port Fairy Folk Festival.

For very large events, the evaluation of the logistics may be contained in the overall evaluation that is put out to tender. In 1997 the Australian Department of Foreign Affairs and Trade launched a multidimensional promotion of Australia in India. It included a series of events throughout India, ranging from trade shows to cultural activities. The logistical problems of such a varied event spread over a large area in a foreign country with a huge population are many. The evaluation report of this promotion was mostly concerned with the business outcomes. However, large sections of the 90-page Buchan Communications Group (1997) report were concerned with the logistics. Areas such as travel, communication and accommodation were evaluated by the participants. Other areas of logistics were 'evaluated' by the fact that they were unseen by the participants and therefore deemed a success. For example, as a result of the security measures put in place as part of the logistics planning, there were no terrorist activities during the promotion. (The day after the promotion had finished a train was blown up.)

■ Figure 10.16
*Extract from
the Port Fairy
Folk Festival
1996
audience
survey*

2.9 Standard of toilet services in camping areas

	Count	Percentage	1994(%)	1995(%)
Good	116	43	46	46.7
Reasonable	114	42	44	44
Poor	41	15	10	9.3
TOTAL	271	100%	100%	100%

2.10 Standard of toilet services in arena

	Count	Percentage	1994(%)	1995(%)
Good	141	35	47	46
Reasonable	196	49	45	46
Poor	65	16	8	8
TOTAL	402	100%	100%	100%

2.11 Respondents' comments about facilities

Category of comment	Count	Percentage
More showers	31	14
Toilets smell/dirty	39	18
Excellent	21	10
Toilets are clean	1	0.5
More ladies toilets	40	18
Better than 1995	14	6
More cleaning needed	16	7
Very clean	7	3
Facilities not large enough	6	3
Food variety needed	22	10
Too crowded	9	4
Table and chairs are good	8	4
More rubbish bins	2	1
Toilets for handicapped inadequate	2	1
TOTAL	218	100%

(**Source**: *Port Fairy Folk Festival 1996*, Audience Survey, *p. 9*)

*T*HE LOGISTICS PLAN

Whether the event is a school class reunion or a multivenued festival, a written logistics plan needs to be part of the communication within the event. It could range from a one-page contact list with approximate arrival times, to a bound folder covering all areas. The folder for a large event would contain:

- a general contact list
- a site map

- schedules, including time lines and bar charts
- the emergency plan
- subcontractor details, including all time constraints
- on-site contacts, including security and volunteers
- evaluation sheets (sample questionnaires).

All of these elements have been described and discussed in this chapter.

SUMMARY

Military logistics is as old as civilisation itself. Business logistics is a recent science. Events logistics has the advantage of building on these areas, using the tools of both and continually improving on them as the events industry in Australia grows.

The event logistics system can be broken down into the procuring and supply of customers, products and facilities. Once on site, the logistics system concerns the flow around the site, communication and requirements of the event. At the conclusion of the event, logistics concerns the breakdown of structures, cleaning and managing the evacuation of the site or venue.

For small events, logistics may be the responsibility of the event manager. However, for larger events a logistics manager may be appointed. Their role within the overall event management was described and their relationship with other managers is vital. The logistics of an event needs to be treated as any other area of management and have in-built evaluation and ongoing control. All of these elements are placed in a plan that is a part of the overall event plan.

Logistics is an invisible part of events. It enables customers to focus completely on the event without being distracted by unnecessary problems. It becomes visible only when it is looked for or when there is a problem. It enables the paying customer, the public, client or sponsor to realise and even exceed their expectations.

Questions

1 What are the logistics areas that need to be contained in initial agreements with the event suppliers?

2 Set out an emergency plan for a small event.

3 List the logistics tasks for (a) a street parade, (b) a product launch and (c) a company party.

4 Create a Gantt chart for a street parade or another event. Identify the critical path.

The Port Fairy
Folk Festival

From a small folk festival specialising in amateur music sessions or get-togethers in 1977, the Port Fairy Folk Festival on the south coast of Victoria has grown to an event that attracted 34 000 people to Port Fairy in 1996. The festival has won many awards, including the Hall of Fame Award and the Australian Tourism Award in 1993, 1994 and 1995. The festival, which is under the management of the Port Fairy Committee, showcases more than 300 international, national and regional artists in 30 venues around town, including the main stages within the festival arena. It is estimated that the festival pumps more than $3 million into the Port Fairy township each year.

The Port Fairy Folk Festival has three advantages over one-off events:
1. a stable and well-connected organising committee
2. a regular venue that is improved each year
3. a well-maintained relationship with the various participating artists and the town.

The festival is managed by a committee of 14 volunteers. The volunteers are local citizens, with professional people and businesses well represented. The members include a health surveyor, a real estate agent, a local shopkeeper, the local fish co-op representative, a retired factory manager, a school principal and a lawyer. The festival director coordinates the festival's content, marketing, staging and performers. The chairman of the festival has a long background in building contracting and project management.

The festival site is the parklands, playing fields and camping ground of Port Fairy. The site is surrounded by a high fence with two entrances. Venues in the township are also used for festival activities. The festival includes free events and a ticketed area called the arena. The arena takes up the area of the local sportsgrounds and contains the four main stages and many smaller venues, including the folk circus which is an area dedicated to children's entertainment. The programming of the stages is the responsibility of the festival director.

In 1997 the PFFF spent only $8000 on publicity. Tickets are sold out four months prior to the start of the three-day festival, which gives the festival a good working capital. The organisers are very conscious of the feedback from participants. For many years an informal feedback sheet from the audience indicated the level of satisfaction with the festival. In 1995 the festival committee commissioned an audience survey on the facilities and program of the festival. The survey also provided demographic information about the audience.

The minimal use of advertising and the complete presale of tickets indicates an audience that has either already attended the festival or has been told about it by friends. This means that the audience is familiar with the festival and is already educated about the logistics that concerns it. For example, people attending the festival will know about how to get there, parking, accommodation, food, toilets, seating and water availability through friends who have been to a previous festival or from attending themselves. One consequence of this is that minimal signage is needed on-site compared to other festivals.

The festival 'product portfolio' contains more than 450 performances, including processions through the town, a craft fair, story telling, instrument making, dancing, competitions and awards. The headline acts come from overseas and are transported by road from Melbourne. Interstate artists generally find their own way to Port Fairy.

The gradual growth of the festival has allowed the organising committee to introduce new facilities and improve them. This improvement has been used as a benchmark for each year. For example, the 1986 festival is noted as the year when the hoeckers were introduced. These large tents are internally supported and do not need the external ropes and pegs that are so dangerous when large crowds are moving around a site. In 1992 the Guinness and wine bars were started, which secured a major sponsor and produced a new source of funds.

Security and rubbish collection, including 80 wheelie bins, are put out to tender. Most of the infrastructure is built up during the year in preparation for future growth. The electricity, water, sewerage and phone lines are all underground. Four large lights were erected by the festival committee in the arena area. The lights have the dual purpose of lighting the festival, allow for night construction work and help the local sports teams who use this area for the rest of the year. This close relationship between the festival and the local community is central to the philosophy of the festival. Many areas of the festival's logistics reflect this relationship. For example, the hoeckers are erected each year by the local farming community of Yambuk. In exchange, the festival provides funds to be distributed as grants to benefit the community.

The festival's critical path is worked out through experience rather than theory. The use of volunteers, community groups and contra deals has resulted in a very personal management style.

The festival has a similar on-site schedule to many of the festivals around Australia. For example, the Northern Rivers Folk Festival, although smaller, is set up and broken down over the same period as the Port Fairy Folk Festival. The following time line is not exhaustive; however, it highlights the milestones that must occur before the next step can happen.

Note how long the festival takes to set up — two weeks — compared to the shut down period — two days. Also note how the security arrives the day before the event begins.

Timing	Day of the week	Milestone task or event	Notes
Fortnight before the festival begins		• pegs set out and surfaces marked	Position of each venue indicated with marking paint. Position of underground power lines are marked on the surface.
Week before the festival begins	Saturday	• marquees and smaller tents arrive	All of the tents are hired and transported from Melbourne.
	Sunday	• tents are erected • electrician constructs power boxes at each venue	Power boxes are needed for on-site construction, particularly for the hydraulic hammers for the hoeckers.
	Monday, Tuesday, Wednesday	• stages, lighting bars, more tents and tables are set up • specially-made fire extinguishers and hoses are set up • the mobile hot water unit arrives • toilets are joined to the sewerage	The extensive underground power is tapped into and the power boards for sound and lighting are connected. This is an advantage of creating an infrastructure for the festival at one site.
	Thursday	• security arrives	Minimal security guards the site Thursday night.
		• Port Fairy Folk Festival events begin at 8.00 p.m.	Full-strength security team on site by 6.00 p.m.
Post-festival	Monday	• flags are taken down • traders leave on Monday night • barbeque dinner, security leaves	The local cycling club organises a barbeque dinner for 5.00 p.m. for all of the workers.
	Wednesday	• committee inspects site	The construction crew have already inspected all equipment, reported any damage and packed the equipment away.

William O'Toole has worked as an entertainment consultant to the Port Fairy Folk Festival supplying performers and event concepts. He has also performed at the festival with the group Sirocco.

Questions

1 Create a Gantt chart that displays the logistics of the Port Fairy Folk Festival.

2 What aspects of the logistics of the festival are 'sensitive' (i.e. a small change in one area will have a large effect on the festival)?

3 Imagine the festival had to change locations to a nearby town. What elements of the logistics would remain the same and what would need changing?

4 Create a risk management list for the festival that would be used as the basis of a 'skull session'.

REFERENCES

Buchan Communications Group, May 1997, *Australia–India New Horizons Evaluation Report*, Department of Foreign Affairs and Trade, Canberra.

Catherwood, D. W. & Van Kirk, R. L. 1992, *The Complete Guide to Special Events Management*, John Wiley and Sons, New York.

CIM Rostrum n.d., *The Comprehensive Convention Planner's Manual*, vol. 32, Rank Publishing Company, St Leonards.

Coyle, John J., Bardi, Edward J. & Langley Jnr, C. John 1988, *The Management of Business Logistics*, 4th edn, West Publishing Company, St Paul.

Dinsmore, P. C. 1990, *Human Factors in Project Management*, AMACOM, New York.

Gilmour, Peter 1993, *Logistics Management, An Australian Framework*, Addison Wesley Longman, Melbourne.

Goldblatt, J. 1997, *Special Events: Best Practices in Modern Event Management*, 2nd edn, Van Nostrand Reinhold.

Graham, S., Goldblatt, J. & Delpy, L. 1995, *The Ultimate Guide to Sports Event Management and Marketing*, Richard Irwin, Chicago.

Lock, Dennis 1988, *Project Management*, Gower Press, England.

Marsh, P. D. V. 1984, *Contract Negotiation Handbook*, 2nd edn, Gower Press, Aldeshot.

Monmonier, Mark 1996, *How to Lie with Maps*, 2nd edn, University of Chicago Press, Chicago.

Neighbourhood Arts Unit 1991, *Community Festival Handbook*, City of Melbourne, Melbourne.

Pagonis, Lt General William G. 1992, *Moving Mountains: Lessons in Leadership and Logistics from the Gulf War*, Harvard Business School Press, Boston.

Queensland Folk Federation Incorporated 1997, *Operational and Site Management Plan 1997*.

Staging

events

LEARNING OBJECTIVES

After studying this chapter, you should be able to:

■ analyse the staging of an event according to its constituent elements

■ demonstrate how these elements relate to each other and to the theme of the event

■ understand the safety elements of each aspect of staging

■ identify the relative importance of the staging elements for different types of events

■ use the tools of staging.

The term 'staging' originates from the presentation of plays at the theatre. It refers to bringing together all the elements of a theatrical production for its presentation on a stage. Most events that use this term take place at a single venue and require organisation similar to that of a theatrical production. However, whereas a play can take place over a season, a special event may take place in one night. Examples of this type of event are product launches, company parties and celebrations, awards ceremonies, conference events, concerts, large weddings, corporate dinners and opening and closing events.

Staging can also refer to the organisation of a venue within a much larger festival. A large festival may have performance areas positioned around a site. Each of these venues may have a range of events with a distinct theme. At the Sydney Royal Easter Show, there are a number of performance areas, each with its own style. Because it is part of a much larger event, one performance area or event has to fit in with the overall planning of the complete event and has to fit in with the festival programming and logistics. However, each performance area is to some extent its own kingdom, with its own micro-logistics, management, staff and individual character. For example, at one of the stages of Sydney's Royal Easter Show the theme was world music and dance. The venue had its own event director, stage manager and light and sound technicians. Although it was part of the overall theme of the Royal Easter Show, it was allowed a certain amount of autonomy by the Show entertainment director.

The main concerns of staging are as follows:
• theming and event design
• choice of venue
• audience and guests
• stage
• power, lights and sound
• audiovisuals and special effects
• catering
• performers
• crew
• hospitality
• the production schedule
• recording the event
• contingencies.

This chapter analyses the staging of an event according to these elements. It demonstrates how these elements revolve around a central event theme. The type of event will determine how important each of these elements is to the others. However, common to the staging of different events are the tools: the stage plan, the contact and responsibility list and the production schedule.

When staging an event, the major artistic and creative decision to be made is that of determining what the theme is to be. The theme of an event differentiates it from other events. In the corporate area, the client may determine the theme of the event. For example, the client holding a corporate party or product launch may want medieval Europe as the theme, or Australiana, complete with native animals and bush band. Outside the corporate area, the theme for one of the stages at a festival may be blues music, debating or a children's circus. Whatever the nature of the event, once the theme is established, the elements of the event must be designed to fit in with the theme. This is straightforward when it comes to deciding on the entertainment and catering. With the medieval corporate party, the entertainment may include jongleurs and jugglers and the catering may be spit roasts and wine. However, audiovisuals may need a lot of thought in order to enhance the theme. The sound and lights must complement the entertainment or they may not fit in with the period theme. Figure 11.1 is a breakdown of the elements of staging, and it emphasises the central role of the theme of the event.

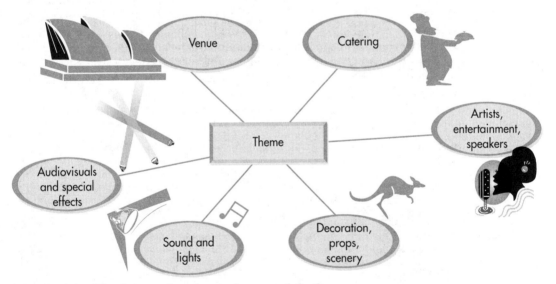

■ **Figure 11.1**   *The elements of staging revolve around the theme.*

The director of the Port Fairy Folk Festival expresses the importance of staging in the following way:

> ■ A great concert experience begins with the excitement built by the advertised program and venue facilities. The audience must be given reasonable comfort and have their expectations met. You must deliver the advertised act, at the advertised place and time and leave them wanting more. This means that the staging will look good, preferably great, the sound production and lighting will be of high quality, the overall presentation will be dignified and professional. ■

An example of event theme and design: *Macquarie Marshes*

The Macquarie Marshes are a wetland system on the Macquarie River in central New South Wales. The marshes filter the river and are a major bird habitat.

As a way of drawing the attention of the public to this area, the music group Sirocco and the local National Parks and Wildlife officers organised an innovative event in the wetlands. The event consisted of:

- a concert of original compositions by Sirocco describing the area in music
- various performances, including a dance by stilt-walkers dressed as sacred ibises
- overnight camping
- a guided walk through the wetlands.

The concert was broadcast live on radio around Australia, Asia and the Pacific by satellite. As the event occurred in a wildlife heritage park not normally open to the public, only 1000 people were allowed into the area.

The three components of the theme decided by the event organisers were:

- the beauty of the Australian environment and the need to conserve it
- high quality cultural performance taking inspiration from the environment
- the latest in Australian technology, in order to demonstrate the world importance of this area and its link to the world.

These elements were combined to produce the Celebration of the Marshes.

It was also important that the event include all the local farming interests — cotton and beef — as well as the environmentalists.

The site was chosen and laid out in accordance with the theme components. The event was staged in the coolabah and river red gum woodland adjacent to the wetland, which allowed ample dry camping space but retained a sense of being within the wetlands. The clear water was next to the stage and the sounds of the bird life enhanced the event. At night, the double splash (one from the legs followed by the tail) of the kangaroos jumping through the wetlands could be clearly heard.

A separate parking area was situated so that it could not be seen from the event area and could not, therefore, detract from the venue environment. The stage was set up so that the audience would see the performers in front of the trees, which were lit from below. Behind this, and quite visible to the audience, was the large ITERRA satellite dish pointing to the stars. At one point in the evening, two four-metre high sacred ibises (stilt-walkers in full costume) came out of the wetlands, to the surprise of the audience, and performed a dance choreographed to the music.

The promotional campaign had to reflect all the elements of the design. The chosen logo was a stunning colour photograph of the wetland plant nardoo. All the artwork was high quality, environmentally friendly and recyclable. An unintended consequence of this was a high demand for the posters of the event. Recycled paper was used for the tickets. (See figure 11.2.) The music used high quality digital recordings of the sounds of the birds and other wildlife in the wetlands. The media launch, one month before the event, was staged in an urban rainforest in Sydney.

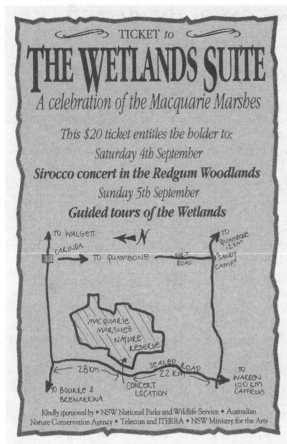

Program
- Saturday 4th September: 7pm Sirocco concert.

8pm Broadcast by ABC–FM and ITERRA Satellite to Asia and the Pacific

Overnight camping (bring a tent)
- Sunday 5th September: tours of the Wetlands every half hour from 8.30am.

Camping suggestions and regulations
- Parking and camping directions provided on entry
- Bring your own tent and camping gear
- Water and toilet facilities provided
- Food and wine on sale
- NO fires
- NO pets
- Beware of snakes
- This is a wildlife sanctuary and the purchase of the ticket implies that you act safely and responsibly — the organisers accept NO responsibility.

The Marshes

The Macquarie Marshes make up a diverse and extensive wetland on the Macquarie River in North West NSW. The Marshes begin where the River breaks into smaller distributive streams. These rejoin and divide many times before the river emerges as a single channel. It then flows into the Darling River and finally into the Southern Ocean.

Prolific in wildlife including a stunning range of waterbirds like the brolga, magpie goose, sacred ibis and spoonbill. The Marshes were a well known meeting place for the Aboriginal tribes.

The Wetlands acts as a filter for the river and has been identified as integral to the health of the inland river systems.

It is VITAL that the Marshes be preserved.

■ **Figure 11.2**   *The Wetlands Suite — a sample ticket for the event*

Food was provided by the local farmers and the profits went to the local schools. To minimise any possible impact on the natural environment, water was brought in by truck and portable toilets were hired. An important design element was that the site be left in pristine condition. The choice of generators was made according to strict guidelines — the latest silent generator was driven up from Sydney. Even the helicopter that was used to film the event for television enhanced the high technology aspect. Indirectly, its presence stressed that the wetlands are of world interest and are not just a local swamp. The audience accommodation was in the bushwalking tradition of small tents scattered through the river red gum woodland. In one sense, the lack of facilities was an element in the event's design.

On the Sunday, the National Parks and Wildlife officers guided small groups through the wetlands. This involved the audience wading waist deep through the clear water. This was an unforgettable part of the event experience.

The products from the event — a video and CD — were themed in much the same way. The nardoo picture was used on the CD cover and the video showed the beauty of the Australian wetlands. It ended with footage of the event.

Designing the event around the theme enabled the audience to be enveloped by the event. All aspects, including publicity, entertainment, arrival, accommodation, food and merchandise, were arranged using the theme as the guide. The sensitive nature of the project, which involved possible conflicting interests, meant that every aspect of the event had to be well thought out in order to celebrate an area that is, ultimately, owned by the world.

CHOICE OF VENUE

The choice of venue is a crucial decision that will ultimately determine many of the elements of staging. Figure 11.3 lists the major factors in the choice of a venue. The venue may be an obvious part of the theme of the event. A corporate party that takes place in a zoo is using the venue as part of the event experience. However, many events take place within 'four walls and a roof', the venue being chosen for other factors. It can be regarded as an empty canvas on which the event is 'painted'. Cameron (1993), in his work on community theatre, describes the events he has staged in disused factories, forests and stages floating on water. He describes how the event manager can utilise the atmosphere and natural beauty of open-air performances. In these situations, the traditional roles of stage manager and event manager become blurred. When the audience and the performers mix together and where they and the venue become the entertainment package, the delineation between stage and auditorium is no longer appropriate.

■ Figure 11.3
The factors in venue selection

- Matching the venue with the theme of the event
- Matching the size of the venue to the size of the event
- Venue configuration, including sight lines and seating configuration
- History of events at that venue, including the venue's reputation
- Availability
- What the venue can provide
- Transport to, from and around the venue; parking
- Access for audience, equipment, performers, VIPs, staff and the disabled
- Toilets and other amenities
- Catering equipment and preferred caterers
- Power (amount available and outlets) and lights
- Communication, including telephone
- Climate, including microclimate and ventilation
- Emergency plans and exits

A special event that uses a purpose-built venue, such as an entertainment centre, will find that much of the infrastructure will be in place. However, because there are so many factors in an event that are dependent on the venue or site, an inspection is absolutely necessary. For conference events, *Rostrum* (vol. 32) suggests that the event manager attends a function at the venue and tests the facilities. They recommend placing a long distance telephone call, trying the food and staying in the approved accommodation.

Two documents that are a good starting point for making an informed choice about the venue are the venue map and the list of facilities. However, *Rostrum* (n.d.) recommends that the event manager meet with the venue management before making any commitment to hire the venue. The principal purpose of this meeting is to check the accuracy of the two documents, since the map, and the list of facilities and the photographs can often be out of date or aimed at promoting the venue rather than imparting detailed information. The photograph of the venue, for example, may be taken with a wide-angle lens so that all the facilities are included. Such a photograph may not give a realistic view of the site if it is being used for event design.

AUDIENCE AND GUESTS

The larger issues of audience (customer) logistics have been described in chapter 10. The event staging considerations concerning the audience are:
• position of entrances and exits
• arrival times — dump or trickle
• seating and sight lines
• facilities.

Goldblatt (1997) emphasises the importance of the entrance and reception area of an event in establishing the event theme, and suggests that the organiser should look at it from the guest's point of view. It is in this area that appropriate signage and meeting and greeting become important to the flow of 'traffic' and to the wellbeing of the guests. An example of a carefully planned entrance area was at the 1998 Woodford Folk Festival, where the children's area was entered through the mouth of a large papier-mâché dragon.

Once the guests have entered the event area, problems can occur that are specific to the type of event. In the case of conferences, audiences immediately head for the back rows. Interestingly, Graham et al. (1995, p. 65) mention the opposite problem occurs at sports events, where the front rows are rushed as soon as the gates open. The solution, therefore, is in the type of admission. For example, organisers can adopt reserved seating methods, using ticket numbers or roped-off sections and a designated seating plan. The style of seating can be chosen to suit the event; theatre, classroom and banquet type seating are three examples. Ultimately, the seating plan has to take into consideration:
• type of seating — fixed or moveable
• the size of the audience

- the method of audience arrival
- safety factors, including emergency exits and fire regulations
- placement and size of the aisles
- sight lines to the performances, speakers or audiovisual displays
- disabled access
- catering needs.

The facilities provided for the guests will depend on the type of event. Referring to figure 11.4, the corporate event will focus on particular audience facilities as they relate to hospitality and catering, whereas a festival event will concentrate on audience facilities as they relate to entertainment. For example, there are no chairs for the audience in some of the Port Fairy Folk Festival performance areas but, because of the nature of the festival, spectators are happy to bring their own or sit on the ground. At the other end of the spectrum, the 1998 Australian Petroleum Production and Exploration Association Conference Dinner, organised by Sing Australia in the Great Hall at Parliament House, Canberra, had high quality furnishings and facilities.

THE STAGE

A stage at an event is rarely the same as a theatrical stage complete with proscenium arch and auditorium. It can range from the back of a truck to a barge in a harbour. It is important to note that, in event management, the term 'stage' can be applied to the general staging area and not just to a purpose built stage. However, all stages require a stage map called the stage plan. The stage plan is simply a bird's-eye view of the performance area, showing the infrastructure, such as lighting fixtures, entrances, exits and power outlets. The stage plan is one of the staging tools (as shown in figure 11.11) and a communication device that enables the event to run smoothly. For large events, the stage plan is drawn in different ways for different people, and supplied on a 'need-to-know basis'. For example, a stage plan for the lighting technician would look different from the plan for the performers. The master stage plan contains all these different plans, each drawn on a separate layer of transparent paper. Other plans that are used in event design are the front elevation and side elevation. In contrast to the bird's-eye view that the stage plan gives, these plans show the staging area as a ground-level view from the front and side, respectively. They assist in establishing the audience's sight lines; that is, the audience's view of the staging area and performers.

An example of when a large stage plan for a special event was used was for the conference of the Société Internationale d'Urologie in Sydney in 1996. The 3000 guests were treated to three streams of entertainment that reflected modern Australia: 'multicultural', including a lion dance and middle eastern dancers; 'land and sea', including a large sailing boat and Aboriginal and Australiana entertainers; and 'cities', with fashion parades and modern dancers.

Figure 11.4
An example of a stage plan

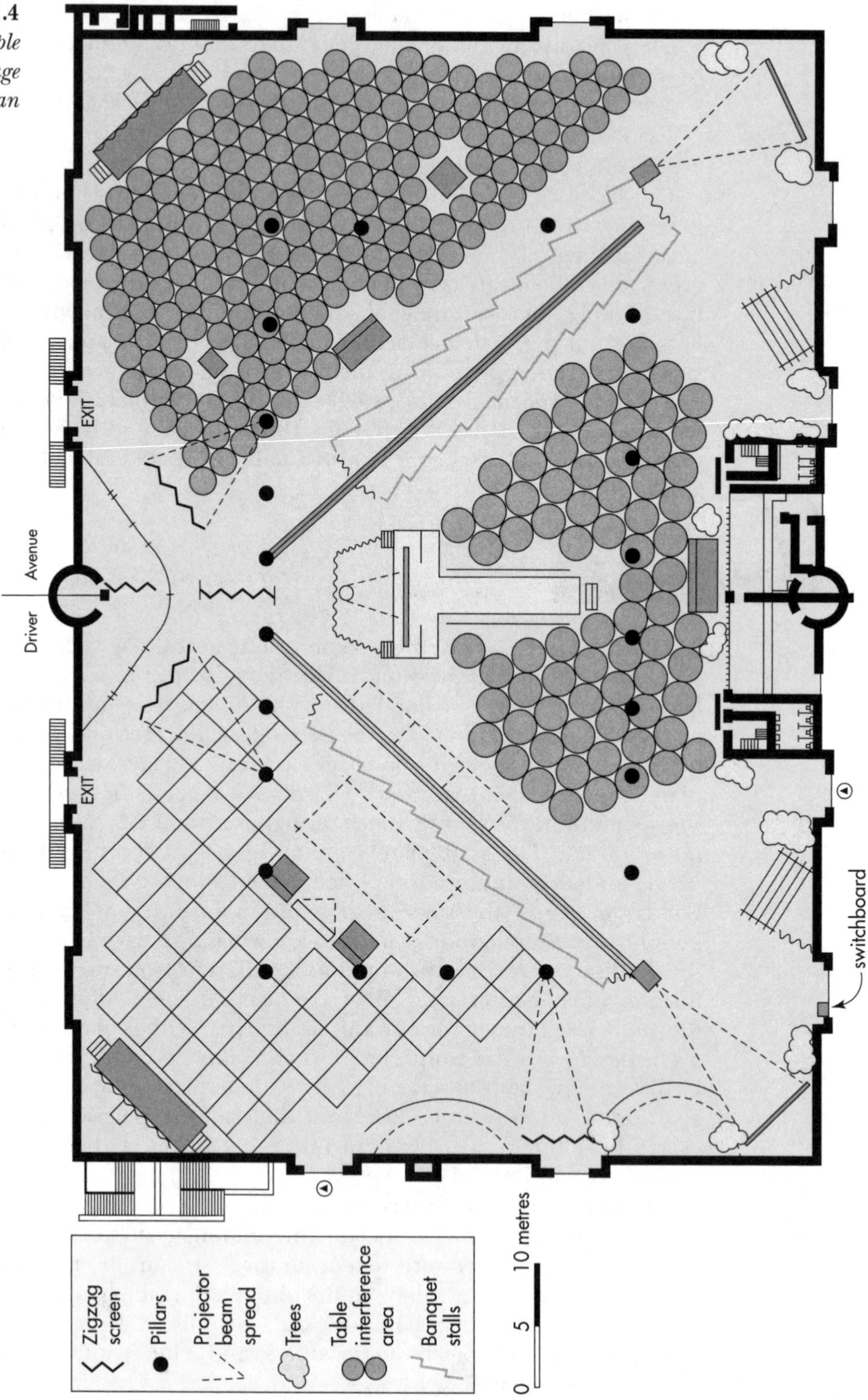

Zigzag screen

Pillars

Projector beam spread

Trees

Table interference area

Banquet stalls

Driver

Avenue

EXIT

EXIT

switchboard

0   5   10 metres

Roger Foley, of Fogg Production, the creator of the Australian Multi-cultural Show, described the stage plan:

■ The stage plan is 100 per cent accurate. I went to the building's architects to get an exact drawing and we used that as the master stage plan. The accuracy of having all the building's peculiarities on a plan allowed all the sub-contractors to anticipate any problems in setting up. [There were] one-metre markings on the building's circumference. All these little things enabled the whole show, including 13 stages and 21 food stalls, to be set up and bumped out in 24 hours. A stage plan for each of the individual stages was created by enlarging that section from the master plan and filling in the necessary information. ■

When the staging of an event includes a large catering component, the stage plan is referred to as the venue layout or floor plan. This is the case in many corporate and conference events, where hospitality and catering become a major part of the staging. Figure 11.5 illustrates how the focus on the elements of staging changes according to the style of event.

■ **Figure 11.5**   *The relationship between types of events and the relative importance of the staging elements*

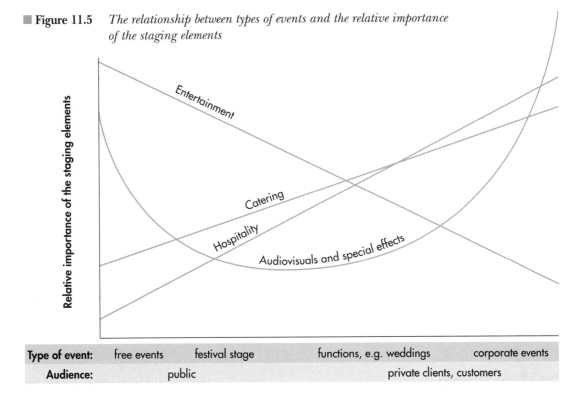

Type of event:	free events	festival stage	functions, e.g. weddings	corporate events
Audience:		public		private clients, customers

The stage manager is the person in control of the performance and for signalling the cues that coordinate the work of the performers. The scheduling of the event on a particular stage is generally the responsibility of the event manager. The stage manager makes sure that this happens according to the plan. The public face of the event may be called the master of ceremonies (MC) or compere. The compere and the stage manager work closely together to ensure that all goes according to the plan. The compere may also make public announcements such as those about lost children and program changes.

The combination of electric wiring, hot lights, special effects, the fast movement of performers and staff in a small space that is perhaps two metres above ground level makes the risk management of the staging area particularly important. At the event, stage safety is generally the responsibility of the stage manager. Figure 11.6 lists a selection of safety considerations.

■ Figure 11.6
Factors to consider in stage safety

- There must be a well-constructed stage, preferably done professionally by a company with adequate insurance.
- There must be clear well-lit access points to the stage.
- All protrusions and steps should be secured and clearly marked.
- Equipment and boxes should be placed out of the way and well marked.
- There should be work lights that provide white lighting before and after the event.
- All electric cabling must be secured.
- A first-aid kit and other emergency equipment should be at hand.
- There must be clear guidelines on who is in authority during an emergency.
- A list of all relevant contact numbers should be made.

The director of the Port Fairy Folk Festival gives this advice for stage managers:

> ■ Make sure you anticipate the many little things that can ruin an otherwise great concert experience. Watch out for distracting buzzes or cracks in the sound (e.g. from powerful fridges); settle out of control children or noisy audiences; ensure all small stage requirements are there (e.g. chair, stool, table, water); ensure you have competent MCs who are well prepared; stop delays before they start. ■

The backstage area is a private room or tent near the performance area and is set aside for the performers and staff. It provides the crew with a place to relax and the performers with a place to prepare for the performance and wind down afterwards. It can be used for storage of equipment and for communication between the stage manager and performers, and it is where the food and drink are kept.

POWER

Staging of any event involves large numbers of people and to service this crowd electricity is indispensable. It should never be taken for granted. Factors that need to be considered concerning power are:
- type of power — three phase or single phase
- amount of power needed, particularly at peak times

- emergency power
- position and number of power outlets
- types of leads and distance from power source to device
- the correct wiring of the venue, since old venues can often be improperly earthed
- the incoming equipment's volt/amp rating
- safety factors, including the covering of leads and the possibility of electricity earth leakage as a result of rain
- local and State regulations regarding power.

LIGHTS

Lighting at a venue has two functions. Pragmatically, lights allow everyone to see what is happening; artistically, they are integral to the design of the event. The general venue or site lighting is important in that it allows all the other aspects of staging to take place. For this reason, it is usually the first item on the check list when deciding on a venue. Indoor lights include signage lights (exit, toilets etc.) as well as those illuminating specific areas such as catering and ticket collection. Outside the venue, lighting is required for venue identification, safety, security and sponsor signs.

Once the general venue or site lighting is confirmed, lighting design needs to be considered. The questions to ask when considering lighting are both practical and aesthetic. They include the following.

- Does it fit in with and enhance the overall event theme?
- Can it be used for ambient lighting as well as performance lighting?
- Is there a back-up?
- What are the power requirements (lights can draw far more power than the sound system)?
- Will it interfere with the electrics of other systems? For example, a dimmer board can create an audible buzz in the sound system.
- Does it come with a light operator, that is, the person responsible for the planning of the lighting with the lighting board?
- What light effects are needed (strobe, cross fading) and can the available lights do this?
- What equipment is needed, (e.g. trees and cans), and is there a place on the site or in the venue to erect it?
- How can the lighting assist in the safety and security of the event?

The lighting plot or lighting plan is a map of the venue that shows the type and position of the lighting. As Reid (1995) points out, the decisions that the event manager has to make when creating a lighting plan are:

- placement of the lights
- the type of lights, including floods and follow spots
- where the light should be pointed
- what colours to use.

The principal reason for having sound equipment at an event is so that all the audience can clearly hear the music, speeches and audio effects. The sound system also is used to:
- communicate between the sound engineer and the stage manager (talk-back or intercom)
- monitor the sound
- create a sound recording of the event
- broadcast the sound to other venues or through other media, including television, radio and the Internet.

This means that the type of equipment used needs to be designed according to the:
- type of sound to be amplified, including spoken word and music
- size and make-up of the audience. An older audience, for example, may like the music at a different volume from a younger audience.
- acoustic properties of the room. Some venues have a bad echo problem, for example.
- theme of the event. A sound system painted bright silver may look out of place at a black tie dinner.

The choice of size, type and location of the sound speakers at an event can make a difference to the guests' experience of the sound. Figure 11.7 shows two simplified plans for speaker positions at a venue. The speakers may all be next to the stage, which is common at music concerts, or distributed around the site. They may also be flown from supports above the audience. At a large site, with speakers widely distributed, the sound engineers need to take into account the natural delay of sound travelling from the various speakers to the members of the audience.

■ **Figure 11.7**
Two examples of audio speaker layout

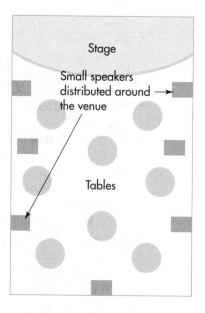

For small events, a simple public address (PA) system may be used. This consists of a microphone, microphone stand and one or two speakers. It is basically the same as a home stereo system with a microphone added, and generally has only enough power to reach a small audience. The quality of sound produced makes such systems suitable for speeches only.

For larger events that have more complex sound requirements, a larger sound system is needed. This would incorporate:

- microphones, which may include lapel mikes and radio mikes
- microphone stands
- cabling, including from the microphones to the mixing desk
- mixing desk, which adjusts the quality and level of the sound coming from the microphones before it goes out the speakers
- amplifier
- speakers, which can vary in size from bass speakers to treble speakers, and which enhance the quality of the sound within a certain sound spectrum
- sound engineer or sound technician, who looks after all aspects of the sound, particularly the sound quality that is heard by the audience
- back-up equipment, including spare leads and microphones.

The next step up from this type of system includes all of the above as well as:

- foldback speakers (are also called monitors) that channel the sound back to the speakers or performers so they can hear themselves over the background sound
- foldback mixing desk
- foldback engineer who is responsible for the quality of sound going through the monitors.

If an event needs a sound system managed by a sound engineer, time must be allocated to tune the sound system. This means that the acoustic qualities of the venue are taken into account by trying out the effect of various sound frequencies within the venue. This is the reason for the often-heard 'testing, one, two, one, two' as a sound system is being prepared. The sound engineer is also looking for any sound feedback problems. Feedback is an unwanted, often high-pitched sound that occurs when the sound coming out of the speakers is picked up by the microphones and comes out of the speakers again, thereby building on the original sound. To avoid the problem of feedback, microphones must be positioned so that they face away from sound speakers. The tuning of a large sound system is one of the main reasons for having a sound check or run-through before an event. Figure 11.8 shows a simplified sound run-through prior to an event.

■ **Figure 11.8** *A simple flow chart for sound systems*

Volume and sound leakage during an event can become a major problem. Local councils can close an event if there are too many complaints from residents. At some venues, for example, there are volume switches that automatically turn off the power if the sound level is too high. At multi-venue events, sound leakage between stages can be minimised by:

- thoughtful placement of the stages
- careful positioning of all sound speakers (including the monitors)
- constant monitoring of the volume level
- careful programming of the events on each stage in a way that avoids interference.

AUDIOVISUAL AND SPECIAL EFFECTS

Many event managers hire lighting and sound from separate companies and integrate their services into the overall design of the event. However, there are suppliers that provide both lighting and sound equipment and act as consultants prior to the event. These audiovisual companies can supply a fully integrated system of film, video, slides and often special effects. However, most audiovisual companies are specialists in flat-screen presentations, and the special effect area is often best left to specialists in this field. For example, pyrotechnics obviously require different skills and licences from ice sculptors. Complex events that use a variety of special effects and audiovisuals require a coordinator who is familiar with the event theme and knows how to link all the specialist areas to each other. This coordinator is called the event producer. Although the terms 'event manager', 'stage manager' and 'event producer' are confusing, they are terms that are used in the industry. The position of event producer is created when there are many different specialists involved in the event. Organisers of corporate events, including product launches and conferences, often sub-contract the audiovisual elements, because the specialist knowledge required means an expert is needed to operate these systems effectively. The decision to use an audiovisual company for an event depends on:

- how the audiovisual presentation fits in with the overall event design
- the budget allocated to the event
- the skills of the audiovisual company, including its technical hardware, software and the abilities of the audiovisual producer and writer.

For large-budget events, the audiovisual company will act as a consultant, with the producer and writer researching and creating a detailed audiovisual script.

Roger Foley of Fogg Production is an expert in the area of 'illuminating art as entertainment and performance'. He regards the essence of an event as the special effects. His aim is to make the event itself a special effect. 'A special effect is anything that is not anticipated or expected. It must heighten the awareness of the viewers and increase their anticipation, sensitivity and receptiveness. The result is to make it easy to get across the message of the event.' Roger emphasises the need to take command completely of all the elements of the special effect. The event producer must know exactly what they are getting when hiring specialists. Fireworks, for example, must be individually listed, fully integrated into the event and not just left to the specialist. The timing of setting off the various devices must be exact, without any gaps.

According to Goldblatt (1997), special effects at an event are used to attract attention, generate excitement and sustain interest. In larger festivals, such as the opening of the Melbourne Festival on the Yarra River, the pyrotechnics become part of the overall logistics planning. Event managers and planners must fully realise the importance of event decoration, scenery and appropriate props as an enhancing tool for the staging of any event.

Because much of the audiovisual and special effects technology is highly complex, it is often 'preprogrammed'. This means that all lighting, audiovisual and sound 'presets' (technical elements positioned prior to the event), including the changing light and sound levels and the cueing of video and slide presentations, can be programmed into the controlling computer. The computer control of much of the audiovisuals means that the whole presentation can be fully integrated and set up well in advance. Because these aspects are prearranged, including all the cue times, the advantage is that few technicians are needed to control these operations during the event. The disadvantages are that spontaneity can be taken from the event and, the more complex the technology, the more things can go wrong. Moreover, the technology becomes the master of the cue times and it is nearly impossible to take advantage of any unforeseen opportunities.

CATERING

Catering can be the major element in staging, depending on the theme and nature of an event. Most purpose-built venues already have catering. For example, Parliament House in Canberra contracts with catering companies. The conference dinners that take place in the Great Hall can only use the in-house caterers. Figure 11.9 illustrates some of the many factors to be considered in catering.

The event producer Reno Dal points out with regard to aspects of catering:

■ My rule for the staff to client ratio at a corporate function is:
silver service, 1 to 10 ratio;
five-star service 1 to 25 ratio;
general catering 1 to 50 ratio.

I emphasise that there should be 'waves of service'. This means that the main course and beverage arrive at the right time and then waiters leave the guests until the appropriate moment for the next course. I like to see each table as a stage, with the placements presented in the same manner as a theatrical stage. The waiters become the performers dressed to the theme. The waiters love it — after all, it's a difficult job at the best of times. ■

Figure 11.9

Issues to be considered when arranging catering for an event

In-house or contracted?

The advantage of in-house catering is the knowledge of the venue. The advantage of contract catering is that the event manager may have a special arrangement with the caterer that has been built up over time; the event manager can choose all aspects of the catering; and the catering can be tendered out and a competitive bid sought.

Quality control factors to consider

- Appropriateness and enhancement of the event theme
- Menu selection and design, including special diets and food displays
- Quality of staff and supervision
- Equipment, including style and quantity, and selection of in-house or hired
- Cleanliness
- Cultural appropriateness — a major consideration in a culturally diverse society
- Staff to guest ratio

Costs

- Are there any guarantees, including those against loss and breakages?
- What are the payment terms?
- Who is responsible for licences and permits: the caterer, the venue or event management?
- What deposits and up front fees are there?
- What is the per capita expenditure? Is each guest getting value commensurate with the client's expenditure?

Waste management

- Must occur before, during and after the event
- Must conform to health regulations and environmental concerns
- Must be appropriate to the event theme

As Graham et al. (1995) stress, the consumption of alcoholic beverages at an event gives rise to many concerns for the event manager. These include the special training of staff, which party holds the licence (venue, event manager or client), and the legal age for consumption. The possible problems that arise from the sale of alcohol, for example, increased audience noise at the end of the event and general behavioural problems, can affect almost all aspects of the event. The decision on whether to allow the sale or consumption of alcohol can be crucial to the success of an event and needs careful thought.

There are a variety of ways that the serving of alcohol can be negotiated with a caterer. The drinks service can be from the bar or may be served at the table by the glass, bottle or jug. A caterer may offer a 'drinks package', which means that the drinks are free for, say, the first hour of the catered event. A subtle result of this type of deal is that the guest can find it hard to find a drinks waiter in the first hour.

PERFORMERS

The 'talent' (as performers are often called) at an event can range from music groups to motivational speakers to specially commissioned shows. A performing group can form a major part of an event's design. The major factors to consider when employing artists are listed below.

- **Contact.** The event's entertainment coordinator needs to establish contact only with the person responsible for the employment of the artist or artists. This could be the artist, an agent representing the artist, or the manager of a group. It is important to establish this line of authority at the beginning when working with the artists.
- **Staging requirements.** A rock band, for example, will have more complex sound requirements than a folk singer. These requirements are usually listed on a document called the spec (specification) sheet. Many groups will also have their own stage plan illustrating the area needed and their preferred configuration of the performance area.
- **Availability for rehearsal, media attention and performance.** The available times given by the artists' management should include the time it takes for the artists to set up on stage as well as the time it takes to vacate the stage or performance area. These are referred to as the time needed for 'set-up' and 'pull-down'. These times need to be considered when, for example, scheduling a series of rehearsals with a number of performing groups.
- **Accompanying personnel.** Many artists travel with an entourage that can include technicians, cooks, stylists and bodyguards. It is important to establish their numbers, and what their roles and needs are.
- **Contracts and legal requirements.** The agreement between the event manager and the performers is described in chapter 9. Of particular importance to the staging are union minimum rates and conditions, the legal structure of the artists and issues such as workers' compensation and public liability. Copyright is also important as its ownership can affect the use of the performance for broadcast and future promotions.
- **Payment.** Most performing groups work on the understanding that they will be paid immediately for their services. Except for 'headline' acts that have a company structure, the 30-, 60- or 90-day invoicing cycle is not appropriate for most performers, who rarely have the financial resources that would allow them to wait for payment.

Performers come from a variety of performance cultural backgrounds. This means that different performers have different expectations about the facilities available for them and how they are to be treated. Theatre performers and concert musicians, for example, expect direct performance guidelines — conducting, scripting or a musical score. Street and outdoor festival performers, on the other hand, are used to less formal conditions and to improvising.

Supervision of performers in a small theatre is generally left to the assistant stage manager, whereas a festival stage may not have this luxury and it may be the stage manager's responsibility. Regardless of who undertakes it, supervision cannot be overlooked. The person responsible needs to make contact with the artists on arrival, give them the appropriate run sheets, introduce them to the relevant crew members and show them the location of the green room (the room in which performers and invited guests are entertained). At the end of the performance, the artists' supervisor needs to assist them in leaving the area.

THE CREW

The chapter on leadership (chapter 5) discussed the role of staff and volunteers at an event. While a large festival or sport event will usually rely on the work of volunteers, staging tends to be handled by professionals. Dealing with cueing, working with complex and potentially dangerous equipment and handling professional performers leaves little room for indecision and inexperience. Professionalism is essential when staging an event. For example, the staging of a concert performance will need skilled sound engineers, roadies, security staff, stage crew, ticket sellers and even ushers. (The roadies are the skilled labourers that assist with the set up and breakdown of the sound and lights.) The crew is selected by matching the tasks involved to the skills of each crew member and ensuring that they all have the ability to work together.

The briefing is the meeting, before the event, at which the crew members are given the briefs, or roles, that match their skills. The names and jobs of the crew members are then kept on a contact and responsibility sheet.

Neil Cameron, the organiser of many events and lantern parades around Australia and overseas, stresses the importance of being 'brief' at the briefing. His events involve large numbers of performers moving near fire sculptures. These sculptures can be over three storeys high and take weeks to build. He first briefs the support organisations, such as St John Ambulance and the Fire Brigade, and emphasises the importance of communication and chain of command. At the crew briefing, Neil is conscious of not overloading the leaders with too much information.

The event producer should also not forget that the crew comes with an enormous amount of experience in staging events. They can provide valuable input into the creation and design of the event.

It is also interesting to note that the changes in the events industry, particularly in the audiovisual area, are reflected in the make-up and number of crew members. As event producer Mark Cavanagh points out:

■ Events in 1998 compared to those as recently as the early 90s require [far fewer] technical staff. When we produced the launch of the *Good Food Guide* for 800 guests, the entire presentation, including rapidly evolving imagery in sync with a variable sound score, only needed two technical staff on the night. ■

HOSPITALITY

A major part of the package offered to sponsors is hospitality (Catherwood & van Kirk 1992). What will the sponsors expect event management to provide for them and their guests? They may require tickets, food and beverages, souvenirs and gifts. As well as the sponsors, the event may benefit in the long term by offering hospitality to stakeholders, VIPs and others, including politicians, media units, media personalities, clients of the sponsor, potential sponsors, partners and local opinion leaders. They are all referred to as the guests of the event.

The invitation may be the first impression of the event that the potential guest receives, and it therefore needs to convey the theme of the event. It should create a desire to attend as well as impart information. Figure 11.10 is a check list for making sure the various elements of hospitality are covered.

In their informative work on sports events, Graham et al. (1995 p. 84) describe the four stages for achieving success in the provision of hospitality to guests. Stage 1 is to know the guests' expectations. Stage 2 is to exceed the guests' expectations, particularly through providing extra amenities. Stage 3 is to be responsive to changes in the guests' needs during the event. Stage 4 is to evaluate the hospitality at the event so that it can be improved next time.

Corporate sponsors may have a variety of reasons for attending the event and these have to be taken into account in hospitality planning. Graham et al. (1995) suggest networking opportunities for business, an incentive for a high sales performance, an opportunity for entertaining possible clients, or just the creation of goodwill from their customers.

The hospitality experience is of particular importance at corporate events. In one sense, such an event is centred around hospitality (see figure 11.5). As it is a private function, there is no public and the members of the audience are the guests. Most of the items on the hospitality check list, from the invitations to the personal service, are applicable to staging these events. For the guests, the hospitality experience is fundamental to the event experience.

Figure 11.10
*Looking after
corporate
sponsors — a
hospitality
check list*

Hospitality check list

Invitations

☐ Is the design of high quality and is it innovative?

☐ Does the method of delivery allow time to reply? Would hand delivery or e-mail be appropriate?

☐ Does the content of the invitation include time, date, name of event, how to RSVP, directions and parking?

☐ Should promotional material be included with the invitation?

Arrival

☐ Has timing been planned so that guests arrive at the best moment?

☐ What are the parking arrangements?

☐ Who will do the meeting and greeting? Will there be someone there to welcome them to the event?

☐ Have waiting times been reduced? For example, will guests receive a welcome cocktail while waiting to be booked into the accommodation?

Amenities

☐ Is there to be a separate area for guests? This can be a marquee, corporate box (at a sporting event) or a club room.

☐ What food and beverages will be provided? Is there a need for a special menu and personal service?

☐ Is there a separate, high-quality viewing area of the performance with good views and facilities?

☐ Has special communication, such as signage or an information desk, been provided?

Gifts

☐ Have tickets to the event, especially for clients, been organised?

☐ What souvenirs (programs, pins, T-shirts, CDs) will there be?

☐ Will there be a chance for guests to meet the 'stars'?

Departure

☐ Has guest departure been timed so that they do not leave at the same time as the rest of the audience?

THE PRODUCTION SCHEDULE

The terms used in the staging of events come from both the theatre and film production. A rehearsal is a run-through of the event, reproducing as closely as possible the actual event. For the sake of 'getting it right on the night', there may also need to be a technical rehearsal and a dress rehearsal. A production meeting, on the other hand, is a get-together of those responsible for producing an event. It involves the stage manager and the event producer, representatives of the lighting and sound crew or audiovisual specialists, representatives of the performers and the master of ceremonies. It is held at the performance site or stage as near to the time of the event as possible. At this crucial meeting:

• final production schedule notes are compared
• possible last-minute production problems are brought up
• the flow of the event is summarised
• emergency procedures are reviewed
• the compere is introduced and familiarised with the production staff
• the communication system is tested (Neighbourhood Arts Unit 1991, p. 50).

The production schedule is the main document for staging. It is the master document from which various other schedules, including the cue or prompt sheet and the run sheets, are created. Goldblatt (1997, p. 143) defines it as the detailed listing of tasks, with specific start and stop times occurring from the set-up of the event's equipment (also known as 'bump-in') to the eventual removal of all the equipment (bump-out or load-out). It is often a written form of the Gantt chart (see page 231, chapter 10) with four columns: time, activity, location and responsibility. Production schedules can also contain a description of the relevant elements of the event.

Two particularly limited times on the schedule are the 'bump-in' and 'bump-out' times. The bump-in is the time when the necessary infrastructure can be brought in, unloaded and set up. The bump-out is the time when the equipment can be dismantled and removed. Although the venue or site may be available to receive the equipment at any time, there are many other factors that set the bump-in time. The hiring cost and availability of equipment are two important limiting factors. In most cases, the larger items must arrive first. These may include fencing, tents, stage, food vans and extra toilets. Next could come the audiovisual equipment and finally the various decorations. Supervision of the arrival and set-up of the equipment can be crucial to minimising problems during the event. The contractor who delivers and assembles the equipment often is not the operator of the equipment. This can mean that once it is set up, it is impossible to change it without recalling the contractor.

Bump-out can be the most difficult time of an event, because the excitement is over, the staff are often tired and everyone is in a hurry to leave. Nevertheless, these are just the times when security and safety are important. The correct order of bump-out needs to be on a detailed schedule.

This is often the reverse of the bump-in schedule. The last item on the checklist for the bump-out is the 'idiot check'. This refers to the check that is done after everything is cleared from the performance area, and some of the staff do a search for anything that may be left.

The run sheets are lists of the order of specific jobs at an event. The entertainers, for example, have one run sheet while the caterers have another. Often the production schedule is a loose-leaf folder that includes all the run sheets. The cue sheets are a list of times that initiate a change of any kind during the event and describe what happens on that change. The stage manager and audiovisual controller use them.

RECORDING THE EVENT

By their very nature, special events are ephemeral. A good quality recording of the event is essential for most event companies, as it demonstrates the ability of the organisation and can be used to promote the event company. It can also help in evaluating the event and, if necessary, in settling later disputes, whether of a legal or other nature. The method of recording the event can be on video, sound recording or as photographs. Making a sound recording can be just a matter of putting a cassette in the sound system and pressing the record button. However, any visual recording of the event will require planning. In particular, the correct lighting is needed for depth of field. Factors that need to be considered for video recording are:

• What is it for — promotion, legal purposes or for sale to the participants?
• What are the costs in time and money?
• How will it affect the event? Will the video cameras be a nuisance? Will they need white lighting?
• What are the best vantage points?

Recording the event is not a decision that should be left to the last minute; it needs to be factored into the planning of the event. Once an event is played out there is no going back.

CONTINGENCIES

As with large festivals and hallmark events, the staging of any event has to make allowances for what might go wrong. 'What if' sessions need to be implemented with the staff. A stage at a festival may face an electricity blackout; performers may not arrive; trouble may arrive instead. Therefore, micro-contingency plans need to be in place. All these must fit in with the overall festival risk-management and emergency plans. At corporate events in well-known venues, the venue will have its own emergency plan that needs to be given to all involved.

The staging of an event can range from presenting a show of multicultural dancers and musicians at a stage in a local park, to the launch of the latest software product at the most expensive hotel in town. All events share common staging elements including sound, lights, food and beverages, performers and special effects. All these elements need to create and enhance the event theme. The importance of each of these elements depends on the type of event. To stage an event successfully a number of tools are used: the production schedule, the stage plan and the contact and responsibility list, all of which are shown in figure 11.11.

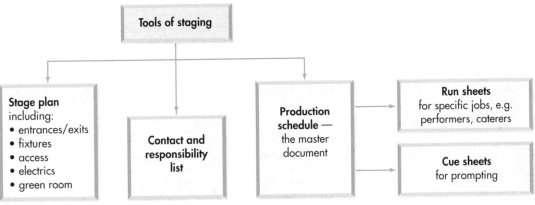

■ **Figure 11.11** *A summary of the tools necessary for staging an event*

Questions

1 Analyse an event into its staging elements and discuss the relationships between each of these elements.

2 Choose a theme for a company's staff party. How would you relate all the elements of staging to the theme?

3 Compile a stage plan, contact responsibility list and production schedule with the relevant run sheets for:
(a) a corporate party for the clients, staff and customers of a company
(b) a fun run with entertainment
(c) a large wedding
(d) one of the stages for a city arts festival.

The Engineering Excellence Awards is an annual event that draws over 800 people to the Sydney Town Hall each September to witness the presentation of citations for excellence, both for projects and individual achievement. Because the event celebrates excellence in engineering, the design and engineering of the event must be of a high standard.

From the initial briefing, it was decided that the ceremony had several purposes. We had to produce an event that provided:
- the right level of dignity
- a way of honouring the entrants and winners
- recognition of the sponsors
- a sense of warmth that would appeal to the 400 partners attending the night
- a reflection of the professional values of the Institution of Engineers and an enhancement of its public image, both for members and the general public.

To satisfy these goals, it was necessary to develop a strategy of shifting emphases while still keeping the main goal in sight — the presentation of the awards. Thus we developed a sequence for the night that offered each of the stakeholders recognition, value and enjoyment.

The following production schedule for the 1997 awards night outlines the basic sequence of events for the rehearsal and the actual show.

PRODUCTION SCHEDULE
Engineering Excellence Awards 97
Sydney Town Hall

SET-UP AND REHEARSAL SCHEDULE

Time	Location/Items	Duration
7:00	Town Hall lighting staff on call (2 people)	
7:00	Load in data projectors and computer systems.	2:00
7:30	Town Hall lighting staff de-rig bar for screen and Sony 1270 data projector.	2:00
8:00	Town Hall staff do room lighting while screen is set	2:00
	NB Screen position: Bar 3	
	NB Screen size: 30 × 40 feet	
	Staging: two lecterns onstage — steps in middle	
	Install follow spots.	1:00
10:00	Install video-camera system.	2:00

Time	Location/Items	Duration
10:30	Tables put in place in main hall.	
11:00	Lighting: general focus lighting — front bars	1:00
11:00	Town Hall staff — sound set-up	1:00
12:01	Lighting break	1:00
12:01	Focus data projectors.	2:00
12:01	Focus video projector.	1:00
14:00	Banquet tables in place	0:30
15:00	Technical rehearsal (with follow spots) and full sound & lighting system operational	1:00
16:00	Dress rehearsal (with MC) Step through entire awards script.	1:00
16:30	Centrepieces in place	0:30
17:00	End dress rehearsal; technical staff meal break (60 mins)	1:00
18:00	Dress rehearsal with finalists	0:30
18:15	Stand by for guests	
	Linear duration in hours — sum:	19:30
	Duration available:	11:15

SHOW SCHEDULE, 24 SEPTEMBER 1997

	Main Hall	
18:00	Stand by for guests	0:01
18:00	Dress rehearsal for finalists (100 pax [people])	0:30
18:25	The organ plays quietly.	
18:30	**Guests arrive**	0:30
	Official party greets guests (till 6:40 p.m.).	
18:30	Caterers serve drinks in vestibule.	0:10
	Entrées *mise en place* [entrées preset]	
18:40	Open Main Hall doors.	0:01
	Caterers open hall doors and cease vestibule service.	
18:41	Quartet plays background music.	0:18
	Caterers stop serving drinks in foyer.	
	Caterers commence drink service in main hall.	
18:45	VIP arrives, greeted by officials.	0:15
	Proceed to separate reception room.	
19:00	MC: (video) 'Ladies & gentlemen, please be upstanding.'	0:01
	Arrival of the official party	
19:01	Play the national anthem.	0:01
	MC: 'Ladies & gentlemen, the Awards Chairman'	
19:02	Awards Chairman welcomes official guests.	0:03
19:05	MC: 'Back soon for Awards of Personal Achievement'	0:01
19:06	Dinner served	0:20
	Caterers note: serve official table first.	
	Video: roll sponsor video (20 min).	
19:20	Young engineers to stand by backstage	

Time	Location/Items		Duration
19:26	**After officials finish their main course**		
19:26	Organ concludes with fanfare.		0:02
	Stage brightens for MC's entry.		
19:28	MC thanks organist and welcomes/settles guests.		0:02
	Invites Sydney Division President onstage.		
	(He comes from his table, as does VIP.)		
	Official proceedings commence.		
19:30	Sydney Division President		0:05
	who asks VIP onstage		
19:35	VIP speech		0:05

PERSONAL ACHIEVEMENT AWARDS

Time	Location/Items		Duration
19:40	MC introduces four engineering students who enter from rear of stage.	1P*	0:01
	MC explains Student Engineer award.		
19:41	Sponsor announces winner.		0:01
19:42	Young Student Engineer speech		0:01
19:43	MC introduces Community & Environment Award.	2P	0:00
19:43	Sponsor announces winner.		0:01
19:44	Winner to lectern		0:01
19:45	Winner speech		0:01
19:46	MC introduces Bachelor of Engineering Final Project Award.	3P	0:00
19:47	Sponsor announces winner.		0:01
19:48	Winner to lectern		0:01
19:49	Winner speech		0:01
19:50	MC introduces B. Tech & FE Project Award.	4P	0:00
19:50	Sponsor announces winner.		0:01
19:51	Winner to lectern		0:01
19:52	Winner speech		0:01
19:53	MC introduces Young Assoc. Engineer Award.	5P	0:00
19:54	Sponsor announces winner.		0:01
19:55	Winner to lectern		0:01
19:56	Winner speech		0:01
19:57	MC introduces Young Professional Engineer Award.	6P	0:01
19:58	Sponsor announces winner.		0:01
19:59	Winner to lectern		0:00
19:59	Winner speech		0:01
20:00	MC introduces journalists' award for best media engineering report.	7P	0:01
20:01	Sponsor announces winner.		0:01
20:02	Winner to lectern		0:00
20:03	Winner speech		0:01
20:04	MC introduces Professional Engineer of the Year Award.	8P	0:01
20:05	Sponsor announces winner.		0:01

Time	Location/Items		Duration
20:06	Winner to lectern		0:00
20:06	Winner speech		0:01
20:07	MC introduces Hollows Award.	9P	0:01
20:08	VIP announces winner.		0:01
20:09	Winner to lectern		0:00
20:10	Hollows Award & speech		0:01
20:11	Awards Chairman thanks VIP etc.		0:02
20:13	MC: 'Thanks, please enjoy meal...'		0:00
20:13	Organ plays (20 min).		0:00
20:13	Clear main course (20 mins).		0:20
20:33	Organ ends.		0:01
20:34	MC welcomes comedian.		0:01
20:35	Entertainment: comedy/music		0:30
21:05	MC thanks; announces dessert, 'back soon with...'		0:20
21:05	Dessert served, coffee cups set in place.		0:20

Caterers make sure every table has a red and a white wine bottle on it.

21:25	MC: 'Ladies & gentlemen please take your seats... The awards are about to commence.'		

PROJECT AWARDS SEQUENCE

Time	Location/Items		Duration
21:25	Opening animation		0:01
21:26	Opening video (3 min)		0:03
	Bring up house lights at end.		
21:29	MC: Intros		0:02
	Asks Sydney Division President & VIP to to present awards.		
21:31	Awards commence	A1 to A11*	
21:31	Intro & finalists (1 min)		
21:31	Finalists av. 7 = 1 min		
21:31	Sponsor speech (1)		
21:31	Winner and text (1)		
21:31	Winner's speech (1)		
21:31	13 awards × 4 mins = 52 mins		0:52
22:23	Introduce Bradfield Award		0:01
22:24	Bradfield video		0:02
22:26	Bradfield award sequence		0:05
22:31	Sydney Division President thanks VIP (Governor of NSW)		0:02
22:33	Credits video (3 mins) & animation (1 min)		0:04
22:37	Awards end		
22:37	MC concludes & introduces organist (or Tina Turner again).		0:01
	Raise screen on his cue to reveal organist.		
22:38	Organist's recital during dessert service		0:20

Time	Location/Items	Duration
22:58	Caterers: serve coffee & beverages as organ plays.	
22:58	Taped music till midnight	0:57
23:55	Lights gradually brighten, music fades...	0:05
0:00	End	0:00
	Pack up immediately after function	

* Annotations such as 1P and A1 are sequence codes.

Reno Dal, B.A. Hons (Sociology)
Executive Producer, Special Event Reno Dal Pty Ltd
© Reno Dal Pty Ltd 1998

Questions

1 Why do you think it is necessary to use sequence codes?

2 From the production schedule, make a list of the major elements in the staging, then devise two back-up plans in case equipment does not arrive at the venue or breaks down. For example, what would you do if the data projector does not arrive?

3 Why was the event set up on the day of the event and not the night before?

4 Why did the guests arrive at 6.30 p.m. and doors open at 6.40 p.m.?

5 What is the benefit of the entrées being preset?

6 Why do event producers use terms such as 'pax' instead of 'people'? Would such a term be understood by everyone in the event industry?

7 Does a production schedule give you a complete picture of an event?

REFERENCES

Cameron, N. 1993, *Fire on the Water*, Currency Press, Sydney.

Catherwood, D. & Van Kirk, R. 1992, *The Complete Guide to Special Event Management*, John Wiley & Sons, New York.

Geldard, E. & Sinclair, L. 1996, *The Sponsorship Manual*, The Sponsorship Unit, Olinda, Victoria.

Goldblatt, J. 1997, *Special Events: Best Practices in Modern Event Management*, 2nd edn, Van Nostrand Reinhold, New York.

Graham, S., Goldblatt, J. & Delpy, L. 1995, *The Ultimate Guide to Sports Event Management and Marketing*, Richard Irwin, Chicago.

Neighbourhood Arts Unit 1991, *Community Festival Handbook*, City of Melbourne.

Reid, F. 1995, *Staging Handbook*, 2nd edn, A & C Black, London.

Rostrum, vol. 32, *The Comprehensive Convention Planner's Manual*, Rank Publishing Company, Sydney.

12

Evaluation

and reporting

LEARNING OBJECTIVES

After studying this chapter, you should be able to:

- understand the role of evaluation in the event management process

- know when to evaluate an event

- understand the evaluation needs of event stakeholders

- create an evaluation plan for an event

- apply a range of techniques, including the conducting of questionnaires and surveys, in evaluating events

- describe and record the intangible impacts of events

- understand the role of economic impact studies in the evaluation of events

- prepare a final evaluation report

- use event profiles to promote the outcomes of events and to seek sponsorship

- apply the knowledge gained by evaluation to the planning of a future event.

WHAT IS EVENT EVALUATION?

Event evaluation is the process of critically observing, measuring and monitoring the implementation of an event in order to assess its outcomes accurately. It enables the creation of an event profile that outlines the basic features and important statistics of an event. It also enables feedback to be provided to event stakeholders, and plays an important role in the event management process by providing a tool for analysis and improvement.

The event management process is a cycle (see figure 12.1) in which inputting and analysing data from an event allows more informed decisions to be made and more efficient planning to be done, and improves event outcomes. This applies to individual repeat events, where the lessons learnt from one event can be incorporated in the planning of the next. It also applies to the general body of events knowledge, where the lessons learnt from individual events contribute to the overall knowledge and effectiveness of the events industry.

■ **Figure 12.1**
Evaluation and the event management process

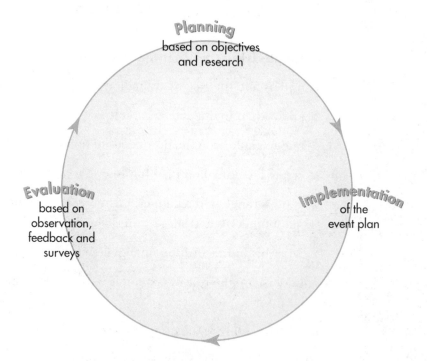

Tamworth, for example, has learnt to cope with an influx of visitors, which doubles the population of the town during the Tamworth Country Music Festival, by applying the lessons learnt each year to the logistics planning of the next year's festival. As discussed in chapter 2, New Year's Eve celebrations in Sydney have also been developed and refined over a period by intelligently feeding back information from one year's celebrations into the planning for the next.

Lessons learnt from one event can also be applied to other events or to the whole events industry. A Taste of Tasmania has solved many of its waste problems by identifying biodegradable containers, which have been adopted by other food festivals around the nation. The Sydney Royal Easter Show was used as a model to test the effectiveness of public transport systems going to and from Homebush Bay and, ultimately, the Sydney Olympics. Similarly, the Disney organisation, by perfecting quieter fireworks suited to the confines of Disneyland in the built-up area of Anaheim in California, has influenced the quality of pyrotechnics used in other markets. Innovations in event communications, products and technologies are constantly spread and refined through the process of event evaluation, which leads to better event planning, implementation and further evaluation. This in turn leads to the improvement of individual events and to an ever-growing and more knowledgeable events industry.

WHEN TO EVALUATE EVENTS

Evaluation is a process that occurs throughout the event management cycle. However, Getz (1997) and others have identified three key periods when it is useful to undertake evaluation.

■ Pre-event *assessment*

Some assessment of the factors governing an event usually takes place in the research and planning stage. This is sometimes called a feasibility study, and is used to determine what level of resources an event is likely to require, and whether or not to proceed with the event. Such a study may involve market research of the probable audience reaction to the event and some research into and prediction of attendance figures, costs and benefits. It will often compare the event with profiles and outcomes of similar previous events. The study may result in establishing targets, or benchmarks, against which the success of the project will be measured.

■ Monitoring *the event*

Event monitoring is the process of tracking the progress of an event through the various stages of implementation, and it enables factors governing the event to be adjusted. For example, ticket sales may be perceived as slow in the lead-up to an event, and this may result in increased advertising or a greater publicity effort. Monitoring the budget may result in the trimming of expenses or the freeing up of money for other areas of expenditure. Observation during the event may lead to changes which improve the delivery of the event, such as adjusting sound volume or altering the dispersal of security and cleaning staff to match changing crowd patterns. This process of monitoring is vital to quality control, and it will also provide valuable information for the final evaluation, and for future planning purposes.

■ Post-event *evaluation*

The most common form of evaluation is post-event evaluation. This involves the gathering of statistics and data on an event and analysing them in relation to the event's mission and objectives. An important aspect is usually a feedback meeting of key participants and stakeholders, at which the strengths and weaknesses of the event are discussed and observations are recorded. Post-event evaluation may also involve some form of questionnaire or survey of the event participants or audience. Such surveys seek to explore participants' opinions of the experience and to measure their levels of satisfaction with the event. They often involve the collection of data on the financial expenditure of the participants, so that the cost can be compared with the revenue generated by the event. The nature of the evaluation will be determined largely by the purpose of the event and audience for which it is intended.

REPORTING TO STAKEHOLDERS

One of the prime reasons that event managers evaluate events is to report to stakeholders.

- The host organisation will want to know what the event achieved. Did the event come in on budget and on time? Did it achieve its objectives? How many people attended and were their expectations met? For future planning purposes, it might be useful to know where they came from, how they heard about it, and whether they intend to return next year.
- The event sponsor may have other measures. Was the level of awareness of the product or service increased? What penetration did the advertising achieve? What media coverage was generated? What was the profile of the people who attended?
- Funding bodies will have grant acquittal procedures to observe, and will usually require audited financial statements of income and expenditure along with a report on the social, cultural or sporting outcomes of the event.
- Councils and government departments may want to know what the impact was on their local or State economies.
- Tourism bodies may want to know the number of visitors attracted to the area and what they spent, not only on the event, but also on travel, shopping and accommodation.

Quantified event outcomes can be very helpful to event organisers in promoting the profile and acceptance of the event. The Sydney Gay and Lesbian Mardi Gras used the 1993 and 1998 studies of the economic benefits of the Mardi Gras very effectively in promoting support for and acceptance of the event. Similarly, the Adelaide Festival has used economic impact studies to underline the contribution of the event to the South Australian economy.

EVALUATION PROCEDURES

In order to meet the many and varied reporting requirements of event stakeholders, it is necessary for the event manager to plan carefully the evaluation of the event. The evaluation will usually be more effective if it is planned from the outset and built into the event management process. Planning should include consideration of:

- what data is needed
- how, when and by whom it is to be gathered
- how it is to be analysed
- what format to use in the final reporting.

■ Data *collection*

The process of implementing the event may provide opportunities for useful data to be collected. For example, participants may be required to fill in an event entry form, which can be designed to provide useful information on numbers, age, gender, point of origin, spending patterns and so on. Ticketed events allow for a ready means of counting spectators, and the ticketing agency may be able to provide further useful information, such as the postcodes of ticket purchasers. For non-ticketed events, figures on the use of public transport and car parks and police crowd estimates can be used in calculating attendance figures. Event managers should look out for and make use of all opportunities for the collection of relevant data.

■ Observation

Staff observation and reports may provide information on a number of aspects of the event, including performance quality, audience reaction, crowd flow and adequacy of catering and toilet facilities. However, staff will provide more accurate and useful data if they are trained to observe and are given a proper reporting format, rather than being left to make casual and anecdotal observations. From the outset, staff should be made aware that observation and reporting on the event are part of their role, and they should be given appropriate guidance and benchmarks. They may be given check lists on which they are asked to evaluate items such as performance quality and audience reaction by using a scale of 1 to 5 or by ticking indicators such as below average, average, good, very good or excellent.

At Sydney's Darling Harbour, stage managers are required to complete a written report on each event, giving their estimates of attendance figures, weather conditions, performance standards and crowd reaction, and commenting on any unusual occurrences or features. Likewise, security staff are required to report on crowd behaviour, incidents, disturbances and injuries, and to estimate the size of crowds with the help of photographs taken at regular intervals by security cameras at strategic locations. By compiling these reports, by using statistics from attraction operators, and by assessing factors such as competition from other major events in the city, management is able to form profiles of individual events and to track trends over time.

Other key players in an event, such as venue owners, councils, sponsors, police and first-aid officers, can often provide valuable feedback from their various perspectives.

- Police may have observed aspects such as crowd behaviour, traffic flow and parking, and may have constructive suggestions for future planning.
- Councils may be aware of disturbance to the local community or of difficulties with street closures or compliance with health regulations.
- Sponsors may have observations based on their own attendance at the event, or may have done their own surveys on audience reaction, awareness levels and media coverage.

■ Feedback *meetings*

All stakeholders should be made aware at the outset that they will be given an opportunity to provide feedback, and that this is a vital part of the event planning process. They should be encouraged to contribute their professional observations and assessment. This may be done at a single 'de-briefing' meeting or at a series of meetings, depending on the complexity of the event. It is often useful for the date and agenda of this meeting to be made known to all parties early in the process, so that if it is not possible for them to communicate their observations during the staging of the event, then they are aware that a suitable forum will be provided during the finalisation of the event. This meeting should ensure that neither congratulations nor recriminations overshadow the important lessons that are to be learnt from the event and the consequent changes to be incorporated in future planning. It is important that all parties are listened to and that their comments are taken into account in the future planning of the event.

The topics to be addressed at the meeting will be determined by the nature and size of the event. However, the following check list is a useful starting point.

Check list for event evaluation

Aspect	Satisfactory	Requires attention	Comments
• Timing of the event • Venue • Ticketing and entry • Staging • Performance standard • Staffing levels and performance of duties • Crowd control • Security • Communications • Information and signage • Transport • Parking • Catering facilities • Toilets • First aid • Lost children • Sponsor acknowledgement • Hosting arrangements • Advertising • Publicity • Media liason			

■ Questionnaires *and surveys*

Questionnaires can range from simple feedback forms targeting event partners to detailed audience or visitor surveys undertaken by trained personnel. The scale of the questionnaire will depend upon the needs and resources of the event. Simple feedback forms can usually be designed and distributed using the event's own internal resources. They may seek to record and quantify basic data, such as the expenditure of event partners, their assessment of event management and outcomes.

Surveys are used to ascertain reliable statistical information on audience profiles and reaction and visitor patterns and expenditure. They may be implemented by direct interviews with participants or may rely on participants filling in written forms. Undertaking effective surveys requires expertise and considerable organisational resources. For event organisers with limited in-house experience and expertise, professional assistance can be called upon for tasks, ranging from the design of survey forms to the full implementation of the survey process.

In the case of repeat events, a single well-designed survey may satisfy the basic research needs of the event. Some event organisers may wish to repeat the survey each year in order to compare successive events and to establish trends, or they may want to embark on more ambitious research programs in order to investigate other aspects of the event. Whatever the scale and approach that is decided on, experts such as Getz (1998) and the publication by the National Centre for Culture and Recreation Statistics (1997) agree on certain basic factors that should be kept in mind. These are listed below.

- *Purpose.* Identify clearly the purpose and objective of the survey. A clearly stated and defined purpose is most likely to lead to a well-targeted survey with effective results.
- *Survey design.* Keep it simple. If too much is attempted in the survey, there is a danger that focus will be lost and effectiveness reduced. Questions should be clear and unambiguous, and should be tested by a 'trial run' before the actual survey.
- *Size of sample.* The number of participants must be large enough to provide an adequate sample of the audience. If in doubt, seek professional advice on the size of the sample.
- *Randomness.* The methodology employed in the selection of participants must avoid biases of age, sex and ethnicity. A procedure such as selecting every tenth person to pass through a turnstile may assist in providing a random selection.
- *Support data.* The calculation of some outcomes will depend on the collection of support data. For example, the calculation of total visitor expenditure will require accurate data on the number of visitors to the event. Then the spending pattern revealed by the survey can be multiplied by the number of visitors to provide an estimate of the total visitor expenditure for the event.

WHAT TO EVALUATE

Events have both tangible and intangible impacts. Surveys most commonly measure tangible impacts such as economic costs and benefits, because these can easily be measured. However, it is also important to evaluate the intangible impacts of events, even if this evaluation needs to be of a narrative or descriptive nature. Some of the intangibles that are hard to measure include the effect on the social life and wellbeing of a community, the sense of pride engendered by an event, and the long-term impact on the image of a place or a tourist destination.

The Survival Day concerts staged by Sydney's Aboriginal community on Australia Day have been a focus of Aboriginal identity and pride. The Festival of International Understanding at Cowra features a different national culture each year, and deliberately fosters racial tolerance. The South Pacific Festival, hosted by a different island nation every four years, has provided a strong focus for South Pacific national identity and independence. While all these events have undoubted social worth, it would be difficult, and perhaps even counterproductive, to quantify them in anything other than descriptive terms.

While the Sydney Gay and Lesbian Mardi Gras has been at the forefront of economic impact studies of events, their 1998 annual report contains a clear statement of the social and cultural values underpinning the event (1998, p. 2)

> ■ Sydney Gay & Lesbian Mardi Gras Ltd is an organisation formed out of the diverse lesbian and gay communities of Sydney to enable us to explore, express and promote the life of our combined community through a cultural focus.
>
> We affirm the pride, joy, dignity and identity of our community and its people through events of celebration.
>
> We are committed to serving our community.
>
> We seek to enable individuals and groups within our community to discover, express and develop their artistic, cultural and political skills and potential.
>
> We strive through our events of celebration to strengthen the lives and rights of gay and lesbian people both nationally and internationally. ■

In her report to Tamworth Council on the Tamworth Country Music Festival, Smyth (1998, p. 2) notes the impact of media reports on the long-term positioning of the city as Country Music Capital which:

> ■ re-inforce the 'this is where it's at' image of a sophisticated Festival which is now the accepted essence of the January event. The growing trend which sees urban dwellers in Australia desiring to embrace the image of their country's identity through clothing and lifestyle (cowboy culture), follows upon that of the United States . . . urban Australia identifies the Festival (hence the city) as almost the heartland of rural Australia. ■

ECONOMIC IMPACT STUDIES

All event managers should be familiar with constructing a simple financial balance statement of the income and expenditure of events. Until recent times, this form of reporting was considered sufficient, because most events were staged for their inherent social, cultural or sporting value to the community. However, the growing involvement of governments, tourism bodies, corporations and sponsors has brought with it an increasing need to consider the wider impacts of events.

Economic impact studies set out to measure the costs and benefits of an event to a State or region by comparing income and visitors' expenditure with the costs of putting on the event. The National Centre for Culture and Recreation Statistics (1997) has published simple guidelines for measuring the impact of festivals, which can be applied to most other events. Their publication outlines a basic methodology, and includes sample questionnaires for visitor and resident surveys.

The visitors' survey form aims to identify expenditure on items such as accommodation, food, festival tickets, other entertainment, transport, personal services, films, books and souvenirs. This survey establishes an average expenditure which can then be multiplied by the number of visitors to obtain the total visitor expenditure. The methodology takes into account the complexity of estimating the number of visitors from outside the region. It seeks to distinguish those visitors attracted by the event or who have extended their visit because of the event from those who would have visited the region anyway.

In the case of a festival that extends for more than one day or that has multiple events, the survey also takes into account the need to identify the number of days or events attended, and to weigh this in calculating the results of the survey.

A residents' survey form is also provided to identify residents who 'holidayed at home' because of the event and 'switched' their expenditure, which can then be legitimately attributed to the event. Since it is difficult to determine what they would have spent if they had gone elsewhere, their expenditure is treated the same as that of visitors to the event.

Having calculated the total visitor expenditure, it is then necessary to identify how much of this is retained in the community. A visitor's expenditure may have flow-on effects; for example, the purchase of a meal benefits not only the restaurateur who provides the meal but also, perhaps, the suppliers such as the local bakery or market gardeners. These flow-on effects are known as the indirect impact, and are calculated by the use of value-added multipliers for specific industry areas. However, the use of these multipliers is controversial, and some authorities prefer to concentrate on direct expenditure figures.

Other expenditure that needs to be taken into account when calculating the total economic impact of an event is payments to performers from outside the region and their expenditure during the event, expenditure by media from outside the region, and sponsorships or grants from outside the region.

■ **Figure 12.3**
An example of a visitor survey

[FESTIVAL NAME] VISITORS' SURVEY

The organising committee of the [Festival name] is conducting this survey to obtain information on the economic importance of the festival.

Information supplied in this survey will be treated confidentially and the results will be presented only in the form of aggregated data.

You may find it easier to complete this questionnaire at the end of your visit to the festival. However, you may wish to complete this questionnaire during your visit. If so, and you are uncertain of the answer to any question, please give what you consider to be your most likely response.

Thank you for your co-operation.

How to complete this questionnaire:

Answer questions by ticking the appropriate box or by writing in the answer.

Please add any comments you feel are necessary to clarify any of your answers.

Do not complete this questionnaire if you are under 15 years of age.

1. Are you: Male? ☐ Female? ☐
2. What is your age? Under 15 years (*no more questions*) ☐
   15–24 ☐   25–44 ☐   45–64 ☐   65 or more ☐
3. How many [festival name] performances and events did you attend?
   number ☐
4. Where do you usually live?
   [Study area] (*no more questions*) ☐
   Elsewhere in Australia ☐   Overseas ☐
5. How many nights did you stay in [study area]?   nights ☐
6. Would you have come to [study area] this year had the [festival name] not been held?
   Yes ☐   No (*go to question 10*) ☐
7. Was your visit to [study area] during the festival an additional visit especially for the festival?
   Yes (*go to question 10*) ☐   No ☐
8. Did you stay longer in [study area] on this visit because of the festival?
   Yes ☐   No (*no more questions*) ☐
9. How many more nights did you stay?   nights ☐
10. *This question is about your estimated expenditure in [study area] during your entire visit.*

    Please include all spending made by you and all members of your family (if another member of your family receives a questionnaire, you should still include their expenditure on your questionnaire).

    Remember to include payments made by cheque, bankcard and credit cards.

    On your visit, how much did you (and your partner/family) spend in [study area] on:

    Accommodation? ☐   Meals, food and drink? ☐
    Festival tickets? ☐
    Other entertainment costs (e.g. nightclubs, movies, museums)? ☐
    Transport (e.g. taxi fares, petrol, car hire)? ☐
    Personal services (e.g. hairdressing, laundry, medical)? ☐
    Other expenditure (e.g. films, souvenirs, books, cigarettes)? ☐
    Total expenditure ☐
11. How many people does this expenditure cover?
    Number of adults ☐   Number of children ☐

If you require any assistance with this questionnaire, please see one of the interviewers who handed it out. Please hand the completed questionnaire back to the interviewer or post it back in the reply paid envelope supplied. Thank you for your assistance.

(**Source:** *National Centre for Culture and Recreation Statistics, Australian Bureau of Statistics 1997,* Measuring the Impact of Festivals: Guidelines for Conducting an Economic Impact Study, *Cultural Ministers Council Statistics Working Group, Canberra*)

The full calculation of economic impacts is best undertaken by experts; it is complex and can be costly. However, by applying the guidelines and the survey shown in figure 12.3, a simple and useful snapshot of the economic impact of an event can be readily obtained.

MEDIA MONITORING AND EVALUATION

Media coverage is an important aspect of an event. This coverage can be either positive or negative depending on the event outcomes, the impact on the community and the kind of relationship built up with the media. It is important to monitor and record this coverage as part of the documentation of the event. If the event is local, it may be possible to do this by keeping a file of newspaper articles and by listening and looking for radio and television interviews and news coverage. For larger events, it may be necessary to employ a professional media-monitoring organisation that can track media coverage from a variety of sources. They will usually provide copies of print media stories and transcripts of radio interviews and news coverage. Audiotapes and videotapes of electronic coverage can be obtained for an additional charge. This coverage provides an excellent record of the event and can be used effectively in profiling the event for potential sponsors and partners.

Some media monitors will attempt to place a monetary value on media coverage, usually valuing it at around three times the cost of equivalent advertising space, on the grounds that editorial coverage is likely to be better trusted by consumers and is therefore worth more. Such valuations should be regarded as approximate only, but may provide a useful comparative assessment of media coverage.

Media coverage of the 1998 Greg Norman Holden International in Sydney was valued by ChangeData (1998) at $3.5 million. This included four days of national coverage by the Seven Network, sold on to international cable television, which opened with a shot of Greg Norman on top of the Sydney Harbour Bridge and included destinational promotion of Sydney in the form of video postcards.

EVENT EVALUATION REPORTS AND PROFILES

Once information has been collated from data collection, observation, feedback meetings and surveys, a final event evaluation report should be completed and distributed to all stakeholders. The information should provide a profile of the event, which can be included in the executive summary of the report. This profile can form the basis of a media release promoting the outcomes of the event, and can be used to begin planning for the next event and approaching sponsors. The following is an example of a media release based on the profile of an event.

■ **Figure 12.4**
*Media release
on economic
impact of
1997 Ford
Australian
Open*

MEDIA RELEASE

OPEN RECORDS UNPRECEDENTED ECONOMIC IMPACT

The record-breaking 1997 Ford Australian Open has resulted in a gross economic impact of $A82.6 million on the Victorian economy, Tennis Australia President Geoff Pollard announced today.

The Economic Impact Study, released today by the National Institute of Economic and Industry Research (NIEIR), indicates a 65 per cent increase on the 1995 figure, and reports that Australia's biggest sporting event boosted gross domestic product by $A50.8 million.

'These figures underline the substantial growth of the Tournament,' Mr Pollard said.

The 1997 record-breaker boasted a patronage of 391 504, with 15 sell-out sessions and 12 record crowd attendances, attracting, as per the NIEIR report, an estimated 21 821 interstate visitors, and 13 788 overseas tourists.

Televised in 169 territories, the 1997 Ford Australian Open had a home reach of 610 million. In addition to the 120 hours of live Australian coverage telecast on the host broadcaster, the Seven network, the Tournament received the following live international coverage: 170 hours throughout Asia; 103 hours throughout the Middle East; 44 hours throughout Africa; 43 hours in Japan; 30 hours throughout Latin America; 96 hours throughout Europe; 148 hours in Italy; 115 hours in Germany; and 42 hours in the USA.

'These statistics are simply staggering and unprecedented in terms of an Australian sporting event,' Tournament Director Paul McNamee said.

The Victorian Government's Community Support Fund assisted the Tournament's tourism marketing drive, resulting in healthy industry figures and expenditure. Overseas and interstate visitors tallied 106 866 visitor nights in Victoria compared to 79 159 in 1995. In addition, the 1819 interstate and international media representatives, players and their entourage, officials, umpires, and other persons associated with the Tournament generated a further 18 732 visitor nights in Victoria.

* The 1995 Victorian economic impact figure has appeared incorrectly in some reports. The correct figure is $A50 million

Lysette Gild
Publicist
1 May, 1997

FINALISATION

Once the event is over and before administration is disbanded and preparation for the next event is begun, it is important to tidy up loose ends and to bring the event management process to a satisfactory conclusion. The following is a useful check list of tasks to be completed in finalising the event.

- Hold a debriefing meeting and provide an opportunity for feedback by all stakeholders.
- Settle accounts and prepare an audited financial statement.
- Fulfil all contractual and statutory obligations.
- Prepare a full report on event outcomes and distribute it to all key stakeholders.
- Make recommendations for future refinements and improvements to the event.
- Thank all staff, participants and stakeholders for their support of the event.

SUMMARY

Event evaluation is a process of measuring and assessing an event throughout the event management cycle. It provides feedback that contributes to the planning and improvement of individual events and to the pool of knowledge of the events industry.

Feasibility studies identify the likely costs and benefits of an event and help to decide whether to proceed with it. Monitoring the event establishes whether it is on track, and enables the event manager to respond to changes and adjust plans. Post-event evaluation measures the outcomes of the event in relation to its objectives. The exact nature of this evaluation will depend on the perspectives and needs of the stakeholders.

A range of techniques is used in event evaluation, including data collection, observation, feedback meetings, questionnaires and surveys. Good evaluation is planned and implemented from the outset of the event management process, with all participants being made aware of its objectives and methodology. As well as tangible impacts, events have intangible benefits that cannot always be quantified and may need to be recorded on a narrative or descriptive basis. These include social and cultural impacts on a community and the long-term profile and positioning of a tourism destination. Calculating the economic impact of an event can be complex and expensive, but a simple methodology is available to carry out a basic study. The media coverage of an event should be monitored in-house or by using professional media monitors. Once information is gathered from all sources, an event evaluation report should be compiled and distributed to all stakeholders. This report can provide the basis of media releases that promote the outcomes of the event, and can be used in planning for the future and seeking sponsorship. In finalising the event, it is important to tidy up loose ends and apply lessons learnt from the event in future event management processes.

Questions

1 Identify an event that you are familiar with. Design an evaluation plan that will provide a profile of the event and form the basis of a report to key stakeholders.

2 Imagine that you are employing staff to work on a particular event. Design a report sheet for them to record their observations of the event. Decide what aspects you want them to observe and what benchmarks you want them to use.

3 Select an event that you are familiar with, and identify the stakeholders that you would invite to a final evaluation meeting. Write an agenda for the meeting that will encourage well-organised feedback on the event.

4 Imagine that you are a tourist officer for your region. Design a questionnaire for a major local event in order to evaluate the impact of the event on local tourism.

5 Obtain copies of three evaluation reports from libraries or from event organisations. Compare and contrast the methodology, style and format of these reports.

6 Choose an event that has a considerable impact, whether positive or negative, on its host community. Describe this impact, and evaluate the social costs and benefits to the community.

7 Using the same event as in question 6, design a brief requiring a professional organisation to carry out an economic impact study of the event.

8 Identify a high-profile event in your region, and monitor as closely as you can the media coverage of the event, including print, radio and television coverage.

9 Choose an event that you have been associated with, and assemble as much data as you can on the event. Using this data, create a written profile of the event. Using this written profile as a basis, draft a media release that outlines the outcomes of the event and the benefits to the local community.

How Tamworth became
the country music capital

Tamworth is widely recognised, both in Australia and overseas, as Australia's 'country music capital'. In January 1997, the city hosted the twenty-fifth anniversary staging of the Toyota Country Music Awards of Australia, the event which was responsible for the birth of the Australasian Country Music Festival, and the development of Tamworth as our country music capital.

So how did this relatively small, inland country town acquire such a reputation, and what effect has the festival had on the modern city of Tamworth and its people?

The modern story of country music and of Tamworth did not begin until the late 1960s, when once-popular Australian country music was relegated to the backblocks by the emerging and all-consuming 'rock 'n' roll'. At that time, commercial radio was smarting from the introduction of television. Radio's evening audiences were decimated, but Tamworth's local station, 2TM, fought back by airing specialist programs of drama, jazz, folk music and even the supposedly despised country and western music in night-time slots.

To everyone's amazement, the listener response to 2TM's country music program was huge. The radio station had a clear transmission frequency which it did not share with stations elsewhere, and at night its signal could be heard all over eastern Australia.

'Hoedown' (as it was called until 1996), hosted by legendary country music personality John Minson, began to attract listeners from all over Australia and became the catalyst for the entire Country Music Capital promotion.

In the late 1960s, a group of executives at 2TM conceived the idea of marketing Tamworth as an Australian centre for country music. In 1969, it was decided to refer to the city as Country Music Capital in all promotional activity undertaken by the station. Despite the fact that the only substance to the title was the 'Hoedown' radio program, the name and concept caught on. In 1972, plans were formulated for a series of awards to be presented to country music songwriters and performing artists, and in January 1973 the first Australasian Country Music Awards were staged.

Once the awards were consolidated, other activities were planned and staged with the deliberate intention of developing a festival out of a single event. Gradually, the period of the festival grew from two days to ten, with individuals and organisations staging events in venues throughout the city and local district.

During Tamworth's country music development period in the 1970s and 1980s, several major factors strongly influenced its growth:

- **Country Music Capital as a marketing concept.** The owners and promoters of the event were not 'fans'. 2TM was concerned only with the establishment of a national promotion which could be developed and marketed widely with financial and social benefits to the station and the City of Tamworth.

- **Professionalism of organisation.** From the first, the awards and the Country Music Capital campaign were run by marketing professionals. Every effort was made to present a highly professional event. This was reflected in everything from the publicity material and attitude to the media to the organisation of the event, the quality and expertise of the people involved and the general approach to the entire promotion.
- **Centralised control.** The entire country music promotion was tightly controlled and coordinated by the Chief Executive of the awards and festival, Max Ellis, who was also the Manager of 2TM and, later, BAL Marketing (until 1984). All major decisions relating to any aspect of the promotion passed through his office.

While Tamworth City Council gradually became more involved with the festival as it grew, the centralised control continued, with council checking all its festival activities with BAL Marketing/2TM as a central reference point.

As other companies and organisations such as talent quest organisers, registered clubs, hotel managers and outside entrepreneurs entered the festival, they voluntarily coordinated their activity through 2TM and BAL Marketing as unofficial, but very effective, festival coordinators. An example of how this worked is the case of the sideshow operators, who voluntarily stayed out of the city for a number of years because 2TM management believed the country music component had to be well established before other elements could safely be introduced into the festival.

- **Strong financial incentive.** 2TM undertook the entire organisation and promotion of the festival at its own expense, setting up and operating the overall activity as a major sales promotion, supported by numerous major national sponsors. Today, the awards are sponsored by Toyota, the festival by Carlton and dozens of other major sponsors are involved in other events.
- **Continuity of management.** One important facet of the festival was the continuity of supervision of the country music promotion (again by Max Ellis through 2TM and BAL), from its inception in the late 1960s and the awards in 1973 until his departure in 1985. Many other key staff members were also deeply involved in setting up and running the promotion over these years. It was a period in which 2TM developed a close relationship with artists, fans and the Australian music industry.

BAL Marketing, under Barry Harley and Jim Hynes, continued its 'unofficial coordination' from 1986 through to the early 90s, finally handing its reduced role and responsibility to the city council in 1994. In recent years ex-BAL marketeers have again become active in the awards and festival management, particularly through their involvement with the Country Music Association of Australia, Prime Television and the new BAL Marketing, which was sold to the Rural Press organisation in 1995.

- **Innovation.** One of the most important factors in the expansion of the festival was innovation — the deliberate on-going creation of complementary new events by 2TM. These events provided the solid foundation of activity which encouraged others to participate. Most of these activities (such as Star Maker, Capital News and Pro-Radio) were created for commercial reasons, but some (such as Hands of Fame, Roll of Renown, Cavalcade) were specifically started to enhance the overall drawing power of the festival.

- **Australian content.** The Australasian Country Music Festival at Tamworth was always promoted strictly as an event for Australian country music and, while major overseas artists were encouraged to visit, they were discouraged from performing. This policy was formulated because 2TM believed its role was to encourage Australian music. Because it had relied on the continuing support of Australian artists such as Slim Dusty to launch the concept, 2TM felt that Australian artists had earned the right to top billing at the festival without the distraction of international stars. Obviously this approach worked because the crowds keep coming back to hear Australian music and Australian artists.

- **Publicity.** The creation of a highly successful visual symbol, the Golden Guitar, provided a powerful public identity for the awards from the start. Publicity was handled by 2TM, and its associated radio and television stations in Tamworth, with the help of professionals in Sydney, Melbourne and Brisbane. Each year, awards executives, with the Mayor, a councillor or a prominent local business person, would visit each capital city and systematically canvas all available national media.

  Over the years, articles appeared in virtually every paper and magazine published in those cities, together with countless appearances on radio and television broadcasts. Every effort was made to facilitate media involvement before and during the festival and, for some years, 2TM flew parties of journalists to Tamworth before the event. Today, council retains a PR firm to handle national publicity, with the firm running a media centre in Tamworth during the festival and holding a launch in December in Sydney. Massive press and television coverage was achieved, with all major networks sending crews to Tamworth for the awards.

  Prime Television covered the awards with news and specials until the late 1980s, when nationwide coverage was organised with the Seven Network. This ceased with a lack of major sponsorship. When the awards were taken over by the Country Music Association of Australia in 1993, Prime directed a massive regional Australian coverage, working with the CMAA and other regional operators.

  In 1996, the awards became the first Australian awards presentations to be featured on national Australian cable television.

  In 1997, the Seven Network carried a delayed telecast of the awards on their capital city and regional stations throughout Australia.

- **Spreading the activity.** Tamworth is unique in that there is no one venue which dominates the festival. This reflects the diverse nature of the event and is a major strength. From the beginning, 2TM worked hard to spread activity throughout the city rather than centralise it in one location. This meant that a diverse range of music could be accommodated and it created a situation where virtually everyone who wished to could become involved in one way or another. It also turned the entire city into an 'attraction' with benefits to all. Over the years various locations have gained a temporary prominence but generally this evens out as new developments occur.

- **The long weekend.** One important factor in building crowds was that the event culminated on the Australia Day long weekend, which, up to 1988, was scheduled on the first Monday on or after 26 January. This enabled organisers and visitors to plan ahead and take advantage of this major cultural celebration.
- **Spin-offs.** As well as the obvious spin-offs of the festival, such as recording studios, artists choosing Tamworth as a home base, printing, publicity and the like, there have been some significant tangible benefits for the city through its country music promotion.

In tourism, having an identity is essential, and country music has given Tamworth an identity second to none. The new Tourist Information Centre is in the shape of a guitar, an obvious tribute to Tamworth's reputation. And of course the Hall of Renown, the Hands of Fame, the giant golden guitar, the Country Collection Wax Museum and the guitar-shaped pool are among dozens of other tourist attractions utilising this famous theme.

Tamworth has become the centre for country music promotion through continued network radio broadcasting, various syndicated television programs emanating from the city, artist management services and publishing. The monthly NFS country music radio sampler service provides new release country music CDs to stations all over Australia. After 23 years, Capital News is still Australia's major country music publication. The Country Music Directory, the industry's 'bible' is also published in Tamworth.

For five years the CMAA (with EMI) has produced its *Winners* CD, containing the music of awards finalists, which now sells well over 30 000 copies annually, as well as the video coverage of the awards.

In 1997 the CMAA, with support from TAFE, established an annual College of Country Music in Tamworth in January, utilising today's top artists to help train tomorrow's country stars.

The Australian Country Music Foundation has been established in Tamworth to build a national archive and resource centre to preserve the heritage of Australian country music.

During 1996 Tourism Tamworth started running a series of high-profile monthly concerts under the banner of the Tamworth Country Theatre and this is generating a lot of interest and tourist visits. Many touring shows also use Tamworth as a base, recruiting talent and organising their tours from the city. And in 1997, the long-awaited Tamworth Regional Entertainment Centre was started by Tamworth City Council with support from the country music industry, State and Federal governments, local business people and public fundraising. This will provide a permanent home for the Country Music Awards each January and lift Tamworth to yet another level of activity by having a first-class, multifunction facility all year round.

It is now over 25 years since the first awards and almost 30 years since the concept of the Country Music Capital was born at 2TM. From the strong foundations laid in the 1970s and early 1980s, the awards and festival have evolved and developed in many ways.

The Country Music Awards of Australia and Australasian Country Music Festival (now the Fosters Tamworth Country Music Festival) are an excellent example of a private enterprise event that has created enormous benefits for the community in which it takes place. With virtually no government assistance prior to the New South Wales State Government's support of the Regional Entertainment Centre, Tamworth and country music have achieved a miraculous transformation of a country town into a nationally — indeed internationally — recognised tourist destination.

The Fosters Tamworth Country Music Festival is also a rare example of a commercially based festival that runs itself through the involvement of a few major entrepreneurs, many smaller operators, self supporting ticket sales, strong sponsorship, a sophisticated visitor-friendly environment, and the support of and professional promotion by the local community through the city council.

Max Ellis
Chief Executive, Australasian Country Music Awards and Festival 1973–84
Chief Executive, CMAA Country Music Awards of Australia 1993–99

Questions

1 From the case study, identify the main stakeholders in the Australasian Country Music Festival.

2 In evaluating the festival, what are the long-term benefits for the city of Tamworth?

3 How has Tamworth used the festival to create an identity for itself?

4 What role does the festival play in selling Tamworth as a tourism destination?

5 Write a brief requiring a consultant to prepare an economic impact study of the Australasian Country Music Festival.

REFERENCES

ChangeData 1998, *Greg Norman Holden International Golf Sponsor Scores© Report*, Manly, NSW.

Getz, Donald 1997, *Event Management and Event Tourism*, Cognizant Communication Corporation, New York.

Gild, L. 1997, 'Open records unprecedented economic impact', media release Australian Open, Melbourne.

Goldblatt, Dr Joe Jeff (1997). *Special Events — Best Practices in Modern Events Management*, Van Rostrand Reinhold, New York.

National Centre for Culture and Recreation Statistics, Australian Bureau of Statistics 1997, *Measuring the Impact of Festivals: Guidelines for Conducting an Economic Impact Study*, Cultural Ministers Council, Statistics Working Group, Canberra.

Smyth, J. 1998, *1998 Foster's Tamworth Country Music Festival, file no. C25*, Business & Corporate Development Department Report no. 98/8 to Tamworth City Council.

Sydney Gay and Lesbian Mardi Gras 1998, *Annual Report*, Sydney.

INDEX

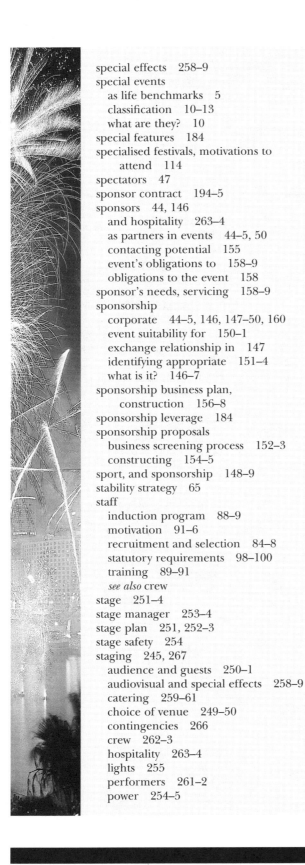